The American story is woven with strong threads of heroism, sacrifice, and compassion. It is a vibrant story of a nation "under God," unshackled from the old chains of oppression, seeking to fulfill a destiny. Sadly, we have since lost that spirit and vigor. No sector of our society feels this loss more keenly than the Christian school and private school movement. It is in response to their requests that we have obtained the rights to reprint *American History in Verse* from the Houghton Mifflin Company.

This collection of poems was originally published for public school use in the 1930's and was well-received. Too many public schools today no longer find patriotism and good literature "relevant" to their goals, but we know this book will find a warm response among those who still love their country. It is the first offering by Bob Jones University Press, Inc., in our Christian Heritage Series. Our hope is that this volume will help give literature and history students a glimpse of the glory they inherit.

Bob Jones
Editor-in-chief

AMERICA

My country, 'tis of thee,
Sweet land of liberty,
 Of thee I sing;
Land where my fathers died,
Land of the pilgrims' pride,
From every mountain-side
 Let freedom ring.

My native country, thee,
Land of the noble free,
 Thy name I love;
I love thy rocks and rills,
Thy woods and templed hills;
My heart with rapture thrills
 Like that above.

Let music swell the breeze,
And ring from all the trees
 Sweet freedom's song;
Let mortal tongues awake,
Let all that breathe partake,
Let rocks their silence break —
 The sound prolong.

Our fathers' God, to Thee,
Author of liberty,
 To Thee we sing;
Long may our land be bright
With freedom's holy light;
Protect us by Thy might,
 Great God, our King.

SAMUEL FRANCIS SMITH

American History in Verse

Burton Stevenson

BOB JONES UNIVERSITY PRESS, INC.
Greenville, South Carolina 29614
1975

BOB JONES UNIVERSITY PRESS, INC.
GREENVILLE, SOUTH CAROLINA 29614
ISBN 0-89084-024-5

PREFACE

THE great events of American history cannot be retold too often, for man's memory is short, and even the recent past soon grows blurred and dim. So with the principles upon which the Republic was founded and the ideals which have grown up about it. They should have frequent restatement, not only because they are admirable in themselves, but because they form the foundation of what has come to be known as Americanism — that devotion to justice and liberty and human rights which has ennobled the country's past and by which its future will be shaped.

Far more than any other form of government, a Republic depends for its existence upon the intelligence and devotion of its citizens. They *are* the government. It consists only of them. They must be proud of their country. They must believe in its destiny and be united in defense of its ideals. It must be first in their hearts. When this is so, it is invincible. Like the towns of ancient Sparta, its citizens are its walls.

No nation exists today of which its people have a better right to be proud than these United States. This book is an effort to show why this is so. It tells again the story of America in terms of poetry, much of it stirring poetry, which sets that story in bold relief and presents it graphically to the imagination. It would be absurd, of course, to pretend that these poems constitute a balanced history, but they do, at least, illumine those gallant and dramatic incidents which appeal most strongly to American patriotism and which Americans have most reason to remember.

Many of them have to do with war, because it is in war that the sort of gallantry and drama which lend themselves to poetry are most conspicuous. But America has no reason to be ashamed of any of her wars, and every reason to be very proud of two of them, which were motivated by a fine ardor for human liberty, and undertaken in complete disregard of selfish gain. They were, in reality, crusades, as has been indicated in the text — the only crusades undertaken by any nation since the Middle Ages — and the fact that the ardor, the passion back of them was to some extent mistaken detracts nothing from its fineness. To pour out blood and treasure in order to free an alien people from oppression, or to send a mighty army across the ocean to join in what seemed to be a struggle for democracy, these are adventures so extraordinary and so exalted that their memory must not be lost.

Especially should American children be made familiar with them. Too often they are permitted to imagine that all countries and governments are alike, and so fail to realize that ours is the only one in the world set up by the people themselves for themselves — largely little bands of people who had fled from other lands, at great toil and peril, in search of a freedom which they could find nowhere else, which they won by long and weary years of warfare, and which they maintained only by ceaseless vigilance. Lowell remarked that American soil was good to be born on, good to live on, good to die for and to be buried in, and perhaps this book can help to bring this home to young Americans, and to make their feeling for their country more passionate and profound. It is with this hope, at least, that it has been compiled.

It is based upon a much larger book by the same editor, *Poems of American History*, published by Houghton Mifflin Company nearly twenty-five years ago, to which reference should be made by anyone interested in the contemporary poems of the various periods. The thread of narrative has been kept as slender as possible, just strong enough to carry the reader understandingly from one poem to the next, but this has been supplemented by rather full notes covering the less familiar allusions. The notes will be found at the back of the book, together with complete indexes of authors, first lines, and titles which should assist in making the poems readily accessible.

CONTENTS

PART I

THE NEW WORLD

CHAPTER I

The Greatest Voyage in History

CHAPTER II

The Virginia Colony

PART II

THE NEW NATION

CHAPTER I

The Bursting of the Storm

CHAPTER II

The War Begins

CHAPTER III

Independence

CHAPTER IV

The First Campaign

CHAPTER V

Victory

CHAPTER VI

First in the Hearts of His Countrymen

PART III

CONQUERING THE CONTINENT

CHAPTER I

The British Again

CHAPTER II

Texas and California

PART IV

THE STRUGGLE FOR THE UNION

CHAPTER I

Civil War

CHAPTER II

The First Campaign

CHAPTER III

The Second Year

CHAPTER IV

The Final Struggle

CONTENTS

PART V

AMERICA GOES CRUSADING

CHAPTER I

The Making of a Giant

CHAPTER II

The Crusade Against Spain

xvi CONTENTS

CHAPTER III

Twenty Years of Peace

CHAPTER IV

The Crusade Against Germany

CONTENTS

PART I
THE NEW WORLD

AMERICA THE BEAUTIFUL

O BEAUTIFUL for spacious skies,
  For amber waves of grain,
For purple mountain majesties
  Above the fruited plain!
    America! America!
  God shed His grace on thee
And crown thy good with brotherhood
  From sea to shining sea!

O beautiful for pilgrim feet,
  Whose stern, impassioned stress
A thoroughfare for freedom beat
  Across the wilderness!
    America! America!
  God mend thine every flaw,
Confirm thy soul in self-control,
  Thy liberty in law!

O beautiful for heroes proved
  In liberating strife,
Who more than self their country loved,
  And mercy more than life!
    America! America!
  May God thy gold refine
Till all success be nobleness,
  And every gain divine!

O beautiful for patriot dream
  That sees beyond the years
Thine alabaster cities gleam
  Undimmed by human tears!
    America! America!
  God shed His grace on thee
And crown thy good with brotherhood
  From sea to shining sea!

            KATHARINE LEE BATES

CHAPTER I

The Greatest Voyage in History

ALTHOUGH it is fairly certain that the Norsemen visited America
about the year 1000, they made no permanent settlement. But in
1451, a boy was born at Genoa, Italy, who was destined to add a
New World to the Old. He was the son of a poor weaver named
Domenico Colombo and was christened Cristoforo. Genoa was a
great port then as now, the boy was soon at sea, and listened to
sailors' talk and studied old maps until he became convinced that
by sailing west from Portugal he could reach Japan and India.

COLUMBUS

Give me white paper!
This which you use is black and rough with smears
Of sweat and grime and fraud and blood and tears,
Crossed with the story of men's sins and fears,
Of battle and of famine all these years,
　　When all God's children had forgot their birth,
　　And drudged and fought and died like beasts of earth.

"Give me white paper!"
One storm-trained seaman listened to the word;
What no man saw he saw; he heard what no man heard.
　　In answer he compelled the sea
　　To eager man to tell
　　The secret she had kept so well!
Left blood and guilt and tyranny behind —
Sailing still West the hidden shore to find;
　For all mankind that unstained scroll unfurled,
　Where God might write anew the story of the World.
　　　　　　　　　　　　EDWARD EVERETT HALE

SPAIN was a great seafaring nation, and its king and queen, Ferdinand and Isabella, were the most enlightened monarchs of the time. Columbus succeeded in gaining admittance to their court, and laid his idea before them.   They were so deeply interested that they commanded the greatest astronomers and map-makers of the kingdom to assemble at the monastery of Saint Stephen, at Salamanca, to examine the project.

COLUMBUS

[January, 1487]

SAINT STEPHEN's cloistered hall was proud
   In learning's pomp that day,
For there a robed and stately crowd
   Pressed on in long array.
A mariner with simple chart
   Confronts that conclave high,
While strong ambition stirs his heart,
And burning thoughts of wonder part
   From lip and sparkling eye.

What hath he said?   With frowning face,
   In whispered tones they speak,
And lines upon their tablets trace,
   Which flush each ashen cheek;
The Inquisition's mystic doom
   Sits on their brows severe,
And bursting forth in visioned gloom,
Sad heresy from burning tomb
   Groans on the startled ear.

Courage, thou Genoese!   Old Time
   Thy splendid dream shall crown;
Yon Western Hemisphere sublime,
   Where unshorn forests frown,
The awful Andes' cloud-wrapt brow,
   The Indian hunter's bow,
Bold streams untamed by helm or prow,

And rocks of gold and diamonds, thou
   To thankless Spain shalt show.

Courage, World-finder! Thou hast need!
   In Fate's unfolding scroll,
Dark woes and ingrate wrongs I read,
   That rack the noble soul.
On! on! Creation's secrets probe,
   Then drink thy cup of scorn,
And wrapped in fallen Cæsar's robe,
Sleep like that master of the globe,
   All glorious — yet forlorn.
                    LYDIA HUNTLEY SIGOURNEY

COLUMBUS explained his project, but the scientists were skeptical and
finally, early in 1491, reported that it was impossible of execution.
Sick at heart with disappointment, Columbus started for Paris
to seek the King of France. He was accompanied by his son Diego,
and stopped one night to ask for food and shelter at the monastery
of La Rabida, near Palos. The prior, Juan Perez de Marchena,
became interested in his idea and finally persuaded Isabella to give
him another hearing.

COLUMBUS AT THE CONVENT

[July, 1491]

DREARY and brown the night comes down,
   Gloomy, without a star.
On Palos town the night comes down;
The day departs with a stormy frown;
   The sad sea moans afar.

A convent-gate is near; 'tis late;
   Ting-ling! the bell they ring.
They ring the bell, they ask for bread —
"Just for my child," the father said.
   Kind hands the bread will bring.

White was his hair, his mien was fair,
    His look was calm and great.
The porter ran and called a friar;
The friar made haste and told the prior;
    The prior came to the gate.

He took them in, he gave them food;
    The traveler's dreams he heard;
And fast the midnight moments flew,
And fast the good man's wonder grew,
    And all his heart was stirred.

The child the while, with soft, sweet smile,
    Forgetful of all sorrow,
Lay soundly sleeping in his bed.
The good man kissed him then, and said:
    "You leave us not tomorrow!

"I pray you rest the convent's guest;
    The child shall be our own —
A precious care, while you prepare
Your business with the court, and bear
    Your message to the throne."

And so his guest he comforted.
    O wise, good prior! to you,
Who cheered the stranger's darkest days,
And helped him on his way, what praise
    And gratitude are due!
                    JOHN TOWNSEND TROWBRIDGE

COLUMBUS stated his case so well that the Queen was convinced and exclaimed: "I undertake the enterprise for my own crown of Castile. I will pledge my jewels to raise the money that is needed." But in the end, Ferdinand's treasurer advanced seventeen thousand florins from the coffers of Aragon, so that Ferdinand paid for the expedition, after all. Columbus secured three little vessels, the Santa Maria, the Pinta, and the Niña, the largest of which displaced only a hundred tons, enlisted a hundred and twenty men, and early on the morning of Friday, August 3, 1492, sailed out from Palos.

STEER, BOLD MARINER, ON!

[August 3, 1492]

STEER, bold mariner, on! albeit witlings deride thee,
And the steersman drop idly his hand at the helm.
Ever and ever to westward! there must the coast be discovered,
If it but lie distinct, luminous lie in thy mind.

Trust to the God that leads thee, and follow the sea that is silent;
Did it not yet exist, now would it rise from the flood.
Nature with Genius stands united in league everlasting;
What is promised by one, surely the other performs.

FRIEDRICH VON SCHILLER

LAND finally sank from sight, and the sailors gave themselves up for lost, but Columbus held steadily westward. Week followed week, and the men were ready to mutiny when, at daybreak on Friday, October 12, land was sighted. The boats were lowered and Columbus, with a large part of his company, went ashore. They found themselves on a small island and Columbus named it San Salvador. It was one of the Bahamas — which one is not certainly known.

COLUMBUS

BEHIND him lay the gray Azores,
  Behind the Gates of Hercules;
Before him not the ghost of shores,
  Before him only shoreless seas.
The good mate said: "Now must we pray,
  For lo! the very stars are gone.
Brave Admiral, speak, what shall I say?"
  "Why, say, 'Sail on! sail on! and on!'"

"My men grow mutinous day by day;
  My men grow ghastly wan and weak."
The stout mate thought of home; a spray
  Of salt wave washed his swarthy cheek.
"What shall I say, brave Admiral, say,
  If we sight naught but seas at dawn?"
"Why, you shall say at break of day,
  'Sail on! sail on! sail on! and on!'"

They sailed and sailed, as winds might blow,
  Until at last the blanched mate said:
"Why, now not even God would know
  Should I and all my men fall dead.
These very winds forget their way,
  For God from these dread seas is gone.
Now speak, brave Admiral, speak and say" —
  He said: "Sail on! sail on! and on!"

They sailed. They sailed. Then spake the mate:
  "This mad sea shows his teeth tonight.
He curls his lip, he lies in wait,
  He lifts his teeth, as if to bite!
Brave Admiral, say but one good word:
  What shall we do when hope is gone?"
The words leapt like a leaping sword:
  "Sail on! sail on! sail on! and on!"

Then, pale and worn, he paced his deck,
  And peered through darkness. Ah, that night
Of all dark nights! And then a speck —
  A light! a light! at last a light!
It grew, a starlit flag unfurled!
  It grew to be Time's burst of dawn.
He gained a world; he gave that world
  Its grandest lesson: "On! sail on!"
                  JOAQUIN MILLER

COLUMBUS reached Spain again March 15, 1493. He was received by the King and Queen with triumphal honors and many distinctions were conferred upon him.

COLUMBUS

VICEROY they made him, Admiral and Don,
    Wishing — good King and Queen! — to honor him
    Whose deeds should make all like distinctions dim.
Columbus!   Other title needs he none.
    And they — in wisdom more than kingship blest —
    Go down to future days, remembered best
For service rendered to that lowly one.

Columbus!   With proud love, yet reverently,
    Pronounce that name — the name of one who heard
    A word of life, and, answering that word,
Braved death, unfearing, on the Shadowy Sea;
    Who — seeking land not known to any chart,
    That land by faith deep graven on his heart —
Found justice, truth, and human liberty!
                   FLORENCE EARLE COATES

BUT Columbus's pretensions and claims for preferment made him many enemies, who finally gained the King's ear.   In 1500 he was arrested in San Domingo, whither he had gone on another voyage, and sent back to Spain in chains.

COLUMBUS IN CHAINS

[August, 1500]

ARE these the honors they reserve for me,
Chains for the man who gave new worlds to Spain!
Rest here, my swelling heart! — O kings, O queens,
Patrons of monsters, and their progeny,
Authors of wrong, and slaves to fortune merely!
Why was I seated by my prince's side,
Honored, caressed like some first peer of Spain?

Was it that I might fall most suddenly
From honor's summit to the sink of scandal?
'Tis done, 'tis done! — what madness is ambition!
What is there in that little breath of men,
Which they call Fame, that should induce the brave
To forfeit ease and that domestic bliss
Which is the lot of happy ignorance,
Less glorious aims, and dull humility? —
Whoe'er thou art that shalt aspire to honor,
And on the strength and vigor of the mind
Vainly depending, court a monarch's favor,
Pointing the way to vast extended empire;
First count your pay to be ingratitude,
Then chains and prisons, and disgrace like mine!
Each wretched pilot now shall spread his sails,
And treading in my footsteps, hail new worlds,
Which, but for me, had still been empty visions.

PHILIP FRENEAU

ISABELLA ordered the chains struck off and promised that he should
be restored to all his dignities, but her death left him without a
patron or protector. The last years of his life were spent in sickness
and poverty, and the end came at Valladolid, May 20, 1506.

COLUMBUS DYING

"*In manus tuas, Domine, commendo spiritum meum.*"
Last words of Columbus

[May 20, 1506]

HARK! do I hear again the roar
    Of the tides by the Indies sweeping down?
Or is it the surge from the viewless shore
    That swells to bear me to my crown?
Life is hollow and cold and drear
    With smiles that darken and hopes that flee;
And, far from its winds that faint and veer,
    I am ready to sail the vaster sea!

Lord, Thou knowest I love Thee best;
  And that scorning peril and toil and pain,
I held my way to the mystic West,
  Glory for Thee and Thy Church to gain.
And Thou didst lead me, only Thou,
  Cheering my heart in cloud and calm,
Till the dawn my glad, victorious prow
  Greeted Thine isles of bloom and balm.

And then, O gracious, glorious Lord,
  I saw Thy face, and all heaven came nigh
And my soul was lost in that rich reward,
  And ravished with hope of the bliss on high,
So, I can meet the sovereign's frown —
  My dear Queen gone — with a large disdain;
For the time will come when his chief renown
  Will be that I sailed from his realm of Spain.

I have found New Lands — a World, maybe,
  Whose splendor will yet the Old outshine;
And life and death are alike to me,
  For earth will honor, and heaven is mine.
Is mine! — What songs of sweet accord!
  What billows that nearer, gentler roll!
Is mine! — Into Thy hands, O Lord,
  Into Thy hands I give my soul!
                              EDNA DEAN PROCTOR

COLUMBUS never saw the North American mainland, and never
realized that he had discovered a New World. He supposed to the
end that he had merely found a western route to Japan and India.

COLUMBUS

How in Heaven's name did Columbus get over
  Is a pure wonder to me, I protest;
Cabot, and Raleigh, too, that well-read rover,
  Frobisher, Dampier, Drake, and the rest.

Bad enough all the same,
For them that after came,
But, in great Heaven's name,
How *he* should ever think
That on the other brink
Of this wild waste, terra firma should be,
Is a pure wonder, I must say, to me.

How a man ever should hope to get thither,
    E'en if he knew that there was another side;
But to suppose he should come any whither,
    Sailing straight on into chaos untried,
        In spite of the motion
        Across the whole ocean,
        To stick to the notion
        That in some nook or bend
        Of a sea without end
He should find North and South America,
Was a pure madness, indeed I must say.

What if wise men had, as far back as Ptolemy,
    Judged that the earth like an orange was round,
None of them ever said, "Come along, follow me,
    Sail to the West and the East will be found."
        Many a day before
        Ever they'd come ashore,
        From the "San Salvador,"
        Sadder and wiser men,
        They'd have turned back again;
And that *he* did not, but did cross the sea
Is a pure wonder, I must say, to me.
                        ARTHUR HUGH CLOUGH

Nor did he suspect that in this New World a New Nation was to rise, founded upon the principles of liberty and equality, and which, four hundred years later, would war against and defeat the proud old kingdom that had sent him forth.

COLUMBUS AND THE MAYFLOWER

O Little fleet! that on thy quest divine
Sailedst from Palos one bright autumn morn,
Say, has old Ocean's bosom ever borne
A freight of faith and hope to match with thine?

Say, too, has Heaven's high favor given again
Such consummation of desire as shone
About Columbus when he rested on
The new-found world and married it to Spain?

Answer — thou refuge of the freeman's need —
Thou for whose destinies no kings looked out,
Nor sages to resolve some mighty doubt —
Thou simple Mayflower of the salt-sea mead!

When thou wert wafted to that distant shore,
Gay flowers, bright birds, rich odors met thee not;
Stern Nature hailed thee to a sterner lot —
God gave free earth and air, and gave no more.

Thus to men cast in that heroic mould
Came empire such as Spaniard never knew,
Such empire as beseems the just and true;
And at the last, almost unsought, came gold.

But He who rules both calm and stormy days,
Can guard that people's heart, that nation's health,
Safe on the perilous heights of power and wealth,
As in the straitness of the ancient ways.

RICHARD MONCKTON MILNES

CHAPTER II

THE VIRGINIA COLONY

NEWS of the discoveries made by Columbus soon spread through Western Europe, and in May, 1497, John Cabot, a Venetian navigator in English employ, sailed from Bristol in a ship called the Matthew, under letters patent from King Henry VII. On June 24, he sighted what he supposed to be the Chinese coast, went ashore, and took possession of the country for England.

THE FIRST VOYAGE OF JOHN CABOT

[1497]

"HE CHASES shadows," sneered the British tars.
"As well fling nets to catch the golden stars
   As climb the surges of earth's utmost sea."
But for the Venice pilot, meagre, wan,
His swarthy sons beside him, life began
With that slipt cable, when his dream rode free.

And Henry, on his battle-wrested throne,
The Councils done, would speak in musing tone
Of Cabot, not the cargo he might bring.
"Man's heart, though morsel scant for hungry crow,
Is greater than a world can fill, and so
Fair fall the shadow-seekers!" quoth the king.

                                              UNKNOWN

BY VIRTUE of Cabot's discoveries, England laid claim to the whole continent, but nearly a century elapsed before she attempted to colonize it. Finally, in 1583, Sir Humphrey Gilbert set out on a voyage of discovery and colonization. He landed at St. John's, Newfoundland, August 5, established there the first English colony in North America, sailed away for England, and was lost in a storm off the Azores. The colony proved a failure.

SIR HUMPHREY GILBERT

[1583]

Southward with fleet of ice
  Sailed the corsair Death;
Wild and fast blew the blast,
  And the East Wind was his breath.

His lordly ships of ice
  Glisten in the sun;
On each side, like pennons wide,
  Flashing crystal streamlets run.

His sails of white sea-mist
  Dripped with silver rain;
But where he passed there were cast
  Leaden shadows o'er the main.

Eastward from Campobello
  Sir Humphrey Gilbert sailed;
Three days or more seaward he bore,
  Then, alas! the land wind failed.

Alas! the land wind failed,
  And ice-cold grew the night;
And nevermore, on sea or shore,
  Should Sir Humphrey see the light.

He sat upon the deck,
  The Book was in his hand;
"Do not fear! Heaven is as near,"
  He said, "by water as by land!"

In the first watch of the night,
  Without a signal's sound,

Out of the sea, mysteriously,
　The fleet of Death rose all around.

The moon and the evening star
　Were hanging in the shrouds;
Every mast, as it passed,
　Seemed to rake the passing clouds.

They grappled with their prize,
　At midnight black and cold!
As of a rock was the shock;
　Heavily the ground swell rolled.

Southward through day and dark,
　They drift in close embrace,
With mist and rain, o'er the open main;
　Yet there seems no change of place.

Southward, forever southward,
　They drift through dark and day;
And like a dream, in the Gulf Stream
　Sinking, vanish all away.

HENRY WADSWORTH LONGFELLOW

IN 1584, an expedition explored Albemarle Sound, naming the region Virginia in honor of Elizabeth, the virgin queen of England, and in 1606, James I sanctioned the formation of two Virginia colonies. The first one sailed on New Year's Day, 1607. Twelve weeks later, the colonists landed at a place they named Point Comfort, proceeded fifty miles up a great river which they named the James, and finally disembarked on a low peninsula, where they started a settlement which they christened Jamestown. Captain John Smith, although not in command, soon proved himself the ablest of the company.

JOHN SMITH'S APPROACH TO JAMESTOWN

[May 13, 1607]

I PAUSE not now to speak of Raleigh's dreams,
Though they might give a loftier bard fit themes:...

But, leaving these and Chesapeake's broad bay,
Resume my story in the month of May,
Where England's cross — Saint George's ensign — flowed
Where ne'er before emblazoned banner glowed;
Where English breasts throbbed fast as English eyes
Looked o'er the waters with a glad surprise —
Looked gladly out upon the varied scene
Where stretched the woods in all their pomp of green;
Flinging great shadows, beautiful and vast
As e'er upon Arcadian lake were cast.
Turn where they would, in what direction rove,
They found some bay, or wild, romantic cove,
On which they coasted through those forests dim,
Wherein they heard the never-ceasing hymn
That swelled from all the tall, majestic pines —
Fit choristers of Nature's sylvan shrines.

For though no priest their solitudes had trod,
The trees were vocal in their praise of God.
And then, when, capes and jutting headlands past,
The sails were furled against each idle mast,
They saw the sunset in its pomp descend,
And sky and water gloriously contend
For gorgeousness of colors, red and gold,
And tints of amethyst together rolled,
Making a scene of splendor and of rest
As vanquished day lit camp-fires in the West.
And when the light grew faint on wave and strand,
New beauties woke in this enchanted land,
For through heaven's lattice-work of crimson bars
Like angels looked the bright eternal stars,
And then, when gathered tints of purplish brown,
A golden sickle, reaping darkness down,
The new moon shone above the lofty trees,
Which made low music in the evening breeze —
The breeze which floating blandly from the shore
The perfumed breath of flowering jasmine bore;

For smiling Spring had kissed its clustering vines,
And breathed her fragrance on the lofty pines.

JAMES BARRON HOPE

CAPTAIN SMITH led numerous expeditions into the country in search
of food, and on one of these was taken prisoner by the Indians and
conducted to the camp of their chief, Powhatan.   According to the
story he sent to England a few months later, he was well treated
and escorted back to Jamestown.   Eight years later, when writing
an account of Powhatan's younger daughter, Pocahontas, for the
entertainment of Queen Anne, he embellished this plain and probably
truthful tale with the romantic incidents so long received as history.

POCAHONTAS

[January 5, 1608]

WEARIED arm and broken sword
    Wage in vain the desperate fight;
Round him press a countless horde,
    He is but a single knight.
Hark! a cry of triumph shrill
    Through the wilderness resounds,
    As, with twenty bleeding wounds,
Sinks the warrior, fighting still.

Now they heap the funeral pyre,
    And the torch of death they light;
Ah! 'tis hard to die by fire!
    Who will shield the captive knight?
Round the stake with fiendish cry
    Wheel and dance the savage crowd,
    Cold the victim's mien and proud,
And his breast is bared to die.

Who will shield the fearless heart?
    Who avert the murderous blade?
From the throng with sudden start
    See, there springs an Indian maid.

Quick she stands before the knight:
"Loose the chain, unbind the ring!
I am daughter of the king,
And I claim the Indian right!"

Dauntlessly aside she flings
Lifted axe and thirsty knife,
Fondly to his heart she clings,
And her bosom guards his life!
In the woods of Powhatan,
Still 'tis told by Indian fires
How a daughter of their sires
Saved a captive Englishman.

WILLIAM MAKEPEACE THACKERAY

His revised story was that he had been dragged before Powhatan and his head forced down upon a stone, when "Pocahontas, the king's dearest daughter, got his head in her arms and laid her own upon his to save him from death: whereat the emperor was contented he should live." Historians are agreed that no such incident ever occurred, but it has always been a favorite with the poets.

POCAHONTAS

Upon the barren sand
A single captive stood;
Around him came, with bow and brand,
The red men of the wood.
Like him of old, his doom he hears,
Rock-bound on ocean's brim —
The chieftain's daughter knelt in tears,
And breathed a prayer for him.

Above his head in air
The savage war-club swung:
The frantic girl, in wild despair,
Her arms about him flung.

Then shook the warriors of the shade,
   Like leaves on aspen limb,
Subdued by that heroic maid
   Who breathed a prayer for him!

"Unbind him!" gasped the chief:
   "It is your king's decree!"
He kissed away the tears of grief,
   And set the captive free!
'Tis ever thus, when in life's storm
   Hope's star to man grows dim,
An angel kneels, in woman's form,
   And breathes a prayer for him.

GEORGE POPE MORRIS

HOWEVER, there really was a Pocahontas, and one of the planters at Jamestown, named John Rolfe, proposed marriage. The Princess was willing, her father consented, though he refused to be present at the ceremony (April 5, 1614), and the bride was given away by her uncle, Opachisco. They had one son, Thomas Rolfe, whose descendants are still living in Virginia.

THE MARRIAGE OF POCAHONTAS

[April 5, 1614]

THAT balmy eve, within a trellised bower,
Rudely constructed on the sounding shore,
Her plighted troth the forest maiden gave
Ere sought the skiff that bore them o'er the wave
To the dark home-bound ship, whose restless sway
Rocked to the winds and waves, impatient of delay....

Short was the word that pledged triumphant love;
That vow, that claims its registry above.
And low the cadence of that hymn of praise
Whose hallowed incense rose, as rose its lays;
And few the worshipers 'neath that pure cope
Which emblems to the soul eternal hope.

One native maiden waited the command
Of the young Princess of Virginia's strand;
And that dark youth, the Page of Cedar Isle,
Who wept her woes, and shared her sad exile,
With his loved bride, who owned the royal blood,
And near the forest Queen majestically stood.

Some others bent beside the rural shrine
In adoration to the Power divine;
When at the altar knelt, with minds serene,
The gallant Soldier and the dark-browed Queen.

These, for the love they bore her guileless youth,
Paid the high fealty of the warm heart's truth;
And with its homage satisfied, gone o'er
Each vision bright that graced their natal shore.

Those, with forebodings dread and brimful eyes,
Bade holy angels guard the destinies
Of one on whom had fallen the chrism of light
With unction pure; the youthful neophyte
Of that fair clime where millions yet unborn
Shall raise the choral hymn from eve till morn.

Mrs. M. M. WEBSTER

IN 1616 Pocahontas was taken to England, where she was received
at court, renewed her acquaintance with Captain John Smith, had
her portrait painted, and led a fashionable life generally. It did
not agree with the wild forest creature, she developed consumption,
and died at Gravesend, March 27, 1617

THE LAST MEETING OF POCAHONTAS AND THE GREAT CAPTAIN

[June, 1616]

IN A stately hall at Brentford, when the English June was green,
Sat the Indian Princess, summoned that her graces might be
seen,
For the rumor of her beauty filled the ear of court and Queen.

There for audience as she waited, with half-scornful, silent
    air
All undazzled by the splendor gleaming round her every-
    where,
Dight in broidered hose and doublet, came a courtier down
    the stair.

As with striding step he hasted, burdened with the Queen's
    command,
Loud he cried, in tones that tingled, "*Welcome, welcome, to
    my land!*"
But a tremor seized the Princess, and she drooped upon her
    hand.

"What! no word, my Sparkling-Water? must I come on
    bended knee?
I were slain within the forest, I were dead beyond the
    sea;
On the banks of wild Pamunkey, I had perished *but for thee.*

"Ah, I keep a heart right loyal, that can nevermore for-
    get!
I can hear the rush, the breathing; I can see the eyelids
    wet;
I can feel the sudden tightening of thine arms about me
    yet.

"Nay, look up. Thy father's daughter never feared the face
    of man,
Shrank not from the forest darkness when her doe-like foot-
    steps ran
To my cabin, bringing tidings of the craft of Powhatan."

With extended arms, entreating, stood the stalwart Captain
    there,
While the courtiers press around her, and the passing pages
    stare;
But no sign gave Pocahontas underneath her veil of hair.

All her lithe and willowy figure quivered like an aspen-leaf,
And she crouched as if she shrivelled, frost-touched by some
 sudden grief,
Turning only on her husband, Rolfe, one glance, sharp,
 searching, brief.

At the Captain's haughty gesture, back the curious courtiers
 fell,
And with soothest word and accent he besought that she
 would tell
Why she turned away, nor greeted him whom she had served
 so well.

But for two long hours the Princess dumbly sat and bowed
 her head,
Moveless as the statue near her.   When at last she spake,
 she said:
"White man's tongue is false.   It told me — told me — *that
 my brave was dead.*

"And I lay upon my deerskins all one moon of falling leaves
(Who hath care for song or corn-dance, when the voice within
 her grieves?),
Looking westward where the souls go, up the path the sunset
 weaves.

"Call me 'child' now.   It is over.   On my husband's arm
 I lean;
Never shadow, *Nenemoosa,* our twain hearts shall come be-
 tween;
Take my hand, and let us follow the great Captain to his
 Queen."

MARGARET JUNKIN PRESTON

MEANWHILE, Jamestown dwindled away, was destroyed by fire
during Bacon's Rebellion, and was never rebuilt.   But a new com-
pany was formed, of which Lord De La Warr was one of the princi-

pals, and he soon infused fresh life into the colony. Many new settlements sprang up, the culture of tobacco was begun, and Virginia was fairly started on the road to prosperity.

TO THE VIRGINIAN VOYAGE

[1611]

You brave heroic minds,
Worthy your country's name,
  That honor still pursue,
  Go and subdue!
Whilst loitering hinds
Lurk here at home, with shame.

Britons, you stay too long:
Quickly aboard bestow you,
  And with a merry gale
  Swell your stretched sail,
With vows as strong
As the winds that blow you.

Your course securely steer,
West and by south forth keep!
  Rocks, lee shores, nor shoals,
  When Eolus scowls,
You need not fear,
So absolute the deep.

And cheerfully at sea,
Success you still entice,
  To get the pearl and gold,
  And ours to hold
Virginia,
Earth's only paradise;

Where Nature hath in store
Fowl, venison, and fish,
  And the fruitful'st soil,
  Without your toil,

Three harvests more,
All greater than your wish.

And the ambitious vine
Crowns with his purple mass
  The cedar reaching high
  To kiss the sky,
The cypress, pine,
And useful sassafras;

To whom the Golden Age
Still Nature's laws doth give,
  No other cares attend,
  But them to defend
From winter's rage,
That long there doth not live.

When as the luscious smell
Of that delicious land,
  Above the seas that flows,
  The clear wind throws,
Your hearts to swell
Approaching the dear strand;

In kenning of the shore
(Thanks to God first given)
  O you the happiest men,
  Be frolic then!
Let cannons roar,
Frighting the wide heaven;

And in regions far
Such heroes bring ye forth
  As those from whom we came,
  And plant our name
Under that star
Not known unto our North. . . .

MICHAEL DRAYTON

CHAPTER III

THE PILGRIMS AND THE PURITANS

IT HAD become evident, of course, that this was a new continent, not Japan or India, but it was still hoped to find a way around it and to reach the East. In 1609, the Dutch East India Company chartered a tiny craft of eighty tons, called the Half Moon, to search for a Northwest passage. It sailed from Amsterdam April 4, under command of Henry Hudson, and after skirting the coast for some distance, dropped anchor inside Sandy Hook September 3. The only result of the voyage was the founding of New Amsterdam, which the British captured in 1664 and renamed New York.

HENRY HUDSON'S QUEST

[1609]

OUT from the harbor of Amsterdam
    The Half Moon turned her prow to sea;
The coast of Norway dropped behind,
    Yet Northward still kept she
Through the drifting fog and the driving snow,
Where never before man dared to go:
"O Pilot, shall we find the strait that leads to the Eastern
    Sea?"
'A waste of ice before us lies — we must turn back," said he.

Westward they steered their tiny bark,
    Westward through weary weeks they sped,
Till the cold gray strand of a stranger-land
    Loomed through the mist ahead.
League after league they hugged the coast,
And their Captain never left his post:
"O Pilot, see you yet the strait that leads to the Eastern Sea?"
"I see but the rocks and the barren shore; no strait is there,"
    quoth he.

They sailed to the North — they sailed to the South —
   And at last they rounded an arm of sand
Which held the sea from a harbor's mouth —
   The loveliest in the land;
They kept their course across the bay,
And the shore before them fell away:
"O Pilot, see you not the strait that leads to the Eastern
   Sea?"
"Hold the rudder true! Praise Christ Jesu! the strait is
   here," said he.

Onward they glide with wind and tide,
   Past marshes gray and crags sun-kist;
They skirt the sills of green-clad hills,
   And meadows white with mist —
But alas! the hope and the brave, brave dream!
For rock and shallow bar the stream:
"O Pilot, can this be the strait that leads to the Eastern Sea?"
"Nay, Captain, nay; 'tis not this way; turn back we must,"
   said he.

Full sad was Hudson's heart as he turned
   The Half Moon's prow to the South once more;
He saw no beauty in crag or hill,
   No beauty in curving shore;
For they shut him away from that fabled main
He sought his whole life long, in vain:
"O Pilot, say, can there be a strait that leads to the Eastern
   Sea?"
"God's crypt is sealed! 'Twill stand revealed in His own
   good time," quoth he.

                             BURTON STEVENSON

MEANWHILE, another settlement had been started farther to the
north by a little band of Separatists from the Church of England,
who have come down through history as the "Pilgrim Fathers."

They had fled from England to Leyden, Holland, in 1609, to escape religious persecution, but they found the Dutch unsympathetic, and finally decided to try their fortunes in the New World.

THE WORD OF GOD TO LEYDEN CAME

[August, 1620]

THE word of God to Leyden came,
    Dutch town by Zuyder Zee:
Rise up, my children of no name,
    My kings and priests to be.
There is an empire in the West,
    Which I will soon unfold;
A thousand harvests in her breast,
    Rocks ribbed with iron and gold.

Rise up, my children, time is ripe!
    Old things are passed away.
Bishops and kings from earth I wipe;
    Too long they've had their day.
A little ship have I prepared
    To bear you o'er the seas;
And in your souls my will declared
    Shall grow by slow degrees.

Beneath my throne the martyrs cry;
    I hear their voice, How long?
It mingles with their praises high,
    And with their victor song.
The thing they longed and waited for,
    But died without the sight;
So, this shall be! I wrong abhor,
    The world I'll now set right.

Leave, then, the hammer and the loom,
    You've other work to do;
For Freedom's commonwealth there's room,
    And you shall build it too.

I'm tired of bishops and their pride,
   I'm tired of kings as well;
Henceforth I take the people's side,
   And with the people dwell.

Tear off the mitre from the priest,
   And from the king, his crown;
Let all my captives be released;
   Lift up, whom men cast down.
Their pastors let the people choose,
   And choose their rulers too;
Whom they select, I'll not refuse,
   But bless the work they do.

The Pilgrims rose, at this, God's word,
   And sailed the wintry seas:
With their own flesh nor blood conferred,
   Nor thought of wealth or ease.
They left the towers of Leyden town,
   They left the Zuyder Zee;
And where they cast their anchor down,
   Rose Freedom's realm to be.

               JEREMIAH EAMES RANKIN

THEY secured a concession from the Northern, or Plymouth, branch of the Virginia Company, a little vessel named the Mayflower was fitted out, and on September 16, 1620, the Pilgrims sailed from Southampton on the most famous voyage in American history, after that of Columbus. The ship was crowded almost to suffocation with one hundred and two persons.

SONG OF THE PILGRIMS

[September 16, 1620]

THE breeze has swelled the whitening sail,
The blue waves curl beneath the gale,
And, bounding with the wave and wind,
We leave Old England's shores behind —

Leave behind our native shore,
Homes, and all we loved before.

The deep may dash, the winds may blow,
The storm spread out its wings of woe,
Till sailors' eyes can see a shroud
Hung in the folds of every cloud;
  Still, as long as life shall last,
  From that shore we'll speed us fast.

For we would rather never be,
Than dwell where mind cannot be free,
But bows beneath a despot's rod
Even where it seeks to worship God.
  Blasts of heaven, onward sweep!
  Bear us o'er the troubled deep!

O see what wonders meet our eyes!
Another land, and other skies!
Columbian hills have met our view!
Adieu! Old England's shores, adieu!
  Here, at length, our feet shall rest,
  Hearts be free, and homes be blessed.

As long as yonder firs shall spread
Their green arms o'er the mountain's head —
As long as yonder cliffs shall stand,
Where join the ocean and the land —
  Shall those cliffs and mountains be
  Proud retreats for liberty.

Now to the King of kings we'll raise
The pæan loud of sacred praise;
More loud than sounds the swelling breeze,
More loud than speak the rolling seas!
  Happier lands have met our view!
  England's shores, adieu! adieu!
                THOMAS COGSWELL UPHAM

On November 19, nine weeks after leaving Plymouth, land was sighted, and in the evening of that day, the "band of exiles moored their bark" behind a sandy peninsula which had already been named Cape Cod.

LANDING OF THE PILGRIM FATHERS

[November 19, 1620]

The breaking waves dashed high
  On the stern and rock-bound coast,
And the woods, against a stormy sky,
  Their giant branches tossed;

And the heavy night hung dark
  The hills and waters o'er,
When a band of exiles moored their bark
  On the wild New England shore.

Not as the conqueror comes,
  They, the true-hearted, came:
Not with the roll of the stirring drums,
  And the trumpet that sings of fame;

Not as the flying come,
  In silence and in fear —
They shook the depths of the desert's gloom
  With their hymns of lofty cheer.

Amidst the storm they sang,
  And the stars heard, and the sea;
And the sounding aisles of the dim woods rang
  To the anthem of the free!

The ocean eagle soared
  From his nest by the white wave's foam,
And the rocking pines of the forest roared:
  This was their welcome home!

There were men with hoary hair
  Amidst that pilgrim band;
Why had they come to wither there,
  Away from their childhood's land?

There was woman's fearless eye,
  Lit by her deep love's truth;
There was manhood's brow, serenely high,
  And the fiery heart of youth.

What sought they thus afar?
  Bright jewels of the mine?
The wealth of seas, the spoils of war? —
  They sought a faith's pure shrine!

Aye, call it holy ground,
  The soil where first they trod!
They have left unstained what there they found —
  Freedom to worship God!
                    FELICIA DOROTHEA HEMANS

Two days later, on Saturday, November 21, the Mayflower dropped her anchor in what is now the harbor of Provincetown, and a force of sixteen, "every one his Musket, Sword and Corslet, under the command of Captaine Myles Standish," went ashore to explore. Sunday was spent on board in prayer and praise, and on the following Monday occurred the first washing-day.

THE FIRST PROCLAMATION OF MILES STANDISH

[November 23, 1620]

"Ho, ROSE!" quoth the stout Miles Standish,
  As he stood on the Mayflower's deck,
And gazed on the sandy coast-line
  That loomed as a misty speck

On the edge of the distant offing —
"See! yonder we have in view
Bartholomew Gosnold's 'headlands.'
'Twas in sixteen hundred and two

"That the Concord of Dartmouth anchored
Just there where the beach is broad,
And the merry old captain named it
(Half swamped by the fish) — Cape Cod.

"And so as his mighty 'headlands'
Are scarcely a league away,
What say you to landing, sweetheart,
And having a washing-day?"...

"Dear heart" — and the sweet Rose Standish
Looked up with a tear in her eye;
She was back in the flag-stoned kitchen
Where she watched, in the days gone by,

Her mother among her maidens
(She should watch them no more, alas!),
And saw as they stretched the linen
To bleach on the Suffolk grass.

In a moment her brow was cloudless,
As she leaned on the vessel's rail,
And thought of the sea-stained garments,
Of coif and of farthingale;

And the doublets of fine Welsh flannel,
The tuckers and homespun gowns,
And the piles of the hosen knitted
From the wool of the Devon downs.

So the matrons aboard the Mayflower
Made ready with eager hand

To drop from the deck their baskets
   As soon as the prow touched land.

And there did the Pilgrim Mothers,
   "On a Monday," the record says,
Ordain for their new-found England
   The first of her washing-days.

And there did the Pilgrim Fathers,
   With matchlock and axe well slung,
Keep guard o'er the smoking kettles
   That propt on the crotches hung.

For the trail of the startled savage
   Was over the marshy grass,
And the glint of his eyes kept peering
   Through cedar and sassafras.

And the children were mad with pleasure
   As they gathered the twigs in sheaves,
And piled on the fire the fagots,
   And heaped up the autumn leaves.

"Do the thing that is next," saith the proverb,
   And a nobler shall yet succeed:
'Tis the motive exalts the action;
   'Tis the doing, and not the deed;

For the earliest act of the heroes
   Whose fame has a world-wide sway
Was — to fashion a crane for a kettle,
   And order a washing-day!
                 MARGARET JUNKIN PRESTON

A SMALL boat which the Pilgrims had brought with them was put together, and in it a party explored the neighboring shores in search of a suitable place for a settlement. They finally selected Plymouth

Harbor, and on Monday, December 21, they "marched into the land and found divers corn-fields and little running brooks — a place (as they supposed) fit for situation." They named the settlement New Plymouth.

THE MAYFLOWER

[December 21, 1620]

Down in the bleak December bay
The ghostly vessel stands away;
Her spars and halyards white with ice,
Under the dark December skies.
A hundred souls, in company,
Have left the vessel pensively —
Have reached the frosty desert there,
And touched it with the knees of prayer
  And now the day begins to dip,
The night begins to lower
    Over the bay, and over the ship
      Mayflower.

Neither the desert nor the sea
Imposes rites: their prayers are free;
Danger and toil the wild imposes,
And thorns must grow before the roses.
And who are these? — and what distress
The savage-acred wilderness
On mother, maid, and child may bring,
Beseems them for a fearful thing;
  For now the day begins to dip,
The night begins to lower
    Over the bay, and over the ship
      Mayflower.

But Carver leads (in heart and health
A hero of the commonwealth)
The axes that the camp requires,
To build the lodge, and heap the fires.

And Standish from his warlike store
Arrays his men along the shore,
Distributes weapons resonant,
And dons his harness militant;
  For now the day begins to dip,
The night begins to lower
    Over the bay, and over the ship
      Mayflower;

And Rose, his wife, unlocks a chest —
She sees a Book, in vellum drest,
She drops a tear and kisses the tome,
Thinking of England and of home:
Might they — the Pilgrims, there and then
Ordained to do the work of men —
Have seen, in visions of the air,
While pillowed on the breast of prayer
  (When now the day began to dip,
The night began to lower
    Over the bay, and over the ship
      Mayflower),

The Canaan of their wilderness
A boundless empire of success;
And seen the years of future nights
Jeweled with myriad household lights;
And seen the honey fill the hive;
And seen a thousand ships arrive;
And heard the wheels of travel go;
It would have cheered a thought of woe,
  When now the day began to dip,
The night began to lower
    Over the bay, and over the ship
      Mayflower.
                ERASTUS WOLCOTT ELLSWORTH

THE colonists planted their fields as soon as spring opened, and were rewarded with a bountiful harvest. "There was great store of wild turkeys, of which they took many," and the governor decreed a festival of thanksgiving. This festival was New England's "First Thanksgiving Day."

THE FIRST THANKSGIVING DAY

[November, 1621]

"AND now," said the Governor, gazing abroad on the piled-up store
Of the sheaves that dotted the clearings and covered the meadows o'er,
"'Tis meet that we render praises because of this yield of grain;
'Tis meet that the Lord of the harvest be thanked for His sun and rain.

"And therefore, I, William Bradford (by the grace of God today,
And the franchise of this good people), Governor of Plymouth, say,
Through virtue of vested power — ye shall gather with one accord,
And hold, in the month November, thanksgiving unto the Lord.

"He hath granted us peace and plenty, and the quiet we've sought so long;
He hath thwarted the wily savage, and kept him from wrack and wrong;
And unto our feast the Sachem shall be bidden, that he may know
We worship his own Great Spirit who maketh the harvests grow.

"So shoulder your matchlocks, masters: there is hunting of all degrees;
And fishermen, take your tackle, and scour for spoil the seas;

And maidens and dames of Plymouth, your delicate crafts
    employ
To honor our First Thanksgiving, and make it a feast of joy!

"We fail of the fruits and dainties — we fail of the old home
    cheer;
Ah, these are the lightest losses, mayhap, that befall us
    here;
But see, in our open clearings, how golden the melons lie;
Enrich them with sweets and spices, and give us the pump-
    kin-pie!"

So, bravely the preparations went on for the autumn feast;
The deer and the bear were slaughtered; wild game from the
    greatest to least
Was heaped in the colony cabins; brown home-brew served
    for wine,
And the plum and the grape of the forest, for orange and
    peach and pine.

At length came the day appointed: the snow had begun to
    fall,
But the clang from the meeting-house belfry rang merrily
    over all,
And summoned the folk of Plymouth, who hastened with
    glad accord
To listen to Elder Brewster as he fervently thanked the
    Lord.

In his seat sate Governor Bradford; men, matrons, and
    maidens fair;
Miles Standish and all his soldiers, with corselet and sword,
    were there;
And sobbing and tears and gladness had each in its turn the
    sway,
For the grave of the sweet Rose Standish o'ershadowed
    Thanksgiving Day.

And when Massasoit, the Sachem, sate down with his hun-
dred braves,
And ate of the varied riches of gardens and woods and waves,
And looked on the granaried harvest — with a blow on his
brawny chest,
He muttered, "The good Great Spirit loves His white children
best!"

MARGARET JUNKIN PRESTON

BUT the period of prosperity was short-lived, and the colony was
pinched with famine through nearly the whole of the next two years.
A crisis was reached in the month of April, 1622, when, so tradition
says, the daily ration for each person was reduced to five kernels
of corn.

FIVE KERNELS OF CORN

[April, 1622]

'TWAS the year of the famine in Plymouth of old,
The ice and the snow from the thatched roofs had rolled;
Through the warm purple skies steered the geese o'er the
seas,
And the woodpeckers tapped in the clocks of the trees;
And the boughs on the slopes to the south winds lay bare,
And dreaming of summer, the buds swelled in the air.
The pale Pilgrims welcomed each reddening morn;
There were left but for rations Five Kernels of Corn.
          Five Kernels of Corn!
          Five Kernels of Corn!
But to Bradford a feast were Five Kernels of Corn!

"Five Kernels of Corn! Five Kernels of Corn!
Ye people, be glad for Five Kernels of Corn!"
So Bradford cried out on bleak Burial Hill,
And the thin women stood in their doors, white and still.
"Lo, the harbor of Plymouth rolls bright in the Spring,
The maples grow red, and the wood robins sing,

The west wind is blowing, and fading the snow,
And the pleasant pines sing, and arbutuses blow.
            Five Kernels of Corn!
            Five Kernels of Corn!
To each one be given Five Kernels of Corn!"

O Bradford of Austerfield haste on thy way.
The west winds are blowing o'er Provincetown Bay,
The white avens bloom, but the pine domes are chill,
And new graves have furrowed Precisioners' Hill!
"Give thanks, all ye people, the warm skies have come,
The hilltops are sunny, and green grows the holm,
And the trumpets of winds, and the white March is gone,
And ye still have left you Five Kernels of Corn.
            Five Kernels of Corn!
            Five Kernels of Corn!
Ye have for Thanksgiving Five Kernels of Corn!

"The raven's gift eat and be humble and pray,
A new light is breaking, and Truth leads your way;
One taper a thousand shall kindle: rejoice
That to you has been given the wilderness voice!"
O Bradford of Austerfield, daring the wave,
And safe through the sounding blasts leading the brave,
Of deeds such as thine was the free nation born,
And the festal world sings the "Five Kernels of Corn."
            Five Kernels of Corn!
            Five Kernels of Corn!
The nation gives thanks for Five Kernels of Corn!
To the Thanksgiving Feast bring Five Kernels of Corn!
                        HEZEKIAH BUTTERWORTH

BETTER times came at last, but Plymouth Colony was soon over-
shadowed by a far more wealthy and vigorous neighbor, founded by
the powerful Puritan party, which had secured a grant for a trading
company, the grant including a strip of land across the continent
from a line three miles north of the Merrimac to another three miles

south of the Charles — no one suspecting that this strip was three thousand miles long! It was into this colony, known as Massachusetts, that the older colony of Plymouth was finally absorbed..

THE PILGRIM FATHERS

THE Pilgrim Fathers — where are they?
　　The waves that brought them o'er
Still roll in the bay, and throw their spray
　　As they break along the shore;
Still roll in the bay, as they rolled that day
　　When the Mayflower moored below;
When the sea around was black with storms,
　　And white the shore with snow.

The mists that wrapped the Pilgrim's sleep
　　Still brood upon the tide;
And his rocks yet keep their watch by the deep
　　To stay its waves of pride.
But the snow-white sail that he gave to the gale,
　　When the heavens looked dark, is gone —
As an angel's wing through an opening cloud
　　Is seen, and then withdrawn.

The pilgrim exile — sainted name!
　　The hill whose icy brow
Rejoiced, when he came, in the morning's flame,
　　In the morning's flame burns now.
And the moon's cold light, as it lay that night
　　On the hillside and the sea,
Still lies where he laid his houseless head —
　　But the Pilgrim! where is he?

The Pilgrim Fathers are at rest:
　　When summer's throned on high,
And the world's warm breast is in verdure drest,
　　Go, stand on the hill where they lie.
The earliest ray of the golden day
　　On that hallowed spot is cast;

And the evening sun, as he leaves the world,
    Looks kindly on that spot last.

The Pilgrim spirit has not fled:
    It walks in noon's broad light;
And it watches the bed of the glorious dead,
    With the holy stars by night.
It watches the bed of the brave who have bled,
    And still guard this ice-bound shore,
Till the waves of the bay, where the Mayflower lay,
    Shall foam and freeze no more.

JOHN PIERPONT

KING CHARLES welcomed the chance to get rid of the Puritans and
confirmed the grant by a royal charter to "The Governor and Com-
pany of the Massachusetts-Bay in New England." John Winthrop
was elected governor, sailed for America April 7, 1630, and arrived
at Salem June 12. It was the beginning of a great emigration. In
the four months that followed, seventeen ships arrived, with nearly
a thousand colonists.

THE THANKSGIVING IN BOSTON HARBOR

[June 12, 1630]

"PRAISE ye the Lord!" The psalm today
    Still rises on our ears,
Borne from the hills of Boston Bay
    Through five times fifty years,
When Winthrop's fleet from Yarmouth crept
    Out to the open main,
And through the widening waters swept,
    In April sun and rain.
        "Pray to the Lord with fervent lips,"
        The leader shouted, "pray";
    And prayer arose from all the ships
        As faded Yarmouth Bay.

They passed the Scilly Isles that day,
　And May-days came, and June,
And thrice upon the ocean lay
　The full orb of the moon.
And as that day, on Yarmouth Bay,
　Ere England sunk from view,
While yet the rippling Solent lay
　In April skies of blue,
　　"Pray to the Lord with fervent lips,"
　　　Each morn was shouted, "pray";
　　And prayer arose from all the ships,
　　　As first in Yarmouth Bay;

Blew warm the breeze o'er Western seas,
　Through Maytime morns, and June,
Till hailed these souls the Isles of Shoals,
　Low 'neath the summer moon;
And as Cape Ann arose to view,
　And Norman's Woe they passed,
The wood-doves came the white mists through,
　And circled round each mast.
　　"Pray to the Lord with fervent lips,"
　　　Then called the leader, "pray";
　　And prayer arose from all the ships,
　　　As first in Yarmouth Bay.

Above the sea the hill-tops fair —
　God's towers — began to rise,
And odors rare breathe through the air,
　Like balms of Paradise.
Through burning skies the ospreys flew,
　And near the pine-cooled shores
Danced airy boat and thin canoe,
　To flash of sunlit oars.
　　"Pray to the Lord with fervent lips,"
　　　The leader shouted, "pray!"
　　Then prayer arose, and all the ships
　　　Sailed into Boston Bay.

The white wings folded, anchors down,
　　The sea-worn fleet in line,
Fair rose the hills where Boston town
　　Should rise from clouds of pine:
Fair was the harbor, summit-walled,
　　And placid lay the sea.
"Praise ye the Lord," the leader called;
　　"Praise ye the Lord," spake he.
　　"Give thanks to God with fervent lips,
　　　　Give thanks to God today,"
　　The anthem rose from all the ships,
　　　　Safe moored in Boston Bay....

　　　　　　　　　　HEZEKIAH BUTTERWORTH

BUT food was soon so scarce that shell-fish served for meat and acorns for bread. Winthrop had foreseen this and had sent Captain William Pierce, with the ship Lion, to Ireland for provisions, but nothing could be obtained there, and Pierce was forced to go on to London. A fast was appointed for February 22, 1631, to implore divine succor. On the 21st, as Winthrop "was distributing the last handful of meal in the barrel unto a poor man distressed with the wolf at the door," a ship sailed into the harbor. It was the Lion, laden with provisions, and the fast-day was changed into a day of feasting and thanksgiving.

THE FIRST THANKSGIVING

[February 22, 1631]

IT WAS Captain Pierce of the Lion who strode the streets of
　　London,
Who stalked the streets in the blear of morn and growled
　　in his grisly beard;
By Neptune! quoth this grim sea-dog, I fear that my master's
　　undone!
'Tis a bitter thing if all for naught through the drench of the
　　deep I've steered!

He had come from out of the ultimate West through the
    spinning drift and the smother,
  Come for a guerdon of golden grain for a hungry land afar;
And he thought of many a wasting maid, and of many a sad-
    eyed mother,
  And how their gaze would turn and turn for a sail at the
    harbor bar.

But famine lay on the English isle, and grain was a hoarded
    treasure,
  So ruddy the coin must gleam to loose the lock of the store-
    house door;
And under his breath the Captain groaned because of his
    meager measure,
  And the grasping souls of those that held the keys to the
    precious store.

But he flung a laugh and a fleer at doubt, and braving the
    roaring city
  He faced them out — those moiling men whose greed had
    grown to a curse —
Till at last he found in the strenuous press a heart that was
    moved to pity,
  And he gave the Governor's bond and word for what he
    lacked in his purse.

So the Lion put her prow to the West in the wild and windy
    weather,
  Her sails all set, though her decks were wet with the
    driving scud and the foam;
Never an hour would the Captain hold his staunch little
    craft in tether,
  For the haunting thought of hungry eyes was the lure that
    called him home.

Sooth, in the streets of Boston-Town was the heavy sound
    of sorrow,
  For an iron frost had bound the wold, and the sky hung
    bleak and dread;

Despair sat dark on the face of him who dared to think of the
     morrow,
   When not a crust could the goodwife give if the children
     moaned for bread.

But hark, from the wintry waterside a loud and lusty cheering,
   That sweeps the sullen streets of the town as a wave the
     level strand!
A sail! a sail! upswelled the cry, speeding the vessel steering
   Out of the vast of the misty sea in to the waiting land.

Turn the dimming page of the past that the dust of the years
     is dry on,
   And see the tears in the eyes of Joy as the ship draws in to
     the shore,
And see the genial glow on the face of Captain Pierce of the
     Lion,
   As the Governor grips his faithful hand and blesses him
     o'er and o'er!

Oh, the rapture of that release! Feasting instead of fasting!
   Happiness in the heart of the home, and hope with its silver
     ray!
Oh, the songs of prayer and praise to the Lord God ever-
     lasting
   That mounted morn and noon and eve on that first Thanks-
     giving Day!
                                        CLINTON SCOLLARD

IN THE four years that followed, the worst hardships of the new
plantation were outlived and nearly four thousand colonists were
distributed among the twenty hamlets along and near the seashore.
The fight for a foothold in the wilderness had been won.

OUR COUNTRY

ON PRIMAL rocks she wrote her name;
   Her towers were reared on holy graves;

The golden seed that bore her came
   Swift-winged with prayer o'er ocean waves.

The Forest bowed his solemn crest,
   And open flung his sylvan doors;
Meek Rivers led the appointed guest
   To clasp the wide-embracing shores;

Till, fold by fold, the broidered land
   To swell her virgin vestments grew,
While sages, strong in heart and hand,
   Her virtue's fiery girdle drew.

O Exile of the wrath of kings!
   O Pilgrim Ark of Liberty!
The refuge of divinest things,
   Their record must abide in thee!

First in the glories of thy front
   Let the crown-jewel, Truth, be found;
Thy right hand fling, with generous wont,
   Love's happy chain to farthest bound!

Let Justice, with the faultless scales,
   Hold fast the worship of thy sons;
Thy Commerce spread her shining sails
   Where no dark tide of rapine runs!

So link thy ways to those of God,
   So follow firm the heavenly laws,
That stars may greet thee, warrior-browed,
   And storm-sped angels hail thy cause!

O Lord, the measure of our prayers,
   Hope of the world in grief and wrong,
Be thine the tribute of the years,
   The gift of Faith, the crown of Song!
                 JULIA WARD HOWE

CHAPTER IV

THE STRUGGLE FOR THE CONTINENT

WHILE England was colonizing the Atlantic seaboard, France was establishing herself along the St. Lawrence, and it was evident that sooner or later there would be a life-and-death struggle for the continent. In 1690 (King William's War), the French, descending from Canada, undertook the conquest of New York, but were finally defeated at La Prairie, south of Montreal.

THE BATTLE OF LA PRAIRIE

[1691]

THAT was a brave old epoch,
　　Our age of chivalry,
When the Briton met the Frenchman
　　At the fight of La Prairie;
And the manhood of New England,
　　And the Netherlanders true
And Mohawks sworn, gave battle
　　To the Bourbon's lilied blue.

That was a brave old governor
　　Who gathered his array,
And stood to meet, he knew not what,
　　On that alarming day.
Eight hundred, amid rumors vast
　　That filled the wild wood's gloom,
With all New England's flower of youth,
　　Fierce for New France's doom....

And those were brave old orders
　　The colonel gave to meet
That forest force with trees entrenched
　　Opposing the retreat:

"De Callière's strength's behind us,
    And in front your Richelieu;
We must go straightforth at them;
    There is nothing else to do."

And then the brave old story comes,
    Of Schuyler and Valrenne,
When "Fight" the British colonel called,
    Encouraging his men,
"For the Protestant Religion
    And the honor of our King!" —
"Sir, I am here to answer you!"
    Valrenne cried, forthstepping.

Were not those brave old races?
    Well, here they still abide;
And yours is one or other,
    And the second's at your side;
So when you hear your brother say,
    "Some loyal deed I'll do,"
Like old Valrenne, be ready with
    "I'm here to answer you!"
        WILLIAM DOUW SCHUYLER-LIGHTHALL

ON AUGUST 29, 1708, a party of French and Indians surprised the town of Haverhill (or Pentucket, as the Indians called it), rushing upon it, as was their custom, just before daylight. They fired the place and murdered some forty of the inhabitants, but were finally driven off after their leader, Hertel de Rouville, had been killed.

PENTUCKET

[August 29, 1708]

How sweetly on the wood-girt town
The mellow light of sunset shone!
Each small, bright lake, whose waters still
Mirror the forest and the hill.

Reflected from its waveless breast
The beauty of a cloudless west,
Glorious as if a glimpse were given
Within the western gates of heaven,
Left, by the spirit of the star
Of sunset's holy hour, ajar!...

Quiet and calm without a fear
Of danger darkly lurking near,
The weary laborer left his plow,
The milkmaid caroled by her cow;
From cottage door and household hearth
Rose songs of praise, or tones of mirth.
At length the murmur died away,
And silence on that village lay.
— So slept Pompeii, tower and hall,
Ere the quick earthquake swallowed all,
Undreaming of the fiery fate
Which made its dwellings desolate!

Hours passed away.   By moonlight sped
The Merrimac along his bed.
Bathed in the pallid luster, stood
Dark cottage-wall and rock and wood,
Silent, beneath that tranquil beam,
As the hushed grouping of a dream.
Yet on the still air crept a sound,
No bark of fox, nor rabbit's bound,
No stir of wings, nor waters flowing,
Nor leaves in midnight breezes blowing.

Was that the tread of many feet,
Which downward from the hillside beat?
What forms were those which darkly stood
Just on the margin of the wood?
Charred tree-stumps in the moonlight dim,
Or paling rude, or leafless limb?
No — through the trees fierce eyeballs glowed,
Dark human forms in moonshine showed,

Wild from their native wilderness,
With painted limbs and battle-dress!

A yell the dead might wake to hear
Swelled on the night air, far and clear;
Then smote the Indian tomahawk
On crashing door and shattering lock;
Then rang the rifle-shot, and then
The shrill death-scream of stricken men —
Sank the red axe in woman's brain,
And childhood's cry arose in vain.
Bursting through roof and window came,
Red, fast, and fierce, the kindled flame,
And blended fire and moonlight glared
On still dead men and scalp-knives bared.

The morning sun looked brightly through
The river willows, wet with dew.
No sound of combat filled the air,
No shout was heard, nor gunshot there;
Yet still the thick and sullen smoke
From smouldering ruins slowly broke;
And on the greensward many a stain,
And, here and there, the mangled slain,
Told how that midnight bolt had sped,
Pentucket, on thy fated head!

Even now the villager can tell
Where Rolfe beside his hearthstone fell,
Still show the door of wasting oak,
Through which the fatal death-shot broke,
And point the curious stranger where
De Rouville's corse lay grim and bare;
Whose hideous head, in death still feared,
Bore not a trace of hair or beard;
And still, within the churchyard ground,
Heaves darkly up the ancient mound,
Whose grass-grown surface overlies
The victims of that sacrifice.

JOHN GREENLEAF WHITTIER

INDECISIVE raids continued for twenty years longer, but finally the British gained a notable victory by capturing the formidable fortress of Louisburg, which the French had built on Cape Breton Island. Louis XV determined on revenge and sent a strong fleet to bombard Boston. The town was panic-stricken, but the fleet was dispersed by a great storm off Cape Sable, October 15, 1746, and such of the ships as survived made their way back to France.

A BALLAD OF THE FRENCH FLEET

[October 15, 1746]

MR. THOMAS PRINCE, *loquitur*

A FLEET with flags arrayed
   Sailed from the port of Brest,
And the Admiral's ship displayed
   The signal: "Steer southwest."
For this Admiral D'Anville
   Had sworn by cross and crown
To ravage with fire and steel
   Our helpless Boston Town.

There were rumors in the street,
   In the houses there was fear
Of the coming of the fleet,
   And the danger hovering near.
And while from mouth to mouth
   Spread the tidings of dismay,
I stood in the Old South,
   Saying humbly: "Let us pray!

"O Lord! we would not advise;
   But if in thy Providence
A tempest should arise
   To drive the French Fleet hence,
And scatter it far and wide,
   Or sink it in the sea,
We should be satisfied,
   And thine the glory be."

This was the prayer I made,
　For my soul was all on flame,
And even as I prayed
　The answering tempest came;
It came with a mighty power,
　Shaking the windows and walls,
And tolling the bell in the tower,
　As it tolls at funerals.

The lightning suddenly
　Unsheathed its flaming sword,
And I cried: "Stand still, and see
　The salvation of the Lord!"
The heavens were black with cloud,
　The sea was white with hail,
And ever more fierce and loud
　Blew the October gale.

The fleet it overtook,
　And the broad sails in the van
Like the tents of Cushan shook,
　Or the curtains of Midian.
Down on the reeling decks
　Crashed the o'erwhelming seas;
Ah, never were there wrecks
　So pitiful as these!

Like a potter's vessel broke
　The great ships of the line;
They were carried away as a smoke,
　Or sank like lead in the brine.
O Lord! before thy path
　They vanished and ceased to be,
When thou didst walk in wrath
　With thine horses through the sea!
HENRY WADSWORTH LONGFELLOW

THE French claimed all the country west of the Alleghanies, and built a string of forts there, among them Fort Duquesne, at the head of the Ohio.   In February, 1755, General Edward Braddock, a celebrated soldier, landed at Hampton, Virginia, and proceeded to organize an expedition to march against Fort Duquesne.   George Washington was made one of his aides.   On May 29 the army began its long journey across the mountains, confident of victory.

THE SONG OF BRADDOCK'S MEN

[May 29, 1755]

To ARMS, to arms! my jolly grenadiers!
   Hark, how the drums do roll it along!
To horse, to horse, with valiant good cheer;
   We'll meet our proud foe before it is long.
     Let not your courage fail you;
      Be valiant, stout and bold;
     And it will soon avail you,
      My loyal hearts of gold.
Huzzah, my valiant countrymen! again I say huzzah!
'Tis nobly done — the day's our own — huzzah, huzzah!

March on, march on, brave Braddock leads the foremost;
   The battle is begun as you may fairly see.
Stand firm, be bold, and it will soon be over;
   We'll soon gain the field from our proud enemy.
     A squadron now appears, my boys;
      If that they do but stand!
     Boys, never fear, be sure you mind
      The word of command!
Huzzah, my valiant countrymen! again I say huzzah!
'Tis nobly done — the day's our own — huzzah, huzzah!

See how, see how, they break and fly before us!
   See how they are scattered all over the plain!
Now, now — now, now our country will adore us!
   In peace and in triumph, boys, when we return again!

Then laurels shall be our glory crown
    For all our actions told:
The hills shall echo all around,
    My loyal hearts of gold.
Huzzah, my valiant countrymen! again I say huzzah!
'Tis nobly done — the day's our own — huzzah, huzzah!

UNKNOWN

BRADDOCK reached the Monongahela July 8, and next morning, with colors flying and drums beating, marched against the fort. The French were ready for flight, but a young captain named Beaujeu obtained permission to take out a small party, mostly Indians, to harass the advancing column. They encountered the British marching along a narrow road which their pioneers had cut through the forest, and opened fire, spreading along either flank. The British soldiers were thrown into confusion. They could not see the enemy, and when they tried to seek shelter, were beaten back into line by Braddock. At last a bullet struck him down, and his troops fled in disorder.

NED BRADDOCK

[July 9, 1755]

SAID the Sword to the Axe, 'twixt the whacks and the hacks,
"Who's your bold Berserker, cleaving of tracks?
Hewing a highway through greenwood and glen,
Foot-free for cattle and heart-free for men?"
— "Braddock of Fontenoy, stubborn and grim,
Carving a cross on the wilderness rim;
In his own doom building large for the Lord,
Steeple and State!" said the Axe to the Sword.

Said the Blade to the Axe, "And shall none say him Nay?
Never a broadsword to bar him the way?
Never a bush where a Huron may hide,
Or the shot of a Shawnee spit red on his side?"
— Down the long trail from the Fort to the ford,
Naked and streaked, plunge a moccasined horde:

Huron and Wyandot, hot for the bout;
Shawnee and Ottawa, barring him out!

Red'ning the ridge, 'twixt a gorge and a gorge,
Bold to the sky, loom the ranks of Saint George;
Braddock of Fontenoy, belted and horsed,
For a foe to be struck and a pass to be forced.
— 'Twixt the pit and the crest, 'twixt the rocks and the
      grass,
Where the bush hides the foe, and the foe holds the pass,
Beaujeu and Pontiac, striving amain;
Huron and Wyandot, jeering the slain!

Beaujeu, bon camarade! Beaujeu the Gay!
Beaujeu and Death cast their blades in the fray.
Never a rifle that spared when they spoke,
Never a scalp-knife that balked in its stroke.
Till the red hillocks marked where the standards had danced,
And the Grenadiers gasped where their sabers had glanced.
— But Braddock raged fierce in that storm by the ford,
And railed at his "curs" with the flat of his sword!

Said the Sword to the Axe, "Where's your Berserker now?
Lo! his bones mark a path for a countryman's cow.
And Beaujeu the Gay? Give him place, right or wrong,
In your tale of a camp, or your stave of a song."
— "But Braddock of Fontenoy, stubborn and grim,
Who but he carved a cross on the wilderness rim?
In his own doom building large for the Lord,
Steeple and State!" said the Axe to the Sword.

JOHN WILLIAMSON PALMER

THREE years later, the British captured Fort Duquesne, renaming
it Fort Pitt, and in 1759, an expedition under General James Wolfe
captured Quebec, ending French dominion in America. The first

act of the drama was finished, but the day was at hand when the New World was to witness the birth of a New Nation.

AMERICA

[*From* "England and America"]

OH, WHO has not heard of the Northmen of yore,
How flew, like the sea-bird, their sails from the shore;
How, westward, they stayed not till, breasting the brine,
They hailed Narragansett, the land of the vine!

Then the war-songs of Rollo, his pennon and glaive,
Were heard as they danced by the moon-lighted wave,
And their golden-haired wives bore them sons of the soil,
While raged with the redskins their feud and turmoil.

And who has not seen, 'mid the summer's gay crowd,
That old pillared tower of their fortalice proud,
How it stands solid proof of the sea chieftains' reign
Ere came with Columbus those galleys of Spain!

'Twas a claim for their kindred: an earnest of sway,
By the stout-hearted Cabot made good in its day;
Of the Cross of St. George, on the Chesapeake's tide,
Where lovely Virginia arose like a bride.

Came the Pilgrims with Winthrop; and, saint of the West,
Came Robert of Jamestown, the brave and the blest;
Came Smith, the bold rover, and Rolfe — with his ring,
To wed sweet Matoäka, child of a king.

Undaunted they came, every peril to dare,
Of tribes fiercer far than the wolf in his lair;
Of the wild irksome woods, where in ambush they lay;
Of their terror by night and their arrow by day.

And so where our capes cleave the ice of the poles,
Where groves of the orange scent sea-coast and shoals,
Where the froward Atlantic uplifts its last crest,
Where the sun, when he sets, seeks the East from the West;

The clime that from ocean to ocean expands,
The fields to the snowdrifts that stretch from the sands,
The wilds they have conquered of mountain and plain —
Those Pilgrims have made them fair Freedom's domain.

And the bread of dependence if proudly they spurned,
'Twas the soul of their fathers that kindled and burned,
'Twas the blood of old Saxon within them that ran;
They held — to be free is the birthright of man.

So oft the old lion, majestic of mane,
Sees cubs of his cave breaking loose from his reign;
Unmeet to be his if they braved not his eye,
He gave them the spirit his own to defy.

ARTHUR CLEVELAND COXE

Harper's Magazine, December, 1876.

PART II
THE NEW NATION

FLAWLESS HIS HEART

[*From* "Ode for the Fourth of July, 1876"]

FLAWLESS his heart and tempered to the core
Who, beckoned by the forward-leaning wave,
First left behind him the firm-footed shore,
And, urged by every nerve of sail and oar,
Steered for the Unknown which gods to mortals gave,
Of thought and action the mysterious door,
Bugbear of fools, a summons to the brave:
Strength found he in the unsympathizing sun,
And strange stars from beneath the horizon won,
And the dumb ocean pitilessly grave:
High-hearted surely he;
But bolder they who first off-cast
Their moorings from the habitable Past
And ventured chartless on the sea
Of storm-engendering Liberty:
For all earth's width of waters is a span,
And their convulsed existence mere repose,
Matched with the unstable heart of man,
Shoreless in wants, mist-girt in all it knows,
Open to every wind of sect or clan,
And sudden-passionate in ebbs and flows.

JAMES RUSSELL LOWELL

CHAPTER I

THE BURSTING OF THE STORM

As soon as the French were disposed of, the British Government set seriously to work to regulate the affairs of the American colonies, which were considered to be sadly lacking in respect for the mother country, if not actually rebellious. In 1768 many new taxes were imposed, among them one on tea. On the night of Tuesday, December 16, 1773, a band of about twenty men, disguised as Indians, boarded three ships laden with tea anchored in Boston Harbor, ripped open the tea-chests and flung their contents into the water.

A BALLAD OF THE BOSTON TEA-PARTY

[December 16, 1773]

No! NEVER such a draught was poured
    Since Hebe served with nectar
The bright Olympians and their Lord,
    Her over-kind protector —
Since Father Noah squeezed the grape
    And took to such behaving
As would have shamed our grandsire ape
    Before the days of shaving —
No! ne'er was mingled such a draught
    In palace, hall, or arbor,
As freemen brewed and tyrants quaffed
    That night in Boston Harbor!...

An evening party — only that,
    No formal invitation,
No gold-laced coat, no stiff cravat,
    No feast in contemplation,
No silk-robed dames, no fiddling band,
    No flowers, no songs, no dancing —
A tribe of red men, axe in hand —
    Behold the guests advancing!...

On — on to where the tea-ships ride!
  And now their ranks are forming —
A rush, and up the Dartmouth's side
  The Mohawk band is swarming!
See the fierce natives! What a glimpse
  Of paint and fur and feather,
As all at once the full grown imps
  Light on the deck together!
A scarf the pigtail's secret keeps,
  A blanket hides the breeches —
And out the cursèd cargo leaps,
  And overboard it pitches!

O woman, at the evening board
  So gracious, sweet, and purring,
So happy while the tea is poured,
  So blest while spoons are stirring,
What martyr can compare with thee,
  The mother, wife, or daughter,
That night, instead of best Bohea,
  Condemned to milk and water!

Ah, little dreams the quiet dame
  Who plies with rock and spindle
The patient flax, how great a flame
  Yon little spark shall kindle!
The lurid morning shall reveal
  A fire no king can smother
Where British flint and Boston steel
  Have clashed against each other!
Old charters shrivel in its track,
  His Worship's bench has crumbled,
It climbs and clasps the union-jack,
  Its blazoned pomp is humbled,
The flags go down on land and sea
  Like corn before the reapers;
So burned the fire that brewed the tea
  That Boston served her keepers!

The waves that wrought a century's wreck
  Have rolled o'er whig and tory;
The Mohawks on the Dartmouth's deck
  Still live in song and story;
The waters in the rebel bay
  Have kept the tea-leaf savor;
Our old North-Enders in their spray
  Still taste a Hyson flavor;
And Freedom's teacup still o'erflows
  With ever fresh libations,
To cheat of slumber all her foes
  And cheer the wakening nations!
           OLIVER WENDELL HOLMES

THIS little insurrection became one of the most famous events in
American history. A hundred years later, its centennial was cele-
brated at Boston, and made memorable by a poem read by the
greatest man of letters in America.

BOSTON

THE rocky nook with hill-tops three
  Looked eastward from the farms,
And twice each day the flowing sea
  Took Boston in its arms;
The men of yore were stout and poor,
And sailed for bread to every shore.

And where they went on trade intent
  They did what freemen can,
Their dauntless ways did all men praise,
  The merchant was a man.
The world was made for honest trade —
To plant and eat be none afraid.

The waves that rocked them on the deep
  To them their secret told;

Said the winds that sung the lads to sleep,
  "Like us be free and bold!"
The honest waves refused to slaves
The empire of the ocean caves.

Old Europe groans with palaces,
  Has lords enough and more; —
We plant and build by foaming seas
  A city of the poor; —
For day by day could Boston Bay
Their honest labor overpay.

We grant no dukedoms to the few,
  We hold like rights, and shall; —
Equal on Sunday in the pew,
  On Monday in the mall,
For what avail the plow or sail,
Or land or life, if freedom fail? ...

Bad news from George on the English throne;
  "You are thriving well," said he;
"Now by these presents be it known
  You shall pay us a tax on tea;
'Tis very small — no load at all —
Honor enough that we send the call."

"Not so," said Boston, "good my lord,
  We pay your governors here
Abundant for their bed and board,
  Six thousand pounds a year.
(Your Highness knows our homely word,)
  Millions for self-government,
But for tribute never a cent."

The cargo came! and who could blame
  If *Indians* seized the tea,
And, chest by chest, let down the same
  Into the laughing sea?

For what avail the plow or sail,
Or land or life, if freedom fail? ...

Kings shook with fear, old empires crave
   The secret force to find
Which fired the little State to save
   The rights of all mankind.

But right is might through all the world;
   Province to province faithful clung,
Through good and ill the war-bolt hurled,
   Till Freedom cheered and joy-bells rung....
              RALPH WALDO EMERSON

THE insurrection enraged the British Government and reprisals were at once undertaken. No ships were to be allowed to enter the port of Boston until the rebellious town had repaid the East India Company for the loss of the tea; the charter of Massachusetts was annulled, and four regiments of British troops, under General Gage, were sent to take possession of the town.

HOW WE BECAME A NATION

[April 15, 1774]

WHEN George the King would punish folk
   Who dared resist his angry will —
Resist him with their hearts of oak
That neither King nor Council broke —
   He told Lord North to mend his quill,
   And sent his Parliament a Bill.

The Boston Port Bill was the thing
   He flourished in his royal hand;
A subtle lash with scorpion sting,
Across the seas he made it swing,
   And with its cruel thong he planned
   To quell the disobedient land.

His minions heard it sing, and bare
　　The port of Boston felt his wrath;
They let no ship cast anchor there,
They summoned Hunger and Despair —
　　And curses in an aftermath
　　Followed their desolating path.

No coal might enter there, nor wood,
　　Nor Holland flax, nor silk from France;
No drugs for dying pangs, no food
For any mother's little brood.
　　"Now," said the King, "we have our chance,
　　We'll lead the haughty knaves a dance."

No other flags lit up the bay,
　　Like full-blown blossoms in the air,
Than where the British war-ships lay;
The wharves were idle; all the day
　　The idle men, grown gaunt and spare,
　　Saw trouble, pall-like, everywhere.

Then in across the meadow land,
　　From lonely farm and hunter's tent,
From fertile field and fallow strand,
Pouring it out with lavish hand,
　　The neighboring burghs their bounty sent,
　　And laughed at King and Parliament.

To bring them succor, Marblehead
　　Joyous her deep-sea fishing sought.
Her trees, with ringing stroke and tread,
Old many-rivered Newbury sped,
　　And Groton in her granaries wrought,
　　And generous flocks old Windham brought.

Rice from the Carolinas came,
　　Iron from Pennsylvania's forge,
And, with a spirit all aflame,
Tobacco-leaf and corn and game

The Midlands sent; and in his gorge
The Colonies defied King George!

And Hartford hung, in black array,
　　Her town-house, and at half-mast there
The flags flowed, and the bells all day
Tolled heavily; and far away
　　In great Virginia's solemn air
　　The House of Burgesses held prayer.

Down long glades of the forest floor
　　The same thrill ran through every vein,
And down the long Atlantic's shore;
Its heat the tyrant's fetters tore
　　And welded them through stress and strain
　　Of long years to a mightier chain.

That mighty chain with links of steel
　　Bound all the Old Thirteen at last,
Through one electric pulse to feel
The common woe, the common weal.
　　And that great day the Port Bill passed
　　Made us a nation hard and fast.
　　　　　　HARRIET PRESCOTT SPOFFORD

THE colonies realized that, in this crisis, they must act together,
and on September 5, 1774, a Continental Congress met at Philadel-
phia. After four weeks' deliberation, it agreed upon a declaration
of rights, protesting against taxation without representation, and
demanding the repeal of eleven oppressive acts of Parliament.

LIBERTY TREE

IN A chariot of light from the regions of day,
　　The Goddess of Liberty came;
Ten thousand celestials directed the way
　　And hither conducted the dame.

A fair budding branch from the gardens above,
    Where millions with millions agree,
She brought in her hand as a pledge of her love,
    And the plant she named *Liberty Tree.*

The celestial exotic struck deep in the ground,
    Like a native it flourished and bore;
The fame of its fruit drew the nations around,
    To seek out this peaceable shore.
Unmindful of names or distinction they came,
    For freemen like brothers agree;
With one spirit endued, they one friendship pursued,
    And their temple was *Liberty Tree.*

Beneath this fair tree, like the patriarchs of old,
    Their bread in contentment they ate,
Unvexed with the troubles of silver and gold,
    The cares of the grand and the great.
With timber and tar they Old England supplied,
    And supported her power on the sea;
Her battles they fought, without getting a groat,
    For the honor of *Liberty Tree.*

But hear, O ye swains, 'tis a tale most profane,
    How all the tyrannical powers,
Kings, Commons, and Lords, are uniting amain
    To cut down this guardian of ours;
From the east to the west blow the trumpet to arms
    Through the land let the sound of it flee,
Let the far and the near, all unite with a cheer,
    In defence of our *Liberty Tree.*

                  THOMAS PAINE

Pennsylvania Magazine, 1775.

MASSACHUSETTS was in a state of ferment. Daily, on every village green, drilled a company of minute-men — so named because they stood ready to respond at a moment's notice to their country's call. It was evident that a single incident might produce a general explosion, and the incident was not long in coming.

"PROPHECY"

[1774]

HAIL, happy Britain, Freedom's blest retreat,
Great is thy power, thy wealth, thy glory great,
But wealth and power have no immortal day,
For all things ripen only to decay.
And when that time arrives, the lot of all,
When Britain's glory, power and wealth shall fall;
Then shall thy sons by Fate's unchanged decree
In other worlds another Britain see,
And what thou art, America shall be.

GULIAN VERPLANCK

ORDERS were sent to General Gage to arrest Samuel Adams and John Hancock on a charge of treason. Gage learned they were to be at Lexington, and on the night of April 18, he dispatched a force of eight hundred men to seize them, and then to proceed to Concord and destroy some munitions collected there. The movement was conducted with great secrecy, but Joseph Warren divined its purpose, and sent Paul Revere by way of Charlestown to give the alarm.

PAUL REVERE'S RIDE

[April 18–19, 1775]

LISTEN, my children, and you shall hear
Of the midnight ride of Paul Revere,
On the eighteenth of April, in Seventy-five;
Hardly a man is now alive
Who remembers that famous day and year.

He said to his friend, "If the British march
By land or sea from the town tonight,
Hang a lantern aloft in the belfry arch
Of the North Church tower as a signal light —

One, if by land, and two, if by sea;
And I on the opposite shore will be,
Ready to ride and spread the alarm
Through every Middlesex village and farm,
For the country folk to be up and to arm."

Then he said, "Good night!" and with muffled oar
Silently rowed to the Charlestown shore,
Just as the moon rose over the bay,
Where swinging wide at her moorings lay
The Somerset, British man-of-war;
A phantom ship, with each mast and spar
Across the moon like a prison bar,
And a huge black hulk, that was magnified
By its own reflection in the tide.

Meanwhile, his friend, through alley and street,
Wanders and watches with eager ears,
Till in the silence around him he hears
The muster of men at the barrack door,
The sound of arms, and the tramp of feet,
And the measured tread of the grenadiers,
Marching down to their boats on the shore.

Then he climbed the tower of the Old North Church,
By the wooden stairs, with stealthy tread,
To the belfry-chamber overhead,
And startled the pigeons from their perch
On the somber rafters, that round him made
Masses and moving shapes of shade —
By the trembling ladder, steep and tall,
To the highest window in the wall,
Where he paused to listen and look down
A moment on the roofs of the town,
And the moonlight flowing over all.

Beneath, in the churchyard, lay the dead,
In their night-encampment on the hill,

Wrapped in silence so deep and still
That he could hear, like a sentinel's tread,
The watchful night-wind, as it went
Creeping along from tent to tent,
And seeming to whisper, "All is well!"
A moment only he feels the spell
Of the place and the hour, and the secret dread
Of the lonely belfry and the dead;
For suddenly all his thoughts are bent
On a shadowy something far away,
Where the river widens to meet the bay —
A line of black that bends and floats
On the rising tide, like a bridge of boats.

Meanwhile, impatient to mount and ride,
Booted and spurred, with a heavy stride
On the opposite shore walked Paul Revere.
Now he patted his horse's side,
Now gazed at the landscape far and near,
Then, impetuous, stamped the earth,
And turned and tightened his saddle-girth;
But mostly he watched with eager search
The belfry-tower of the Old North Church,
As it rose above the graves on the hill,
Lonely and spectral and somber and still.
And lo! as he looks, on the belfry's height
A glimmer, and then a gleam of light!
He springs to the saddle, the bridle he turns,
But lingers and gazes, till full on his sight
A second lamp in the belfry burns!

A hurry of hoofs in a village street,
A shape in the moonlight, a bulk in the dark,
And beneath, from the pebbles, in passing, a spark
Struck out by a steed flying fearless and fleet:
That was all! And yet, through the gloom and the light,
The fate of a nation was riding that night;
And the spark struck out by that steed, in his flight,
Kindled the land into flame with its heat.

He has left the village and mounted the steep,
And beneath him, tranquil and broad and deep,
Is the Mystic, meeting the ocean tides;
And under the alders that skirt its edge,
Now soft on the sand, now loud on the ledge,
Is heard the tramp of his steed as he rides.

It was twelve by the village clock,
When he crossed the bridge into Medford Town.
He heard the crowing of the cock,
And the barking of the farmer's dog,
And felt the damp of the river fog,
That rises after the sun goes down.

It was one by the village clock,
When he galloped into Lexington.
He saw the gilded weathercock
Swim in the moonlight as he passed,
And the meeting-house windows, blank and bare,
Gaze at him with a spectral glare,
As if they already stood aghast
At the bloody work they would look upon.

It was two by the village clock,
When he came to the bridge in Concord Town.
He heard the bleating of the flock,
And the twitter of birds among the trees,
And felt the breath of the morning breeze
Blowing over the meadows brown.
And one was safe and asleep in his bed
Who at the bridge would be first to fall,
Who that day would be lying dead,
Pierced by a British musket-ball.

You know the rest.   In the books you have read,
How the British Regulars fired and fled —
How the farmers gave them ball for ball,
From behind each fence and farm-yard wall,

Chasing the red-coats down the lane,
Then crossing the fields to emerge again
Under the trees at the turn of the road,
And only pausing to fire and load.

So through the night rode Paul Revere;
And so through the night went his cry of alarm
To every Middlesex village and farm —
A cry of defiance and not of fear,
A voice in the darkness, a knock at the door,
And a word that shall echo forevermore!
For, borne on the night wind of the Past,
Through all our history, to the last,
In the hour of darkness and peril and need,
The people will waken and listen to hear
The hurrying hoof-beats of that steed,
And the midnight message of Paul Revere.

HENRY WADSWORTH LONGFELLOW

REVERE galloped to Lexington and warned Hancock and Adams who left the town at daybreak. Meanwhile, the minute-men of the village had gathered, and when the vanguard of the British column came up, it was confronted by about fifty colonials under command of Captain John Parker. The British commander ordered them to disperse, and, as they stood motionless, gave the command to fire. His troops hesitated, but he discharged his own pistol and repeated the order, whereupon a deadly volley killed eight of the minute-men and wounded ten. At that moment the main body of the British arrived, and Captain Parker, seeing the folly of resistance, ordered his men to retire.

LEXINGTON

[April 19, 1775]

SLOWLY the mist o'er the meadow was creeping,
  Bright on the dewy buds glistened the sun,
When from his couch, while his children were sleeping,
  Rose the bold rebel and shouldered his gun.

Waving her golden veil
Over the silent dale,
Blithe looked the morning on cottage and spire;
Hushed was his parting sigh,
While from his noble eye
Flashed the last sparkle of liberty's fire.

On the smooth green where the fresh leaf is springing
Calmly the first-born of glory have met;
Hark! the death-volley around them is ringing!
Look! with their life-blood the young grass is wet!
Faint is the feeble breath,
Murmuring low in death,
"Tell to our sons how their fathers have died";
Nerveless the iron hand,
Raised for its native land,
Lies by the weapon that gleams at its side.

Over the hillsides the wild knell is tolling,
From their far hamlets the yeomanry come;
As through the storm-clouds the thunder-burst rolling,
Circles the beat of the mustering drum.
Fast on the soldier's path
Darken the waves of wrath —
Long have they gathered and loud shall they fall;
Red glares the musket's flash,
Sharp rings the rifle's crash,
Blazing and clanging from thicket and wall.

Gayly the plume of the horseman was dancing,
Never to shadow his cold brow again;
Proudly at morning the war-steed was prancing,
Reeking and panting he droops on the rein;
Pale is the lip of scorn,
Voiceless the trumpet horn,
Torn is the silken-fringed red cross on high;
Many a belted breast
Low on the turf shall rest
Ere the dark hunters the herd have passed by.

Snow-girdled crags where the hoarse wind is raving,
  Rocks where the weary floods murmur and wail,
Wilds where the fern by the furrow is waving,
  Reeled with the echoes that rode on the gale;
    Far as the tempest thrills
    Over the darkened hills,
Far as the sunshine streams over the plain,
    Roused by the tyrant band,
    Woke all the mighty land,
Girdled for battle, from mountain to main.

Green be the graves where her martyrs are lying!
  Shroudless and tombless they sunk to their rest,
While o'er their ashes the starry fold flying
  Wraps the proud eagle they roused from his nest.
    Borne on her Northern pine,
    Long o'er the foaming brine
Spread her broad banner to storm and to sun;
    Heaven keep her ever free,
    Wide as o'er land and sea
Floats the fair emblem her heroes have won!
OLIVER WENDELL HOLMES

THE British pressed on to Concord, but the greater part of the stores
had been hidden. Minute-men were gathering from all directions,
and the British, realizing the danger of their position, started to
retreat to Boston, but the minute-men, taking advantage of every
tree and hillock by the roadside, poured into the enemy a fire so
deadly that the retreat soon became a disorderly flight.

LEXINGTON

[1775]

No BERSERK thirst of blood had they,
  No battle-joy was theirs, who set
  Against the alien bayonet
Their homespun breasts in that old day.

Their feet had trodden peaceful ways;
    They loved not strife, they dreaded pain;
    They saw not, what to us is plain,
That God would make man's wrath His praise.

No seers were they, but simple men;
    Its vast results the future hid:
    The meaning of the work they did
Was strange and dark and doubtful then.

Swift as their summons came they left
    The plow mid-furrow standing still,
    The half-ground corn grist in the mill,
The spade in earth, the axe in cleft.

They went where duty seemed to call,
    They scarcely asked the reason why;
    They only knew they could but die,
And death was not the worst of all!

Of man for man the sacrifice,
    All that was theirs to give, they gave.
    The flowers that blossomed from their grave
Have sown themselves beneath all skies.

Their death-shot shook the feudal tower,
    And shattered slavery's chain as well;
    On the sky's dome, as on a bell,
Its echo struck the world's great hour.

That fateful echo is not dumb:
    The nations listening to its sound
    Wait, from a century's vantage-ground,
The holier triumphs yet to come —

The bridal time of Law and Love,
    The gladness of the world's release,
    When, war-sick, at the feet of Peace
The hawk shall nestle with the dove! —

The golden age of brotherhood
   Unknown to other rivalries
   Than of the mild humanities,
And gracious interchange of good,

When closer strand shall lean to strand,
   Till meet, beneath saluting flags,
   The eagle of our mountain-crags,
The lion of our Motherland!

JOHN GREENLEAF WHITTIER

SIXTY years later, a monument was raised to mark the spot where the first battle of the Revolution was fought, and in a poem composed for the occasion, Ralph Waldo Emerson coined the famous phrase, "the shot heard round the world."

CONCORD HYMN:

SUNG AT THE COMPLETION OF THE BATTLE MONUMENT APRIL 19, 1836

BY THE rude bridge that arched the flood,
   Their flag to April's breeze unfurled,
Here once the embattled farmers stood,
   And fired the shot heard round the world.

The foe long since in silence slept;
   Alike the conqueror silent sleeps;
And Time the ruined bridge has swept
   Down the dark stream which seaward creeps.

On this green bank, by this soft stream,
   We set today a votive stone;
That memory may their deed redeem,
   When, like our sires, our sons are gone.

Spirit that made those heroes dare
   To die, and leave their children free,
Bid Time and Nature gently spare
   The shaft we raise to them and thee.

RALPH WALDO EMERSON

CHAPTER II

The War Begins

THE news of the fight at Lexington thrilled the whole country, and a rustic army of twenty thousand men quickly gathered about Boston to besiege General Gage. Benedict Arnold suggested that expeditions be sent against the fortresses at Ticonderoga and Crown Point, the suggestion was adopted, and Arnold set out to raise a regiment among the Berkshire Hills. There he found that Ethan Allen, at the head of a force of Vermonters called the Green Mountain Boys, had already started for Ticonderoga.

THE GREEN MOUNTAIN BOYS

[May 9, 1775]

HERE halt we our march, and pitch our tent
    On the rugged forest-ground,
And light our fire with the branches rent
    By winds from the beeches round.
Wild storms have torn this ancient wood,
    But a wilder is at hand,
With hail of iron and rain of blood,
    To sweep and waste the land.

How the dark wood rings with voices shrill,
    That startle the sleeping bird!
Tomorrow eve must the voice be still,
    And the step must fall unheard.
The Briton lies by the blue Champlain,
    In Ticonderoga's towers,
And ere the sun rise twice again,
    Must they and the lake be ours.

Fill up the bowl from the brook that glides
    Where the fire-flies light the brake:
A ruddier juice the Briton hides
    In his fortress by the lake.

Build high the fire, till the panther leap
   From his lofty perch in flight,
And we'll strengthen our weary arms with sleep
   For the deeds of tomorrow night.
                     WILLIAM CULLEN BRYANT

ARNOLD overtook Allen on May 9, and accompanied the expedition
as a volunteer. At daybreak of the 10th, the two leaders, with
eighty-three men, crossed Lake Champlain and entered Ticonderoga
side by side. The garrison was completely surprised and surrend-
ered the stronghold without a blow.

THE SURPRISE AT TICONDEROGA

[May 10, 1775]

'TWAS May upon the mountains, and on the airy wing
Of every floating zephyr came pleasant sounds of spring —
Of robins in the orchards, brooks running clear and warm,
Or chanticleer's shrill challenge from busy farm to farm.

But, ranged in serried order, attent on sterner noise,
Stood stalwart Ethan Allen and his "Green Mountain
     Boys" —
Two hundred patriots listening, as with the ears of one,
To the echo of the muskets that blazed at Lexington!

"My comrades" — thus the leader spake to his gallant
     band —
"The key of all the Canadas is in King George's hand,
Yet, while his careless warders our slender armies mock,
Good Yankee swords — God willing — may pick his rusty
     lock!"

At every pass a sentinel was set to guard the way,
Lest the secret of their purpose some idle lip betray,
As on the rocky highway they marched with steady feet
To the rhythm of the brave hearts that in their bosoms beat.

The curtain of the darkness closed 'round them like a tent,
When, travel-worn and weary, yet not with courage spent,
They halted on the border of slumbering Champlain,
And saw the watch-lights glimmer across the glassy plain.

O proud Ticonderoga, enthroned amid the hills!
O bastions of old Carillon, the "Fort of Chiming Rills"!
Well might your quiet garrison have trembled where they
     lay,
And, dreaming, grasped their sabers against the dawn of
     day!

In silence and in shadow the boats were pushed from shore,
Strong hands laid down the musket to ply the muffled oar;
The startled ripples whitened and whispered in their wake,
Then sank again, reposing, upon the peaceful lake.

Fourscore and three they landed, just as the morning gray
Gave warning on the hilltops to rest not or delay;
Behind, their comrades waited, the fortress frowned before,
And the voice of Ethan Allen was in their ears once more:

"Soldiers, so long united — dread scourge of lawless power!
Our country, torn and bleeding, calls to this desperate hour.
One choice alone is left us, who hear that high behest —
To quit our claims to valor, or put them to the test!

"I lead the storming column up yonder fateful hill,
Yet not a man shall follow save at his ready will!
There leads no pathway backward — 'tis death or victory!
Poise each his trusty firelock, ye that will come with me!"

From man to man a tremor ran at their captain's word
(Like the "going" in the mulberry-trees that once King
     David heard) —
While his eagle glances sweeping adown the triple line,
Saw, in the glowing twilight, each even barrel shine!

"Right face, my men, and forward!" Low-spoken, swift-
    obeyed!
They mount the slope unfaltering — they gain the esplanade!
A single drowsy sentry beside the wicket-gate,
Snapping his aimless fusil, shouts the alarm — too late!

They swarm before the barracks — the quaking guards take
    flight,
And such a shout exultant resounds along the height,
As rang from shore and headland scarce twenty years ago,
When brave Montcalm's defenders charged on a British foe!

Leaps from his bed in terror the ill-starred Delaplace,
To meet across his threshold a wall he may not pass!
The bayonets' lightning flashes athwart his dazzled eyes,
And, in tones of sudden thunder, "Surrender!" Allen cries.

"Then in whose name the summons?" the ashen lips reply.
The mountaineer's stern visage turns proudly to the sky —
"In the name of great Jehovah!" he speaks with lifted
    sword,
"And the Continental Congress, who wait upon His word!"

Light clouds, like crimson banners, trailed bright across the
    east,
As the great sun rose in splendor above a conflict ceased,
Gilding the bloodless triumph for equal rights and laws.
As with the smile of heaven upon a holy cause

Still, wave on wave of verdure, the emerald hills arise,
Where once were heroes mustered from men of common guise,
And still, on Freedom's roster, through all her glorious years,
Shine the names of Ethan Allen and his bold volunteers!

MARY A. P. STANSBURY

THE Continental army, meanwhile, had established itself at Cam-
bridge, just outside of Boston, and was busy day and night drilling

and getting into shape.   It was at this time that a "gentleman of Connecticut," whose name, it is said, was Edward Bangs, described his visit to the camp in verses destined to become famous.

THE YANKEE'S RETURN FROM CAMP

[June, 1775]

FATHER and I went down to camp,
　　Along with Captain Gooding,
And there we see the men and boys,
　　As thick as hasty pudding.

Chorus — Yankee Doodle, keep it up,
　　　　Yankee Doodle, dandy,
　　　　Mind the music and the step,
　　　　And with the girls be handy.

And there we see a thousand men,
　　As rich as 'Squire David;
And what they wasted every day
　　I wish it could be savèd....

And there we see a swamping gun,
　　Large as a log of maple,
Upon a deucèd little cart,
　　A load for father's cattle.

And every time they shoot it off,
　　It takes a horn of powder,
And makes a noise like father's gun,
　　Only a nation louder....

I see a little barrel, too,
　　The heads were made of leather,
They knocked upon 't with little clubs
　　And called the folks together.

And there was Captain Washington,
    And gentlefolks about him,
They say he's grown so tarnal proud
    He will not ride without 'em.

He got him on his meeting clothes,
    Upon a strapping stallion,
He set the world along in rows,
    In hundreds and in millions....

I see another snarl of men
    A-digging graves, they told me,
So tarnal long, so tarnal deep,
    They 'tended they should hold me.

It scared me so, I hooked it off,
    Nor stopped, as I remember,
Nor turned about, till I got home,
    Locked up in mother's chamber.
                  EDWARD BANGS (?)

HEAVY British reënforcements were hurried to Boston and plans were made to extend the lines to cover the heights of Charlestown and Dorchester. The Americans heard of this, and during the night of June 16, a force of twelve hundred men under Colonel William Prescott, took possession of Bunker Hill, in Charlestown, and then pushed on to Breed's Hill, and threw up rude entrenchments there.

THE EVE OF BUNKER HILL

[June 16, 1775]

'TWAS June on the face of the earth, June with the rose's
    breath,
When life is a gladsome thing, and a distant dream is death;
There was gossip of birds in the air, and a lowing of herds
    by the wood,
And a sunset gleam in the sky that the heart of a man holds
    good;

Then the nun-like Twilight came, violet-vestured and still,
And the night's first star outshone afar on the eve of Bunker
Hill.

There rang a cry through the camp, with its word upon
rousing word;
There was never a faltering foot in the ranks of those that
heard; —
Lads from the Hampshire hills, and the rich Connecticut
vales,
Sons of the old Bay Colony, from its shores and its inland
dales;
Swiftly they fell in line; no fear could their valor chill;
Ah, brave the show as they ranged a-row on the eve of
Bunker Hill!

Then a deep voice lifted a prayer to the God of the brave and
the true,
And the heads of the men were bare in the gathering dusk
and dew;
The heads of a thousand men were bowed as the pleading
rose —
Smite Thou, Lord, as of old Thou smotest Thy people's foes!
Oh, nerve Thy servants' arms to work with a mighty will!
A hush, and then a loud *Amen!* on the eve of Bunker Hill!

Now they are gone through the night with never a thought
of fame,
Gone to the field of a fight that shall win them a deathless
name;
Some shall never again behold the set of the sun,
But lie like the Concord slain, and the slain of Lexington,
Martyrs to Freedom's cause. Ah, how at their deeds we
thrill,
The men whose might made strong the height on the eve of
Bunker Hill!

CLINTON SCOLLARD

THE entrenchments were discovered at dawn by the British, and a force of three thousand veterans was ordered forward to rout out the "peasants." At three o'clock in the afternoon, they were ready to attack, and advanced steadily up the hill, only to be met by so terrific a fire that they gave way and retreated in disorder.

WARREN'S ADDRESS TO THE AMERICAN SOLDIERS

[June 17, 1775]

STAND! the ground's your own, my braves!
Will ye give it up to slaves?
Will ye look for greener graves?
    Hope ye mercy still?
What's the mercy despots feel?
Hear it in that battle-peal!
Read it on yon bristling steel!
    Ask it — ye who will.

Fear ye foes who kill for hire?
Will ye to your homes retire?
Look behind you! they're a-fire!
    And, before you, see
Who have done it! — From the vale
On they come! — And will ye quail? —
Leaden rain and iron hail
    Let their welcome be!

In the God of battles trust!
Die we may — and die we must;
But, oh, where can dust to dust
    Be consigned so well,
As where Heaven its dews shall shed
On the martyred patriot's bed,
And the rocks shall raise their head,
    Of his deeds to tell!

JOHN PIERPONT

GENERAL HOWE re-formed his men and a second time sent them forward to the assault. Again the Americans held their fire, and then, at thirty yards, poured into the British so deadly a volley that again they broke and fled.

THE BALLAD OF BUNKER HILL

WE LAY in the Trenches we'd dug in the Ground
 While *Phœbus* blazed down from his glory-lined Car,
And then from the lips of our Leader renown'd,
 These lessons we learn'd in the *Science of War:*
   "Let the Foeman draw nigh,
   Till the white of his Eye
Is in range with your Rifles, and then, Lads, let fly!
And shew to *Columbia*, to *Britain*, and *Fame*,
How *Justice* smiles aweful, when *Freemen* take *aim!*"

The Regulars from Town to the Foot of the Hill
 Came in Barges and Rowboats, some great and some small,
But they potter'd and dawdl'd, and twaddled, until
 We fear'd there would be no *Attack* after all!
   Two men in red Coats
   Talk'd to one in long Boots,
And all of them *pinted* and *gestur'd* like *Coots*,
And we said — as the Boys do upon *Training-Day* —
"If they waste all their *Time* so, the *Sham fight* won't pay."

But when they got Ready, and All came along,
 The way they march'd up the *Hillside* wasn't slow,
But we were not a-fear'd, and we welcomed 'em strong,
 Held our *Fire* till the Word, and then laid the Lads low!
   ... But who shall declare
   The *End* of the Affair?
At Sundown there wasn't a Man of us there!
But we didn't depart till we'd given them *Some!*
When we burned up our Powder, we had to go *Home!*
       EDWARD EVERETT HALE

THERE was a long pause, but the British finally decided to make a third attempt, and at five o'clock it was ordered. Prescott, meanwhile, had discovered to his dismay that his supply of powder and ball was nearly exhausted. One volley was sent into the advancing British, the last cartridges were spent, and at the point of the bayonet the Americans were driven from their works and forced to retreat.

BUNKER HILL

"NOT yet, not yet; steady, steady!"
On came the foe, in even line:
Nearer and nearer to thrice paces nine.
We looked into their eyes. "Ready!"
A sheet of flame! A roll of death!
They fell by scores; we held our breath!
Then nearer still they came;
Another sheet of flame!
And brave men fled who never fled before.
Immortal fight!
Foreshadowing flight
Back to the astounded shore.

Quickly they rallied, reënforced.
'Mid louder roar of ship's artillery,
And bursting bombs and whistling musketry
And shouts and groans, anear, afar,
All the new din of dreadful war,
Through their broad bosoms calmly coursed
The blood of those stout farmers, aiming
For freedom, manhood's birthright claiming.
Onward once more they came;
Another sheet of deathful flame!
Another and another still:
They broke, they fled:
Again they sped
Down the green, bloody hill.

Howe, Burgoyne, Clinton, Gage,
Stormed with commander's rage.

Into each emptied barge
They crowd fresh men for a new charge
          Up that great hill.
Again their gallant blood we spill:
          That volley was the last:
              Our powder failed.
              On three sides fast
The foe pressed in; nor quailed
A man. Their barrels empty, with musket-stocks
          They fought, and gave death-dealing knocks,
              Till Prescott ordered the retreat.
Then Warren fell; and through a leaden sleet,
          From Bunker Hill and Breed,
Stark, Putnam, Pomeroy, Knowlton, Read,
Led off the remnant of those heroes true,
The foe too shattered to pursue.
          The ground they gained; but we
              The victory.

          The tidings of that chosen band
              Flowed in a wave of power
          Over the shaken, anxious land,
          To men, to man, a sudden dower.
          From that stanch, beaming hour
          History took a fresh, higher start;
And when the speeding messenger, that bare
          The news that strengthened every heart,
              Met near the Delaware
              Riding to take command,
          The leader, who had just been named,
              Who was to be so famed,
          The steadfast, earnest Washington
              With hand uplifted cries,
          His great soul flashing to his eyes,
"Our liberties are safe; the cause is won."
          A thankful look he cast to heaven, and then
His steed he spurred, in haste to lead such noble men.
                              GEORGE H. CALVERT

THE British had gained the victory, but the moral advantage was wholly with the Americans — they had proved that they could stand against British regulars. An irreparable loss, however, was the death of General Joseph Warren, who was shot through the head as he lingered on the field, loath to join in the retreat. He had hastened to the battle-field in the early morning, replying to the remonstrance of a friend, with the famous line from Horace, "*Dulce et decorum est pro patria mori.*"

THE DEATH OF WARREN

[June 17, 1775]

WHEN the war-cry of Liberty rang through the land,
To arms sprang our fathers the foe to withstand;
On old Bunker Hill their entrenchments they rear,
When the army is joined by a young volunteer.
"Tempt not death!" cried his friends; but he bade them
    good-bye,
Saying, "Oh! it is sweet for our country to die!"

The tempest of battle now rages and swells,
'Mid the thunder of cannon, the pealing of bells;
And a light, not of battle, illumes yonder spire —
Scene of woe and destruction; — 'tis Charlestown on fire!
The young volunteer heedeth not the sad cry,
But murmurs, "'Tis sweet for our country to die!"

With trumpets and banners the foe draweth near:
A volley of musketry checks their career!
With the dead and the dying the hillside is strown,
And the shout through our lines is, "The day is our own!"
"Not yet," cries the young volunteer, "do they fly!
Stand firm! — it is sweet for our country to die!"

Now our powder is spent, and they rally again; —
"Retreat!" says our chief, "since unarmed we remain!"
But the young volunteer lingers yet on the field,
Reluctant to fly, and disdaining to yield.
A shot! Ah! he falls! but his life's latest sigh
Is, "'Tis sweet, oh, 'tis sweet for our country to die!"

And thus Warren fell! Happy death! noble fall!
To perish for country at Liberty's call!
Should the flag of invasion profane evermore
The blue of our seas or the green of our shore,
May the hearts of our people reëcho that cry —
"'Tis sweet, oh, 'tis sweet for our country to die!"

EPES SARGENT

Two weeks after the battle of Bunker Hill, George Washington, who had been appointed commander-in-chief of the Continental army by the Congress then assembled at Philadelphia, arrived at Cambridge, and on the following day, under the shade of a great elm near Cambridge Common, took command of the sixteen thousand men composing the American forces.

THE NEW-COME CHIEF

[From "Under the Old Elm"]

[July 3, 1775]

BENEATH our consecrated elm
A century ago he stood,
Famed vaguely for that old fight in the wood
Whose red surge sought, but could not overwhelm
The life foredoomed to wield our rough-hewn helm: —
From colleges, where now the gown
To arms had yielded, from the town,
Our rude self-summoned levies flocked to see
The new-come chief and wonder which was he.
No need to question long; close-lipped and tall,
Long trained in murder-brooding forests lone
To bridle others' clamors and his own,
Firmly erect, he towered above them all,
The incarnate discipline that was to free
With iron curb that armed democracy.

A motley rout was that which came to stare,
In raiment tanned by years of sun and storm,

Of every shape that was not uniform,
Dotted with regimentals here and there;
An army all of captains, used to pray
And stiff in fight, but serious drill's despair,
Skilled to debate their orders, not obey;
Deacons were there, selectmen, men of note
In half-tamed hamlets ambushed round with woods,
Ready to settle Freewill by a vote,
But largely liberal to its private moods;
Prompt to assert by manners, voice, or pen,
Or ruder arms, their rights as Englishmen,
Nor much fastidious as to how and when:
Yet seasoned stuff and fittest to create
A thought-staid army or a lasting state:
Haughty they said he was, at first; severe;
But owned, as all men own, the steady hand
Upon the bridle, patient to command,
Prized, as all prize, the justice pure from fear,
And learned to honor first, then love him, then revere.
Such power there is in clear-eyed self-restraint
And purpose clean as light from every selfish taint....

JAMES RUSSELL LOWELL

ON THE night of March 4, 1776, Washington seized and fortified Dorchester Heights. The British realized that Boston was untenable unless the Americans could be dislodged, but, with the memory of Bunker Hill before them, decided to abandon the town. On March 17, the British troops sailed away for Halifax, and Washington took possession of the city.

OFF FROM BOSTON

SONS of valor, taste the glories
  Of celestial liberty,
Sing a triumph o'er the Tories,
  Let the pulse of joy beat high.

Heaven hath this day foiled the many
  Fallacies of George the King;
Let the echo reach Britan'y,
  Bid her mountain summits ring.

See yon navy swell the bosom
  Of the late enragèd sea;
Where'er they go, we shall oppose them,
  Sons of valor must be free.

Should they touch at fair Rhode Island,
  There to combat with the brave,
Driven from each dale and highland,
  They shall plow the purple wave.

Should they thence to fair Virginia,
  Bend a squadron to Dunmore,
Still with fear and ignominy,
  They shall quit the hostile shore.

To Carolina or to Georg'y,
  Should they next advance their fame,
This land of heroes shall disgorge the
  Sons of tyranny and shame....

In New York State, rejoined by Clinton,
  Should their standards mock the air,
Many a surgeon shall put lint on
  Wounds of death receivèd there.

War, fierce war, shall break their forces,
  Nerves of Tory men shall fail,
Seeing Howe, with altered courses,
  Bending to the western gale.

Thus from every bay of ocean,
  Flying back with sails unfurled,

Tossed with ever-troubled motion,
　They shall quit this smiling world.

Like Satan banishèd from heaven,
　Never see the smiling shore;
From this land, so happy, driven,
　Never stain its bosom more.

UNKNOWN

CHAPTER III

INDEPENDENCE

ON JUNE 8, 1776, Richard Henry Lee submitted to the Continental Congress a motion "That these United Colonies are, and of a right ought to be, free and independent States; that they are absolved from all allegiance to the British Crown; and that all political connection between them and the state of Great Britain is, and ought to be, totally dissolved." The debate on the motion began July 1.

RODNEY'S RIDE

[July 3, 1776]

IN THAT soft mid-land where the breezes bear
The North and South on the genial air,
Through the county of Kent, on affairs of state,
Rode Cæsar Rodney, the delegate.

Burly and big, and bold and bluff,
In his three-cornered hat and coat of snuff,
A foe to King George and the English State,
Was Cæsar Rodney, the delegate.

Into Dover village he rode apace,
And his kinsfolk knew, from his anxious face,
It was matter grave that brought him there,
To the counties three on the Delaware.

"Money and men we must have," he said,
"Or the Congress fails and our cause is dead;
Give us both and the King shall not work his will.
We are men, since the blood of Bunker Hill!"

Comes a rider swift on a panting bay:
"Ho, Rodney, ho! you must save the day,
For the Congress halts at a deed so great,
And your vote alone may decide its fate."

Answered Rodney then: "I will ride with speed;
It is Liberty's stress; it is Freedom's need.
When stands it?" "Tonight. Not a moment to spare,
But ride like the wind from the Delaware."

"Ho, saddle the black! I've but half a day,
And the Congress sits eighty miles away —
But I'll be in time, if God grants me grace,
To shake my fist in King George's face."

He is up; he is off! and the black horse flies
On the northward road ere the "God-speed" dies;
It is gallop and spur, as the leagues they clear,
And the clustering milestones move a-rear.

It is two of the clock; and the fleet hoofs fling
The Fieldboro's dust with a clang and a cling;
It is three; and he gallops with slack rein where
The road winds down to the Delaware.

Four; and he spurs into New Castle Town,
From his panting steed he gets him down —
'A fresh one, quick! not a moment's wait!"
And off speeds Rodney, the delegate.

It is five; and the beams of the western sun
Tinge the spires of Wilmington gold and dun;
Six; and the dust of Chester Street
Flies back in a cloud from the courser's feet.

It is seven; the horse-boat broad of beam,
At the Schuylkill ferry crawls over the stream —
And at seven-fifteen by the Rittenhouse clock,
He flings his reins to the tavern jock.

The Congress is met; the debate's begun,
And Liberty lags for the vote of one —
When into the hall, not a moment late,
Walks Cæsar Rodney, the delegate.

Not a moment late! and that half-day's ride
Forwards the world with a mighty stride;
For the act was passed; ere the midnight stroke
O'er the Quaker City its echoes woke.

At Tyranny's feet was the gauntlet flung;
"We are free!" all the bells through the colonies rung,
And the sons of the free may recall with pride
The day of Delegate Rodney's ride.

ELBRIDGE STREETER BROOKS

On July 2, the motion was put to a vote and carried, a committee
was appointed to draw up a paper which should be worthy the
occasion, and Thomas Jefferson, its chairman, was chosen to draft
the document. On the evening of July 4, 1776, the Declaration of
Independence was unanimously adopted.

THE FOURTH OF JULY

Day of glory! Welcome day!
Freedom's banners greet thy ray;
See! how cheerfully they play
　　With thy morning breeze,
On the rocks where pilgrims kneeled,
On the heights where squadrons wheeled,
When a tyrant's thunder pealed
　　O'er the trembling seas.

God of armies! did thy stars
On their courses smite his cars;
Blast his arm, and wrest his bars
　　From the heaving tide?
On our standard, lo! they burn,
And, when days like this return,
Sparkle o'er the soldier's urn
　　Who for freedom died.

God of peace! whose spirit fills
All the echoes of our hills,
All the murmur of our rills,
    Now the storm is o'er,
O let freemen be our sons,
And let future Washingtons
Rise, to lead their valiant ones
    Till there's war no more!

                        JOHN PIERPONT

THE sessions of the Congress had been held in the State House at
Philadelphia, and a few minutes after the Declaration was adopted,
so the story goes, the great bell in the State House tower was boom-
ing forth the news. This bell, the Liberty Bell, is still preserved
there, and the State House is now known as Independence Hall.

INDEPENDENCE BELL

THERE was tumult in the city,
    In the quaint old Quaker town,
And the streets were thronged with people
    Passing restless up and down —
People gathering at the corners,
    Where they whispered lip to ear,
While the sweat stood on their temples,
    With the stress of hope and fear.

As the bleak Atlantic currents
    Lash the wild Newfoundland shore,
So they beat about the State House,
    So they surged against the door;
And the mingling of their voices
    Swelled in harmony profound,
Till the quiet street of Chestnut
    Was all turbulent with sound.

"Will they do it?" "Dare they do it?"
    "Who is speaking?" "What's the news?"

"What of Adams?"   "What of Sherman?"
    "Oh, God grant they won't refuse!"
"Make some way, there!"   "Let me nearer!"
    "I am stifling!"   "Stifle then!
When a nation's life's at hazard
    We've no time to think of men!"

So they surged against the State House,
    While all solemnly inside
Sat the Continental Congress,
    Truth and reason for their guide;
O'er a simple scroll debating:
    Which, though simple it might be,
Yet should shake the cliffs of England
    With the thunders of the free.

Far aloft in the high steeple
    Sat the bellman, old and gray;
He was weary of the tyrant
    And his iron-sceptered sway.
So he sat with one hand ready
    On the clapper of the bell,
Till his eye should catch the signal,
    The expected news to tell.

See! See! the dense crowd quivers
    As beside the door a boy
Looks forth with hands uplifted,
    His eyes alight with joy.
Hushed the people's swelling murmur
    As they listen breathlessly —
"Ring!" he shouts; "ring, grandpapa!
    Ring! oh, ring for liberty!"

Quickly at the welcome signal
    The old bellman lifts his hand;
Forth he sends the good news, making
    Iron music through the land.

How they shouted! What rejoicing!
  How the old bell shook the air,
Till the clang of freedom echoed
  From the belfries everywhere.

The old State House bell is silent,
  Hushed is now its clamorous tongue,
But the spirit it awakened
  Still is living, ever young.
And we'll ne'er forget the bellman
  Who, that great day in July,
Hailed the birth of Independence,
  Which, please God, shall never die.

UNKNOWN

A NEW nation, the United States of America, had been born — the only country in the world to have such a birthday. Henceforth the people of the New World were not British but American.

COLUMBIA

COLUMBIA, Columbia, to glory arise,
The queen of the world, and the child of the skies;
Thy genius commands thee; with rapture behold,
While ages on ages thy splendor unfold,
Thy reign is the last, and the noblest of time,
Most fruitful thy soil, most inviting thy clime;
Let the crimes of the east ne'er encrimson thy name,
Be freedom, and science, and virtue thy fame.

To conquest and slaughter let Europe aspire:
Whelm nations in blood, and wrap cities in fire;
Thy heroes the rights of mankind shall defend,
And triumph pursue them, and glory attend.
A world is thy realm: for a world be thy laws,
Enlarged as thine empire, and just as thy cause;
On Freedom's broad basis, that empire shall rise,
Extend with the main, and dissolve with the skies.

Fair Science her gates to thy sons shall unbar,
And the east see the morn hide the beams of her star.
New bards, and new sages, unrivaled shall soar
To fame unextinguished, when time is no more;
To thee, the last refuge of virtue designed,
Shall fly from all nations the best of mankind;
Here, grateful to Heaven, with transport shall bring
Their incense, more fragrant than odors of spring....

Thy fleets to all regions thy power shall display,
The nations admire and the ocean obey;
Each shore to thy glory its tribute unfold,
And the east and the south yield their spices and gold.
As the day-spring unbounded, thy splendor shall flow,
And earth's little kingdoms before thee shall bow;
While the ensigns of union, in triumph unfurled,
Hush the tumult of war and give peace to the world.

Thus, as down a lone valley, with cedars o'er-spread,
From war's dread confusion I pensively strayed,
The gloom from the face of fair heaven retired;
The winds ceased to murmur; the thunders expired;
Perfumes as of Eden flowed sweetly along,
And a voice as of angels, enchantingly sung:
"Columbia, Columbia, to glory arise,
The queen of the world, and the child of the skies."

TIMOTHY DWIGHT

CHAPTER IV

THE FIRST CAMPAIGN

ENGLAND did not propose to lose her colonies without a struggle, and General Howe, with an army of twenty-five thousand men, prepared to attack New York. Washington had only eighteen thousand undisciplined levies, but on August 27, 1776, he made a stand on Brooklyn Heights. Howe prepared to besiege the position, and after nightfall of August 29, Washington succeeded in ferrying his entire force over to the New York side.

THE MARYLAND BATTALION

[August 27, 1776]

SPRUCE Macaronis, and pretty to see,
Tidy and dapper and gallant were we;
Blooded fine gentlemen, proper and tall,
Bold in a fox-hunt and gay at a ball;
Prancing soldados, so martial and bluff,
Billets for bullets, in scarlet and buff —
But our cockades were clasped with a mother's low prayer.
And the sweethearts that braided the swordknots were fair.

There was grummer of drums humming hoarse in the hills,
And the bugles sang fanfaron down by the mills,
By Flatbush the bagpipes were droning amain,
And keen cracked the rifles in Martense's lane;
For the Hessians were flecking the hedges with red,
And the Grenadiers' tramp marked the roll of the dead.

Three to one, flank and rear, flashed the files of Saint George,
The fierce gleam of their steel as the glow of a forge.
The brutal boom-boom of their swart cannoneers
Was sweet music compared with the taunt of their cheers —

For the brunt of their onset, our crippled array,
And the light of God's leading gone out in the fray!

Oh, the rout on the left and the tug on the right!
The mad plunge of the charge and the wreck of the flight!
When the cohorts of Grant held stout Stirling at strain,
And the mongrels of Hesse went tearing the slain;
When at Freeke's Mill the flumes and the sluices ran red,
And the dead choked the dyke and the marsh choked the
     dead!

"Oh, Stirling, good Stirling! How long must we wait?
Shall the shout of your trumpet unleash us too late?
Have you never a dash for brave Mordecai Gist,
With his heart in his throat, and his blade in his fist?
Are we good for no more than to prance in a ball,
When the drums beat the charge and the clarions call?"

Tralára! Tralára! Now praise we the Lord,
For the clang of His call and the flash of His sword!
Tralára! Tralára! Now forward to die;
For the banner, hurrah! and for sweethearts, good-bye!
"Four hundred wild lads!" Maybe so. I'll be bound
'Twill be easy to count us, face up, on the ground.
If we hold the road open, though Death take the toll,
We'll be missed on parade when the States call the roll —
When the flags meet in peace and the guns are at rest,
And fair Freedom is singing Sweet Home in the West.

                         JOHN WILLIAMSON PALMER

ON SEPTEMBER 16, the British took possession of New York, and
Washington withdrew to the line of the Harlem River. It was
important that he should obtain accurate information as to the
enemy position, and Captain Nathan Hale volunteered for the
dangerous service and passed into the British lines in disguise. He
was captured and taken before Sir William Howe, who at once

ordered him to be hanged. He was executed shortly after sunrise, September 22, 1776. His last words were the famous, "I only regret that I have but one life to lose for my country."

NATHAN HALE

[September 22, 1776]

To DRUM-BEAT and heart-beat,
　A soldier marches by;
There is color in his cheek,
　There is courage in his eye,
Yet to drum-beat and heart-beat
　In a moment he must die.

By the starlight and moonlight,
　He seeks the Briton's camp;
He hears the rustling flag
　And the armèd sentry's tramp;
And the starlight and moonlight
　His silent wanderings lamp.

With slow tread and still tread,
　He scans the tented line;
And he counts the battery guns,
　By the gaunt and shadowy pine;
And his slow tread and still tread
　Gives no warning sign.

The dark wave, the plumed wave,
　It meets his eager glance;
And it sparkles 'neath the stars,
　Like the glimmer of a lance —
A dark wave, a plumed wave,
　On an emerald expanse.

A sharp clang, a still clang,
　And terror in the sound!

For the sentry, falcon-eyed,
  In the camp a spy hath found;
With a sharp clang, a steel clang,
  The patriot is bound.

With calm brow, and steady brow,
  He listens to his doom;
In his look there is no fear,
  Nor a shadow-trace of gloom;
But with calm brow and steady brow,
  He robes him for the tomb.

In the long night, the still night,
  He kneels upon the sod;
And the brutal guards withhold
  E'en the solemn word of God!
In the long night, the still night,
  He walks where Christ hath trod.

'Neath the blue morn, the sunny morn,
  He dies upon the tree;
And he mourns that he can lose
  But one life for Liberty;
And in the blue morn, the sunny morn,
  His spirit wings are free.

But his last words, his message-words,
  They burn, lest friendly eye
Should read how proud and calm
  A patriot could die,
With his last words, his dying words,
  A soldier's battle-cry.

From Fame-leaf and Angel-leaf,
  From monument and urn,
The sad of earth, the glad of heaven
  His tragic fate shall learn;
But on Fame-leaf and Angel-leaf
  The name of HALE shall burn!
                    FRANCIS MILES FINCH

Washington soon found himself unable to cope with Howe's superior force, and retreated across New Jersey, hotly pursued by the enemy. On December 8, he succeeded in crossing the Delaware River. The British came up next day and took a position on the east bank, with their center at Trenton. The British soldiers, thinking the war virtually ended, grew careless, and Howe and Cornwallis returned to New York to celebrate Christmas. It was at this juncture that Washington decided to attack. More than ten hours were consumed in getting across the river, which was blocked with ice, but at daybreak of the 26th, Washington entered Trenton and attacked the enemy.

ACROSS THE DELAWARE

[December 26, 1776]

The winter night is cold and drear,
    Along the river's sullen flow;
The cruel frost is camping here —
    The air has living blades of snow.
Look! pushing from the icy strand,
    With ensigns freezing in the air,
There sails a small but mighty band,
    Across the dang'rous Delaware.

Oh, wherefore, soldiers, would you fight
    The bayonets of a winter storm?
In truth it were a better night
    For blazing fire and blankets warm!
We seek to trap a foreign foe,
    Who fill themselves with stolen fare;
We carry freedom as we go
    Across the storm-swept Delaware!

The night is full of lusty cheer
    Within the Hessians' merry camp;
And faint and fainter on the ear
    Doth fall the heedless sentry's tramp.
O hirelings, this new nation's rage
    Is something 'tis not well to dare;

You are not fitted to engage
These men from o'er the Delaware!

A rush — a shout — a clarion call,
Salute the early morning's gray:
Now, roused invaders, yield or fall:
The refuge-land has won the day!
Soon shall the glorious news be hurled
Wherever men have wrongs to bear;
For freedom's torch illumes the world,
And God has crossed the Delaware!

WILL CARLETON

THE surprise was complete. Eighteen of the British were killed,
over a thousand captured, and the remainder fled in disorder to
Princeton, leaving their sick and wounded and all their heavy arms
and baggage in the hands of the Americans. So elated were the
latter by this great victory, coming as it did at the darkest hour
of the war, that it may well be called the turning-point of the
struggle. There were miseries and defeats still to be endured, but
the patriots never again lost heart.

THE BATTLE OF TRENTON

On Christmas Day in seventy-six,
Our ragged troops, with bayonets fixed,
For Trenton marched away.
The Delaware see! the boats below!
The light obscured by hail and snow!
But no signs of dismay.

Our object was the Hessian band,
That dared invade fair freedom's land,
And quarter in that place.
Great Washington he led us on,
Whose streaming flag, in storm or sun,
Had never known disgrace.

In silent march we passed the night,
Each soldier panting for the fight,
        Though quite benumbed with frost.
Greene on the left at six began,
The right was led by Sullivan
        Who ne'er a moment lost.

Their pickets stormed, the alarm was spread,
That rebels risen from the dead
        Were marching into town.
Some scampered here, some scampered there,
And some for action did prepare;
        But soon their arms laid down.

Twelve hundred servile miscreants,
With all their colors, guns, and tents,
        Were trophies of the day.
The frolic o'er, the bright canteen,
In center, front, and rear was seen
        Driving fatigue away.

Now, brothers of the patriot bands,
Let's sing deliverance from the hands
        Of arbitrary sway.
And as our life is but a span,
Let's touch the tankard while we can,
        In memory of that day.

                                    UNKNOWN

AT PRINCETON, Cornwallis rallied the retreating British, and on
January 2, 1777, advanced against Trenton at the head of eight
thousand men. Washington had withdrawn his force beyond a
little stream called the Assunpink, where he repelled two assaults.
That night he marched toward Princeton, routed a detachment of
two thousand, and took up a strong position on the heights at

Morristown.   But the British had had enough, and retreated to
New York.

ASSUNPINK AND PRINCETON
[January 3, 1777]

GLORIOUS the day when in arms at Assunpink,
    And after at Princeton the Briton we met:
Few in both armies — they'd skirmishes call them,
    Now hundreds of thousands in battle are set.
But for the numbers engaged, let me tell you,
    Smart brushes they were, and two battles that told;
There 'twas I first drew a bead on a foeman —
    I, a mere stripling, not twenty years old....

Ranged for a mile on the banks of Assunpink,
    There, southward of Trenton, one morning we lay,
When, with his red-coats all marshaled to meet us,
    Cornwallis came fiercely at close of the day —
Driving some scouts who had gone out with Longstreet,
    From where they were crossing at Shabbaconk Run —
Trumpets loud blaring, drums beating, flags flying —
    Three hours, by the clock, before setting of sun.

Two ways were left them by which to assail us,
    And neither was perfectly to their desire —
One was the bridge we controlled by our cannon,
    The other the ford that was under our fire.
"Death upon one side, and Dismal on t'other,"
    Said Sambo, our cook, as he gazed on our foes:
Cheering and dauntless they marched to the battle,
    And, doubtful of choice, both the dangers they chose.

Down at the ford, it was said, that the water
    Was reddened with blood from the soldiers who fell:
As for the bridge, when they tried it, their forces
    Were beaten with terrible slaughter, as well.
Grape-shot swept causeway, and pattered on water,
    And riddled their columns, that broke and gave way;

Thrice they charged boldly, and thrice they retreated;
  Then darkness came down, and so ended the fray....

Early that night, when the leaders held council,
  Both St. Clair and Reed said our action was clear;
Useless to strike at the van of our foeman —
  His force was too strong; we must fall on his rear.
Washington thought so, and bade us replenish
  Our watch-fires till nearly the dawn of the day;
Setting some more to make feint of entrenching,
  While swiftly in darkness the rest moved away.

Marching by Sandtown, and Quaker Bridge crossing,
  We passed Stony Creek a full hour before dawn,
Leaving there Mercer with one scant battalion
  Our foes to amuse, should they find we were gone;
Then the main force pushed its way into Princeton,
  All ready to strike those who dreamed of no blow;
Only a chance that we lost not our labor,
  And slipped through our fingers, unknowing, the foe.

Mawhood's brigade, never feeling its danger,
  Had started for Trenton at dawn of the day,
Crossed Stony Creek, after we had gone over,
  When Mercer's weak force they beheld on its way;
Turning contemptuously back to attack it,
  They drove it with ease in disorder ahead —
Firelocks alone were no match for their cannon —
  A fight, and then flight, and brave Mercer lay dead....

Hearing the firing, we turned and we met them,
  Our cannon replying to theirs with a will;
Fiercely with grape and with canister swept them,
  And chased them in wrath from the brow of the hill.
Racing and chasing it was into Princeton,
  Where, seeking the lore to be taught in that hall,
Redcoats by scores entered college, but stayed not —
  We rudely expelled them with powder and ball.

Only a skirmish, you see, though a sharp one —
  It did not last over the fourth of an hour;
But 'twas a battle that did us this service —
  No more, from that day, had we fear of their power.
Trenton revived us, Assunpink encouraged,
  But Princeton gave hope that we held to the last;
Flood-tide had come on the black, sullen water
  And ebb-tide for ever and ever had passed.

THOMAS DUNN ENGLISH

"THUS in a brief campaign of three weeks, Washington had rallied
the fragments of a defeated and broken army, fought two successful
battles, taken nearly two thousand prisoners, and recovered the
State of New Jersey." Frederick the Great is said to have pro-
nounced this campaign the most brilliant in military history.

SEVENTY-SIX

WHAT heroes from the woodland sprung,
  When, through the fresh-awakened land,
The thrilling cry of freedom rung
And to the work of warfare strung
  The yeoman's iron hand!

Hills flung the cry to hills around,
  And ocean-mart replied to mart,
And streams, whose springs were yet unfound,
Pealed far away the startling sound
  Into the forest's heart.

Then marched the brave from rocky steep,
  From mountain river swift and cold;
The borders of the stormy deep,
The vales where gathered waters sleep,
  Sent up the strong and bold —

As if the very earth again
  Grew quick with God's creating breath,

And, from the sods of grove and glen,
Rose ranks of lion-hearted men
    To battle to the death.

The wife, whose babe first smiled that day,
    The fair fond bride of yestereve,
And agèd sire and matron gray,
Saw the loved warriors haste away,
    And deemed it sin to grieve.

Already had the strife begun;
    Already blood on Concord's plain,
Along the springing grass had run,
And blood had flowed at Lexington,
    Like brooks of April rain.

That death-stain on the vernal sward
    Hallowed to freedom all the shore;
In fragments fell the yoke abhorred —
The footstep of a foreign lord
    Profaned the soil no more.

WILLIAM CULLEN BRYANT

IT WAS at this time that the question of a national flag was finally
settled. There is a tradition that in June, 1776, General Washington and a committee of the Congress had called upon Mrs. John
Ross, of Philadelphia, and requested her to make a flag after a design
which Washington furnished, which she did, producing the first
"Stars and Stripes."

BETSY'S BATTLE-FLAG

FROM dusk till dawn the livelong night
She kept the tallow dips alight,
And fast her nimble fingers flew
To sew the stars upon the blue.
With weary eyes and aching head
She stitched the stripes of white and red,

And when the day came up the stair
Complete across a carven chair
    Hung Betsy's battle-flag.

Like shadows in the evening gray
The Continentals filed away,
With broken boots and ragged coats,
But hoarse defiance in their throats;
They bore the marks of want and cold,
And some were lame and some were old,
And some with wounds untended bled,
But floating bravely overhead
    Was Betsy's battle-flag.

When fell the battle's leaden rain,
The soldier hushed his moans of pain
And raised his dying head to see
King George's troopers turn and flee.
Their charging column reeled and broke,
And vanished in the rolling smoke,
Before the glory of the stars,
The snowy stripes, and scarlet bars
    Of Betsy's battle-flag.

The simple stone of Betsy Ross
Is covered now with mould and moss,
But still her deathless banner flies,
And keeps the color of the skies.
A nation thrills, a nation bleeds,
A nation follows where it leads,
And every man is proud to yield
His life upon a crimson field
    For Betsy's battle-flag!

                                MINNA IRVING

IT WAS really not until Saturday, June 14, 1777, that a flag was
formally adopted by the Congress. On that day, it "Resolved,

That the flag of the thirteen United States be thirteen stripes alternate red and white; that the union be thirteen stars, white in a blue field, representing a new constellation."

THE AMERICAN FLAG

When Freedom from her mountain height
    Unfurled her standard to the air,
She tore the azure robe of night,
    And set the stars of glory there;
She mingled with its gorgeous dyes
The milky baldric of the skies,
And striped its pure, celestial white
With streakings of the morning light;
Then from his mansion in the sun
She called her eagle bearer down,
And gave into his mighty hand
The symbol of her chosen land.

Majestic monarch of the cloud!
    Who rear'st aloft thy regal form,
To hear the tempest-trumpings loud,
    And see the lightning lances driven,
    When strive the warriors of the storm,
And rolls the thunder-drum of heaven —
Child of the sun! to thee 'tis given
    To guard the banner of the free,
To hover in the sulphur smoke,
To ward away the battle-stroke,
And bid its blendings shine afar,
Like rainbows on the cloud of war,
    The harbingers of victory!

Flag of the brave! thy folds shall fly,
The sign of hope and triumph high,
When speaks the signal trumpet tone,
And the long line comes gleaming on;
Ere yet the life-blood, warm and wet,

Has dimmed the glistening bayonet,
Each soldier eye shall brightly turn
To where thy sky-born glories burn,
And, as his springing steps advance,
Catch war and vengeance from the glance
And when the cannon-mouthings loud
Heave in wild wreaths the battle-shroud
And gory sabers rise and fall,
Like shoots of flame on midnight's pall;
Then shall thy meteor-glances glow,
    And cowering foes shall sink beneath
Each gallant arm that strikes below
    That lovely messenger of death.

Flag of the seas! on ocean wave
Thy stars shall glitter o'er the brave;
When death, careering on the gale,
Sweeps darkly round the bellied sail,
And frighted waves rush wildly back
Before the broadside's reeling rack,
Each dying wanderer of the sea
Shall look at once to heaven and thee,
And smile to see thy splendors fly
In triumph o'er his closing eye.

Flag of the free heart's hope and home,
    By angel hands to valor given;
Thy stars have lit the welkin dome,
    And all thy hues were born in heaven.
Forever float that standard sheet!
    Where breathes the foe but falls before us,
With Freedom's soil beneath our feet,
    And Freedom's banner streaming o'er us?
                    JOSEPH RODMAN DRAKE

SAVE for the addition of a star for each new state admitted to the
Union, this is the flag of the United States today, and each year on

June 14, the anniversary of its adoption, it is honored in every one of the forty-eight states which have grown from the original thirteen.

THE FLOWER OF LIBERTY

WHAT flower is this that greets the morn,
Its hues from Heaven so freshly born?
With burning star and flaming band
It kindles all the sunset land:
Oh tell us what the name may be —
Is this the Flower of Liberty?
    It is the banner of the free,
    The starry Flower of Liberty!

In savage Nature's far abode
Its tender seed our fathers sowed;
The storm-winds rocked its swelling bud,
Its opening leaves were streaked with blood,
Till lo! earth's tyrants shook to see
The full-blown Flower of Liberty!
    Then hail the banner of the free,
    The starry Flower of Liberty!

Behold its streaming rays unite,
One mingling flood of braided light —
The red that fires the Southern rose,
With spotless white from Northern snows,
And, spangled o'er its azure, see
The sister Stars of Liberty!
    Then hail the banner of the free,
    The starry Flower of Liberty!

The blades of heroes fence it round,
Where'er it springs is holy ground;
From tower and dome its glories spread;
It waves where lonely sentries tread;
It makes the land as ocean free,
And plants an empire on the sea!

Then hail the banner of the free,
The starry Flower of Liberty!

Thy sacred leaves, fair Freedom's flower,
Shall ever float on dome and tower,
To all their heavenly colors true,
In blackening frost or crimson dew, —
And God love us as we love thee,
Thrice holy Flower of Liberty!
    Then hail the banner of the free,
    The starry Flower of Liberty!

OLIVER WENDELL HOLMES

CHAPTER V

VICTORY

DEFEATED in Jersey, the British determined to cut the colonies in two by securing the line of the Hudson, and early in June, 1777, an army of eight thousand men under General John Burgoyne started from Canada to march to Albany. It soon ran out of supplies, and on August 13, Burgoyne sent a force of Hessians under General Baum to seize horses and stores which the Americans had collected at Bennington, Vermont. Bennington was warned, and on August 15, Colonel John Stark, with eight hundred yeomen, set out to meet the enemy.

THE MARCHING SONG OF STARK'S MEN

[August 15, 1777]

MARCH! March! March! from sunrise till it's dark,
    And let no man straggle on the way!
March! March! March! as we follow old John Stark,
    For the old man needs us all today.

Load! Load! Load! Three buckshot and a ball,
    With a hymn-tune for a wad to make them stay!
But let no man dare to fire till he gives the word to all,
    Let no man let the buckshot go astray.

Fire! Fire! Fire! Fire all along the line,
    When we meet those bloody Hessians in array!
They shall have every grain from this powder-horn of mine,
    Unless the cowards turn and run away.

Home! Home! Home! When the fight is fought and won,
    To the home where the women watch and pray!
To tell them how John Stark finished what he had begun,
    And to hear them thank our God for the day.

EDWARD EVERETT HALE

STARK found the Hessians intrenched in a strong position six miles from Bennington, and decided to storm it next day. During the night a company of Berkshire militia arrived, and with them the warlike parson of Pittsfield, Thomas Allen.

PARSON ALLEN'S RIDE

[August 15, 1777]

THE "Catamount Tavern" is lively tonight,
　　The boys of Vermont and New Hampshire are here,
Assembled and grouped in the lingering light,
　　To greet Parson Allen with shout and with cheer.

Over mountain and valley, from Pittsfield green,
　　Through the driving rain of that August day,
The "Flock" marched on with martial mien,
　　And the Parson rode in his "one-hoss shay."

"Three cheers for old Berkshire!" the General said,
　　As the boys of New England drew up face to face,
"Baum bids us a breakfast tomorrow to spread,
　　And the Parson is here to say us the 'grace.'"

"The lads who are with me have come here to fight,
　　And we know of no grace," was the Parson's reply,
"Save the name of Jehovah, our country and right,
　　Which your own Ethan Allen pronounced at Fort Ti."

"Tomorrow," said Stark, "there'll be fighting to do,
　　If you think you can wait for the morning light,
And, Parson, I'll conquer the British with you,
　　Or Molly Stark sleeps a widow at night."

What the Parson dreamed in that Bennington camp,
　　Neither Yankee nor Prophet would dare to guess;
A vision, perhaps, of the King David stamp,
　　With a mixture of Cromwell and good Queen Bess.

But we know the result of that glorious day,
    And the victory won ere the night came down;
How Warner charged in the bitter fray,
    With Rossiter, Hobart, and old John Brown:

And how in the lull of the three hours' fight,
    The Parson harangued the Tory line,
As he stood on a stump, with his musket bright,
    And sprinkled his texts with the powder fine: —

"The sword of the Lord is our battle-cry,
    A refuge sure in the hour of need,
And freedom and faith can never die,
    Is article first of the Puritan creed."

"Perhaps the 'occasion' was rather rash,"
    He remarked to his comrades after the rout,
"For behind a bush I saw a flash,
    But I fired that way and put it out."

And many the sayings, eccentric and queer,
    Repeated and sung through the country side,
And quoted in Berkshire for many a year,
    Of the Pittsfield march and the Parson's ride.

All honor to Stark and his resolute men,
    To the Green Mountain Boys all honor and praise,
While with shout and with cheer we welcome again,
    The parson who came in his one-horse chaise.
                        WALLACE BRUCE

AUGUST 16 dawned clear and bright, and during the morning Stark managed to place half his force on the enemy's rear and flanks. Early in the afternoon, he attacked on all sides. The Hessians stood their ground and fought desperately, but were soon thrown into disorder, and at the end of two hours were all either killed or captured.

THE BATTLE OF BENNINGTON

[August 16, 1777]

UP THROUGH a cloudy sky, the sun
  Was buffeting his way,
On such a morn as ushers in
  A sultry August day.
Hot was the air — and hotter yet
  Men's thoughts within them grew:
They Britons, Hessians, Tories saw —
  They saw their homesteads too....

The night before, the Yankee host
  Came gathering from afar,
And in each belted bosom glowed
  The spirit of the war.
As full of fight, through rainy storm,
  Night, cloudy, starless, dark,
They came, and gathered as they came,
  Around the valiant Stark.

There was a Berkshire parson — he
  And all his flock were there,
And like true churchmen militant
  The arm of flesh made bare.
Out spake the Dominie and said,
  "For battle have we come
These many times, and after this
  We mean to stay at home."...

The morning came — there stood the foe,
  Stark eyed them as they stood —
Few words he spake — 'twas not a time
  For moralizing mood.

"See there the enemy, my boys!
  Now strong in valor's might,
Beat them, or Molly Stark will sleep
  In widowhood tonight."...

Brief eloquence was Stark's — nor vain —
  Scarce uttered he the words,
When burst the musket's rattling peal
  Out-leaped the flashing swords;
And when brave Stark in after time
  Told the proud tale of wonder,
He said the battle din was one
  "Continual clap of thunder."

Two hours they strove — then victory crowned
  The gallant Yankee boys.
Naught but the memory of the dead
  Bedimmed their glorious joys;
Aye — there's the rub — the hour of strife,
  Though follow years of fame,
Is still in mournful memory linked
  With some death-hallowed name.

The cypress with the laurel twines —
  The pæan sounds a knell,
The trophied column marks the spot
  Where friends and brothers fell.
Fame's mantle a funereal pall
  Seems to the grief-dimmed eye,
For ever where the bravest fall
  The best beloved die.

                              THOMAS P. RODMAN

BURGOYNE soon found himself hemmed in by an American force
which was rapidly increasing in numbers, and after some hesitation
decided to press on to Albany. A desperate attempt was made to
break through the American lines, but the British were routed by

Benedict Arnold's superb generalship, and forced to retreat to Sara-
toga, where they were again surrounded. On October 17, 1777,
Burgoyne hoisted the white flag and surrendered his entire army.

CARMEN BELLICOSUM

IN THEIR ragged regimentals
Stood the old Continentals,
    Yielding not,
When the grenadiers were lunging,
And like hail fell the plunging
    Cannon-shot;
    When the files
    Of the isles,
From the smoky night encampment, bore the banner of the
    rampant
    Unicorn,
And grummer, grummer, grummer, rolled the roll of the
    drummer,
    Through the morn!

Then with eyes to the front all,
And with guns horizontal,
    Stood our sires;
And the balls whistled deadly,
And in streams flashing redly
    Blazed the fires:
    As the roar
    Of the shore,
Swept the strong battle-breakers o'er the green-sodded acres
    Of the plain;
And louder, louder, louder, cracked the black gunpowder,
    Cracking amain!

Now like smiths at their forges
Worked the red Saint George's
    Cannoneers;
And the "villainous saltpeter"

Rung a fierce, discordant meter
    Round their ears;
    As the swift
    Storm-drift,
With hot sweeping anger, came the horseguards' clangor
    On our flanks:
Then higher, higher, higher, burned the old-fashioned fire
    Through the ranks!

Then the bareheaded Colonel
Galloped through the white infernal
    Powder-cloud;
And his broadsword was swinging
And his brazen throat was ringing
    Trumpet-loud.
    Then the blue
    Bullets flew,
And the trooper-jackets redden at the touch of the leaden
    Rifle-breath;
And rounder, rounder, rounder, roared the iron six-pounder,
    Hurling Death.

            GUY HUMPHREYS MCMASTER

INSTEAD of coming to Burgoyne's assistance, as had been planned, Howe set off across New Jersey to capture Philadelphia, and after an ineffectual attempt to prevent this, Washington retired to winter quarters at Valley Forge. There, through the neglect and misman-agement of the Congress, the patriot army was so ill-provided with food, clothing, and shelter, and endured sufferings so intense, that it dwindled at times, from disease and desertion, to less than two thousand effective men.

VALLEY FORGE

[*From* "The Wagoner of the Alleghanies"]

[1777–78]

O'ER town and cottage, vale and height,
Down came the Winter, fierce and white,

And shuddering wildly, as distraught
At horrors his own hand had wrought.

His child, the young Year, newly born,
    Cheerless, cowering, and affrighted,
Wailed with a shivering voice forlorn,
    As on a frozen heath benighted.
In vain the hearths were set aglow,
    In vain the evening lamps were lighted,
To cheer the dreary realm of snow:
Old Winter's brow would not be smoothed,
Nor the young Year's wailing soothed.

How sad the wretch at morn or eve
Compelled his starving home to leave,
Who, plunged breast-deep from drift to drift,
Toils slowly on from rift to rift,
Still hearing in his aching ear
The cry his fancy whispers near,
Of little ones who weep for bread
Within an ill-provided shed!

But wilder, fiercer, sadder still,
    Freezing the tear it caused to start,
Was the inevitable chill
    Which pierced a nation's agued heart —
A nation with its naked breast
Against the frozen barriers prest,
Heaving its tedious way and slow
Through shifting gulfs and drifts of woe,
Where every blast that whistled by
Was bitter with its children's cry.

Such was the winter's awful sight
For many a dreary day and night,
What time our country's hope forlorn,
Of every needed comfort shorn,

Lay housed within a hurried tent,
Where every keen blast found a rent,
And oft the snow was seen to sift
Along the floor its piling drift,
Or, mocking the scant blankets' fold,
Across the night-couch frequent rolled;
Where every path by a soldier beat,
    Or every track where a sentinel stood,
Still held the print of naked feet,
    And oft the crimson stains of blood;
Where Famine held her spectral court,
    And joined by all her fierce allies:
She ever loved a camp or fort
    Beleaguered by the wintry skies —
But chiefly when Disease is by,
To sink the frame and dim the eye,
Until, with reeking forehead bent,
    In martial garments cold and damp,
Pale Death patrols from tent to tent,
    To count the charnels of the camp.

Such was the winter that prevailed
    Within the crowded, frozen gorge;
Such were the horrors that assailed
    The patriot band at Valley Forge.

It was a midnight storm of woes
    To clear the sky for Freedom's morn;
And such must ever be the throes
    The hour when Liberty is born.
                    THOMAS BUCHANAN READ

EARLY in May, Sir Harry Clinton succeeded Howe in command of
the British, and on June 18, evacuated Philadelphia and started
with his whole army for New York. Washington hastened in pur-
suit, and on June 28, fell upon the British at Monmouth Court-
House. They were defeated, but managed to get away under cover

of darkness. The most famous incident of the fight was the exploit of Molly Pitcher, who, so the story goes, was carrying water to her husband, a cannoneer, and when a bullet killed him, seized his rammer and served his gun until the battle was won.

MOLLY PITCHER

[June 28, 1778]

'Twas hurry and scurry at Monmouth Town,
  For Lee was beating a wild retreat;
The British were riding the Yankees down,
  And panic was pressing on flying feet.

Galloping down like a hurricane
  Washington rode with his sword swung high,
Mighty as he of the Trojan plain
  Fired by a courage from the sky.

"Halt, and stand to your guns!" he cried,
  And a bombardier made swift reply.
Wheeling his cannon into the tide,
  He fell 'neath the shot of a foeman nigh.

Molly Pitcher sprang to his side,
  Fired as she saw her husband do.
Telling the king in his stubborn pride
  Women like men to their homes are true.

Washington rode from the bloody fray
  Up to the gun that a woman manned.
"Molly Pitcher, you saved the day,"
  He said, as he gave her a hero's hand.

He named her sergeant with manly praise,
  While her war-brown face was wet with tears —
A woman has ever a woman's ways,
  And the army was wild with cheers.
                    KATE BROWNLEE SHERWOOD

NEXT morning, General Greene presented Molly Pitcher to Washington, who complimented her upon her bravery, and gave her a sergeant's commission in the army. She was afterwards awarded a pension by the Pennsylvania Legislature.

MOLLY PITCHER

PITCHER the gunner is brisk and young;
He's a lightsome heart and a merry tongue;
The ear of a fox, the eye of a hawk,
A foot that would sooner run than walk,
And a hand that can touch the linstock home
As the lightning darts from the thunder-dome.
He hates a Tory — he loves a fight —
The roll of the drum is his heart's delight,
And three things rule the gunner's life,
His country, his gun, and his Irish wife.

Oh! Molly, with your eyes so blue;
Oh! Molly, Molly, here's to you!
Sure, honor's roll will aye be richer
For the bright name of Molly Pitcher.

The sun shoots down on Monmouth fight
His brazen arrows broad and bright.
They strike on sabers' glittering sheen,
On rifle-stock and bay'net keen;
They pierce the smoke-cloud gray and dim
Where stand the gunners swart and grim,
Firing fast as balls can flee
At the foe they neither hear nor see.
Where all are brave the bravest one,
Pitcher the gunner, serves his gun.

Oh! Molly, Molly, haste and bring
The sparkling water from the spring,
To drive the heat and thirst away,
And keep your soldier glad and gay!

A bullet comes singing over the brow,
And Pitcher's gun is silent now.
The brazen throat that roared his will,
The shout of his warlike joy, is still;
The black lips gape, but they shoot no flame,
And the voice that falters the gunner's name
Brings only its echo where he lies
With his ghastly face turned up to the skies.

Oh! Molly, Molly, where he lies,
    His last look meets your faithful eyes;
His last thought sinks from love to love
    Of your darling face that bends above.

"No one to serve in Pitcher's stead?
Wheel back the gun," the Captain said.
When like a flash before him stood
A figure, dashed with smoke and blood,
With streaming hair, with eyes of flame,
And lips that cry out the gunner's name.
"Wheel back his gun, who never yet
His fighting duty would forget?
His voice shall speak, though he lie dead.
I'll serve my husband's gun!" she said.

Oh! Molly, now your hour is come.
    Up, girl, and send the linstock home!
Leap out, swift ball, away, away!
    Avenge the gunner's death today!

All day the great guns barked and roared;
All day the big balls screeched and soared;
All day, 'mid the sweating gunners grim,
Who toiled in their smoke-shroud dense and dim,
Sweet Molly labored with courage high,
With steady hand and watchful eye,

Till day was o'er, and the setting sun
Looked down on the field of Monmouth won,
And Molly standing beside her gun.

Now, Molly, rest your weary arm!
 Safe, Molly, all is safe from harm.
Now, woman, bow your aching head,
 And weep in sorrow o'er your dead!

Next day on that field so hardly won,
Stately and calm stands Washington,
And looks where the gallant Greene doth lead
A figure clad in motley weed —
A soldier's cap and a soldier's coat
Masking a woman's petticoat.
He greets our Molly in kindly wise;
He bids her raise her fearful eyes;
And now he hails her before them all
Comrade and soldier, whate'er befall,
"And since she has played a man's full part,
A man's reward for her loyal heart,
And Sergeant Molly Pitcher's name
Be writ henceforth on the shield of fame!"

Oh, Molly, with your eyes so blue,
 Oh, Molly, Molly, here's to you!
Sweet honor's roll is aye the richer
 For the bright name of Molly Pitcher.
                    LAURA E. RICHARDS

FOR nearly a year, Clinton remained inactive in New York, under
Washington's attentive eye. Then, on May 30, 1779, he captured
the fortress at Stony Point on the Hudson, garrisoned it heavily and
so strengthened its fortifications that it was almost impregnable.
Washington, nevertheless, determined to recapture it, and intrusted
the task to General Anthony Wayne. At midnight of July 15, 1779,

the Americans crossed the swamp which divided the fort from the mainland, reached the outworks before they were discovered, and carried the fort by storm.

WAYNE AT STONY POINT

[July 16, 1779]

'Twas the heart of the murky night, and the lowest ebb of the
　　tide,
Silence lay on the land, and sleep on the waters wide,
Save for the sentry's tramp, or the note of a lone night bird,
Or the sough of the haunted pines as the south wind softly
　　stirred.
Gloom above and around, and the brooding spirit of rest;
Only a single star over Dunderberg's lofty crest.

Through the drench of ooze and slime at the marge of the
　　river fen
File upon file slips **by.** See! are they ghosts or men?
Fast do they forward press, on by a track unbarred;
Now is the causeway won, now have they throttled the guard;
Now have they parted line to storm with a rush on the height,
Some by a path to the left, some by a path to the right.

Hark — the peal of a gun! and the drummer's rude alarms!
Ringing down from the height there soundeth the cry, *To arms!*
Thundering down from the height there cometh the cannon's
　　blare;
Flash upon blinding flash lightens the livid air:
Look! do the stormers quail? Nay, for their feet are set
Now at the bastion's base, now on the parapet:

Urging the vanguard on prone doth the leader fall,
Smitten sudden and sore by a foeman's musket-ball;
Waver the charging lines; swiftly they spring to his side —
Madcap Anthony Wayne, the patriot army's pride!
Forward, my braves! he cries, and the heroes hearten again;
Bear me into the fort, I'll die at the head of my men!

Die! — did he die that night, felled in his lusty prime?
Answer many a field in the stormy aftertime!
Still did his prowess shine, still did his courage soar,
From the Hudson's rocky steep to the James's level shore;
But never on Fame's fair scroll did he blazon a deed more
    bright
Than his charge on Stony Point in the heart of the murky
    night.

CLINTON SCOLLARD

THE STORMING OF STONY POINT

[July 16, 1779]

HIGHLANDS of Hudson! ye saw them pass,
    Night on the stars of their battle-flag,
Threading the maze of the dark morass
    Under the frown of the Thunder Crag;

Flower and pride of the Light Armed Corps,
    Trim in their trappings of buff and blue,
Silent, they skirted the rugged shore,
    Grim in the promise of work to do.

"Cross ye the ford to the moated rock!
    Let not a whisper your march betray!
Out with the flint from the musket lock!
    Now! let the bayonet find the way!"

"Halt!" rang the sentinel's challenge clear.
    Swift came the shot of the waking foe.
Bright flashed the axe of the Pioneer
    Smashing the abatis, blow on blow.

Little they tarried for British might!
    Lightly they recked of the Tory jeers!
Laughing, they swarmed to the craggy height,
    Steel to the steel of the Grenadiers!

Storm King and Dunderberg! wake once more
    Sentinel giants of Freedom's throne,
Massive and proud! to the Eastern shore
    Bellow the watchword: "The fort's our own!"

Echo our cheers for the Men of old!
    Shout for the Hero who led his band
Braving the death that his heart foretold
    Over the parapet, "spear in hand!"

                                ARTHUR GUITERMAN

ANOTHER year passed, with various indecisive operations, one of
which was a raid against Springfield in June, 1780. On their way to
Springfield, the British passed through a village called Connecticut
Farms. They set it on fire, and a chance shot killed the wife of the
Reverend James Caldwell, as she was kneeling at prayer in her bed-
room. Her husband took the revenge described in Bret Harte's
poem.

CALDWELL OF SPRINGFIELD

[June 23, 1780]

HERE's the spot. Look around you. Above on the height
Lay the Hessians encamped. By that church on the right
Stood the gaunt Jersey farmers. And here ran a wall —
You may dig anywhere and you'll turn up a ball.
Nothing more. Grasses spring, waters run, flowers blow,
Pretty much as they did ninety-three years ago.

Nothing more, did I say? Stay one moment; you've heard
Of Caldwell, the parson, who once preached the Word
Down at Springfield? What, No? Come — that's bad; why,
        he had
All the Jerseys aflame. And they gave him the name
Of the "rebel high priest." He stuck in their gorge,
For he loved the Lord God — and he hated King George!

He had cause, you might say!   When the Hessians that day
Marched up with Knyphausen, they stopped on their way
At the "Farms," where his wife, with a child in her arms,
Sat alone in the house.   How it happened none knew
But God — and that one of the hireling crew
Who fired the shot!   Enough! — there she lay,
And Caldwell, the chaplain, her husband, away!

Did he preach — did he pray?   Think of him as you stand
By the old church today; — think of him and his band
Of militant plowboys!   See the smoke and the heat
Of that reckless advance, of that straggling retreat!
Keep the ghost of that wife, foully slain, in your view —
And what could you, what should you, what would *you* do:

Why, just what *he* did!   They were left in the lurch
For the want of more wadding.   He ran to the church,
Broke the door, stripped the pews, and dashed out in the road
With his arms full of hymn-books, and threw down his load
At their feet!   Then above all the shouting and shots,
Rang his voice: "Put Watts into 'em! Boys, give 'em Watts!"

And they did.   That is all.   Grasses spring, flowers blow
Pretty much as they did ninety-three years ago.
You may dig anywhere and you'll turn up a ball —
But not always a hero like this — and that's all.

BRET HARTE

THEN came the second great personal tragedy of the war.   The
Americans relied for the defense of the Hudson upon the impregna-
ble position at West Point, commanded by Benedict Arnold.   Arnold
was a brilliant officer, but believed that he had been treated unjustly
by the Congress, and determined to revenge himself by betraying
West Point into the hands of the British.   He opened communica-
tion with Clinton, and on September 21, Major John André, Adju-
tant-General of the British Army, was sent to confer with him.

While returning the following night, André was captured by an American outpost, who searched him, discovered the papers giving the details of the plot, and took him back to the American lines.

BRAVE PAULDING AND THE SPY

[September 23, 1780]

Come all you brave Americans,
    And unto me give ear,
And I'll sing you a ditty
    That will your spirits cheer,
Concerning a young gentleman
    Whose age was twenty-two;
He fought for North America,
    His heart was just and true....

He with a scouting-party
    Went down to Tarrytown,
Where he met a British officer,
    A man of high renown,
Who says unto these gentlemen,
    "You're of the British cheer,
I trust that you can tell me
    If there's any danger near?"

Then up stept this young hero,
    John Paulding was his name,
"Sir, tell us where you're going,
    And, also, whence you came?"
"I bear the British flag, sir;
    I've a pass to go this way,
I'm on an expedition,
    And have no time to stay."

Then round him came this company,
    And bid him to dismount;
"Come, tell us where you're going,
    Give us a strict account;

For we are now resolvèd
  That you shall ne'er pass by."
Upon examination
  They found he was a spy.

He beggèd for his liberty,
  He pled for his discharge,
And oftentimes he told them,
  If they'd set him at large,
"Here's all the gold and silver
  I have laid up in store,
But when I reach the city,
  I'll give you ten times more."

"I scorn the gold and silver
  You have laid up in store,
And when you get to New York,
  You need not send us more;
But you may take your sword in hand
  To gain your liberty,
And if that you do conquer me,
  Oh, then you shall be free."

"The time it is improper
  Our valor for to try,
For if we take our swords in hand,
  Then one of us must die;
I am a man of honor,
  With courage true and bold,
And I fear not the man of clay,
  Although he's clothed in gold."

He saw that his conspiracy
  Would soon be brought to light;
He begged for pen and paper,
  And askèd leave to write
A line to General Arnold,
  To let him know his fate,

And beg for his assistance;
  But now it was too late.

When the news it came to Arnold,
  It put him in a fret;
He walked the room in trouble,
  Till tears his cheek did wet;
The story soon went through the camp,
  And also through the fort;
And he callèd for the Vulture
  And sailèd for New York.

Now Arnold to New York has gone,
  A-fighting for his king,
And left poor Major André
  On the gallows for to swing;
When he was executed,
  He looked both meek and mild;
He looked upon the people,
  And pleasantly he smiled.

It moved each eye with pity,
  Caus'd every heart to bleed,
And everyone wished him released
  And Arnold in his stead.
He was a man of honor,
  In Britain he was born;
To die upon the gallows
  Most highly he did scorn.

A bumper to John Paulding!
  Now let your voices sound,
Fill up your flowing glasses,
  And drink his health around;
Also to those young gentlemen
  Who bore him company;
Success to North America,
  Ye sons of liberty!

                              UNKNOWN

ARNOLD learned of André's capture just in time to escape to a British
ship in the Hudson.   André was tried by court-martial September
29, and condemned to be hanged as a spy.   Clinton made a desper-
ate effort to save him, but in vain; and a petition from André himself,
that he might be shot instead of hanged, was rejected by Washing-
ton, who, though deeply moved, remembered the fate which had
been meted out to Nathan Hale.

ANDRÉ'S REQUEST TO WASHINGTON

[October 1, 1780]

IT IS not the fear of death
    That damps my brow,
It is not for another breath
    I ask thee now;
I can die with a lip unstirred
    And a quiet heart —
Let but this prayer be heard
    Ere I depart.

I can give up my mother's look —
    My sister's kiss;
I can think of love — yet brook
    A death like this!
I can give up the young fame
    I burned to win —
All — but the spotless name
    I glory in.

Thine is the power to give,
    Thine to deny,
Joy for the hour I live —
    Calmness to die.
By all the brave should cherish,
    By my dying breath,
I ask that I may perish
    By a soldier's death!

                        NATHANIEL PARKER WILLIS

ACCORDINGLY, on Monday, October 2, 1780, André was led to the gallows, and shared the fate which had befallen Nathan Hale four years before. In 1821 his body was removed to Westminster Abbey.

ANDRÉ

THIS is the place where André met that death
Whose infamy was keenest of its throes,
And in this place of bravely yielded breath
His ashes found a fifty years' repose;

And then, at last, a transatlantic grave,
With those who have been kings in blood or fame,
As Honor here some compensation gave
For that once forfeit to a hero's name.

But whether in the Abbey's glory laid,
Or on so fair but fatal Tappan's shore,
Still at his grave have noble hearts betrayed
The loving pity and regret they bore.

In view of all he lost — his youth, his love,
And possibilities that wait the brave,
Inward and outward bound, dim visions move
Like passing sails upon the Hudson's wave.

The country's Father! how do we revere
His justice — Brutus-like in its decree —
With André-sparing mercy, still more dear
Had been his name — if that, indeed, could be!

CHARLOTTE FISKE BATES

ANDRÉ's death was a great blow to Clinton, and he never thereafter took the offensive. The scene of activity switched to the South, and it was here that the war was decided. Georgia and South Carolina had been overrun by the British and organized resistance was impossible, but there soon sprang up a number of partisan, or guerrilla, leaders, foremost among whom was Francis Marion, known as the Swamp Fox, perhaps the most picturesque figure of the Revolution.

THE SWAMP FOX

WE FOLLOW where the Swamp Fox guides,
　His friends and merry men are we;
And when the troop of Tarleton rides,
　We burrow in the cypress-tree.
The turfy hammock is our bed,
　Our home is in the red deer's den,
Our roof, the tree-top overhead,
　For we are wild and hunted men.

We fly by day and shun its light,
　But, prompt to strike the sudden blow,
We mount and start with early night,
　And through the forest track our foe.
And soon he hears our chargers leap,
　The flashing saber blinds his eyes,
And ere he drives away his sleep,
　And rushes from his camp, he dies.

Free bridle-bit, good gallant steed,
　That will not ask a kind caress
To swim the Santee at our need,
　When on his heels the foemen press —
The true heart and the ready hand,
　The spirit stubborn to be free,
The twisted bore, the smiting brand —
　And we are Marion's men, you see.

Now light the fire and cook the meal,
　The last perhaps that we shall taste;
I hear the Swamp Fox round us steal,
　And that's a sign we move in haste.
He whistles to the scouts, and hark!
　You hear his order calm and low.

Come, wave your torch across the dark,
   And let us see the boys that go....

Now pile the brush and roll the log;
   Hard pillow, but a soldier's head
That's half the time in brake and bog
   Must never think of softer bed.
The owl is hooting to the night,
   The cooter crawling o'er the bank,
And in that pond the flashing light
   Tells where the alligator sank.

What! 'tis the signal! start so soon,
   And through the Santee swamp so deep,
Without the aid of friendly moon,
   And we, Heaven help us! half asleep!
But courage, comrades! Marion leads,
   The Swamp Fox takes us out tonight;
So clear your swords and spur your steeds,
   There's goodly chance, I think, of fight.

We follow where the Swamp Fox guides,
   We leave the swamp and cypress-tree,
Our spurs are in our coursers' sides,
   And ready for the strife are we.
The Tory camp is now in sight,
   And there he cowers within his den;
He hears our shouts, he dreads the fight,
   He fears, and flies from Marion's men.
WILLIAM GILMORE SIMMS

No ACT of wanton cruelty, such as the British were too often guilty
of, ever sullied the brightness of Marion's fame, but no partisan
leader surpassed him in ability to harass the enemy in legitimate
warfare.

SONG OF MARION'S MEN

OUR band is few, but true and tried,
   Our leader frank and bold;

The British soldier trembles
   When Marion's name is told.
Our fortress is the good greenwood,
   Our tent the cypress-tree;
We know the forest round us
   As seamen know the sea.
We know its walls of thorny vines,
   Its glades of reedy grass,
Its safe and silent islands
   Within the dark morass.

Woe to the English soldiery,
   That little dread us near!
On them shall light at midnight
   A strange and sudden fear:
When, waking to their tents on fire,
   They grasp their arms in vain,
And they who stand to face us
   Are beat to earth again;
And they who fly in terror deem
   A mighty host behind,
And hear the tramp of thousands
   Upon the hollow wind....

Well knows the fair and friendly moon
   The band that Marion leads —
The glitter of their rifles,
   The scampering of their steeds.
'Tis life to guide the fiery barb
   Across the moonlight plain;
'Tis life to feel the night-wind
   That lifts his tossing mane.
A moment in the British camp —
   A moment — and away,
Back to the pathless forest
   Before the peep of day.

Grave men there are by broad Santee,
   Grave men with hoary hairs;

Their hearts are all with Marion,
  For Marion are their prayers.
And lovely ladies greet our band
  With kindliest welcoming,
With smiles like those of summer,
  And tears like those of spring.
For them we wear these trusty arms,
  And lay them down no more
Till we have driven the Briton
  Forever, from our shore.

WILLIAM CULLEN BRYANT

THE British forces in the South were commanded by Lord Corn-
wallis, and after defeating the Americans at Camden, he started a
raid into North Carolina. He soon found himself almost surrounded,
retreated rapidly northward to Virginia, and established himself
(safely as he thought), at Yorktown, with an army of seven thousand
men. But Washington, with a daring worthy of Cæsar or Napoleon,
marched his army from the Hudson to Virginia, caught Cornwallis in
a trap, with the assistance of a French fleet under De Grasse, and
compelled his surrender, October 17, 1781.

THE RIDE OF TENCH TILGHMAN

[October 17, 1781]

THEY'VE marched them out of old Yorktown, the vanquished
    red-coat host —
The grenadiers and fusiliers, Great Britain's pride and boast;
They've left my Lord Cornwallis sitting gnawing at his nails,
With pale chagrin from brow to chin that grim defeat
    prevails.
Their banners cased, in sullen haste their pathway they
    pursue
Between the lilied lines of France, the boys in Buff and Blue;
At last their arms away are cast, with muttering and frown,
The while the drums roll out the tune *The World Turned
    Upside Down!*

It's up, Tench Tilghman, you must ride,
    Yea, you must ride straightway,
And bear to all the countryside
    The glory of this day,
Crying amain the glad refrain,
    This world by field and town —
"Cornwallis' ta'en! Cornwallis' ta'en!
    The World Turned Upside Down!"

Roused Williamsburgh to hear the hoofs
    That loud a tattoo played,
While back from doorways, windows, roofs,
    Rang cheers from man and maid.
His voice, a twilight clarion, spoke
    By slow Pamunkey's ford;
In Fredericksburg to all the folk
    'Twas like a singing sword.

It thrilled while Alexandria slept
    By broad Potomac's shore,
And, like a forest-fire, it swept
    The streets of Baltimore.
With it Elk Tavern's rafters shook
    As though the thunder rolled;
It stirred the brigs off Marcus Hook
    From lookout to the hold.

When midnight held the autumn sky,
    Again and yet again
It echoed through the way called High
    Within the burg of Penn.
The city watch adjured in vain, —
    "Cease! cease! you tipsy clown!"
Flung Tilghman out — "Cornwallis' ta'en!
    The World Turned Upside Down!"

Where wrapt in virtuous repose
    The head of Congress lay,

A clamor welled as though there rose
　　The Trump of Judgment Day.
"What madness this?" fierce called McKean,
　　In white nightcap and gown;
The answer came — "Cornwallis' ta'en!
　　The World Turned Upside Down!"

Then forth into the highways poured
　　A wild, exultant rout,
And till the dawn there swelled and soared
　　Tench Tilghman's victory shout;
Then bells took up the joyous strain,
　　And cannon roared to drown
The triumph cry — "Cornwallis' ta'en!
　　The World Turned Upside Down!"

In dreams, Tench Tilghman, still you ride,
　　As in the days of old,
And with your horse's swinging stride
　　Your patriot tale is told;
It rings by river, hill, and plain,
　　Your memory to crown —
"Cornwallis' ta'en! Cornwallis' ta'en!
　　The World Turned Upside Down!"

　　　　　　　　　　　CLINTON SCOLLARD

"EARLY on a dark morning of the fourth week in October, an honest old German, slowly pacing the streets of Philadelphia on his night watch, began shouting, 'Past two o'clock, and Cornwallis is taken!' and light sleepers sprang out of bed and threw up their windows." The whole country burst into jubilation at the news, for the war was won.

NEWS FROM YORKTOWN

[October 23, 1781]

"PAST two o'clock and Cornwallis is taken."
　　How the voice rolled down the street

Till the silence rang and echoed
　With the stir of hurrying feet!
In the hush of the Quaker city,
　As the night drew on to morn,
How it startled the troubled sleepers,
　Like the cry for a man-child born!

"Past two o'clock and Cornwallis is taken."
　How they gathered, man and maid,
Here the child with a heart for the flint-lock,
　There the trembling grandsire staid!
From the stateliest homes of the city,
　From hovels that love might scorn,
How they followed that ringing summons,
　Like the cry for a king's heir born!

"Past two o'clock and Cornwallis is taken."
　I can see the quick lights flare,
See the glad, wild face at the window,
　Half dumb in a breathless stare.
In the pause of an hour portentous,
　In the gloom of a hope forlorn,
How it throbbed to the star-deep heavens,
　Like the cry for a nation born!

"Past two o'clock and Cornwallis is taken."
　How the message is sped and gone
To the farm and the town and the forest
　Till the world was one vast dawn!
To distant and slave-sunk races,
　Bowed down in their chains that morn,
How it swept on the winds of heaven,
　Like a cry for God's justice born!

　　　　　　　　LEWIS WORTHINGTON SMITH

KING GEORGE threatened and blustered, and declared he would abdi-
cate before he would recognize the independence of America, but he
thought better of it in the end, and on December 5, 1782, recom-
mended that peace be made with the American colonies, and that
they be declared free and independent.

ENGLAND AND AMERICA IN 1782

O THOU, that sendest out the man
　　To rule by land and sea,
Strong mother of a Lion-line,
Be proud of those strong sons of thine
　　Who wrenched their rights from thee!

What wonder if in noble heat
　　Those men thine arms withstood,
Retaught the lesson thou had'st taught,
And in thy spirit with thee fought —
　　Who sprang from English blood!

But thou rejoice with liberal joy,
　　Lift up thy rocky face,
And shatter, when the storms are black,
In many a streaming torrent back,
　　The seas that shock thy base!

Whatever harmonies of law
　　The growing world assume,
Thy work is thine — the single note
From that deep chord which Hampden smote
　　Will vibrate to the doom.

ALFRED TENNYSON

CHAPTER VI

FIRST IN THE HEARTS OF HIS COUNTRYMEN

GEORGE WASHINGTON was to render even greater service to his country. The war was ended, liberty was won, but thirteen proud and jealous States must be bound together into a Nation. It was Washington who presided over the Convention which accomplished this by evolving a Constitution knitting them together, and when the first Presidential election was held in January, 1789, George Washington, of Virginia, received every one of the sixty-nine electoral votes.

WASHINGTON

GOD wills no man a slave. The man most meek,
Who saw Him face to face on Horeb's peak,
Had slain a tyrant for a bondman's wrong,
And met his Lord with sinless soul and strong.
But when, years after, overfraught with care,
His feet once trod doubt's pathway to despair,
For that one treason lapse, the guiding hand
That led so far now barred the promised land.
God makes no man a slave, no doubter free;
Abiding faith alone wins liberty.

No angel led our Chieftain's steps aright;
No pilot cloud by day, no flame by night;
No plague nor portent spake to foe or friend;
No doubt assailed him, faithful to the end.

Weaklings there were, as in the tribes of old,
Who craved for fleshpots, worshipped calves of gold,
Murmured that right would harder be than wrong,
And freedom's narrow road so steep and long;
But he who ne'er on Sinai's summit trod,
Still walked the highest heights and spake with God;

Saw with anointed eyes no promised land
By petty bounds or pettier cycles spanned,
Its people curbed and broken to the ring,
Packed with a caste and saddled with a King, —
But freedom's heritage and training school,
Where men unruled should learn to wisely rule,
Till sun and moon should see at Ajalon
King's heads in dust and freemen's feet thereon.

His work well done, the leader stepped aside,
Spurning a crown with more than kingly pride,
Content to wear the higher crown of worth,
While time endures, First Citizen of earth.

JAMES JEFFREY ROCHE

WASHINGTON was at his estate, Mount Vernon, at the time. He was
apprised of his election and proceeded to New York, where, on April
30, 1789, he took the oath of office as the first President of the United
States of America.

THE VOW OF WASHINGTON

[April 30, 1789]

THE sword was sheathed: in April's sun
Lay green the fields by Freedom won;
And severed sections, weary of debates,
Joined hands at last and were United States.

O City sitting by the Sea!
How proud the day that dawned on thee,
When the new era, long desired, began,
And, in its need, the hour had found the man!

One thought the cannon salvos spoke,
The resonant bell-tower's vibrant stroke,
The voiceful streets, the plaudit-echoing halls,
And prayer and hymn borne heavenward from Saint Paul's!

How felt the land in every part
The strong throb of a nation's heart,
As its great leader gave, with reverent awe,
His pledge to Union, Liberty, and Law!

That pledge the heavens above him heard,
That vow the sleep of centuries stirred;
In world-wide wonder listening peoples bent
Their gaze on Freedom's great experiment.

Could it succeed? Of honor sold
And hopes deceived all history told.
Above the wrecks that strewed the mournful past,
Was the long dream of ages true at last?

Thank God! the people's choice was just,
The one man equal to his trust,
Wise beyond lore, and without weakness good,
Calm in the strength of flawless rectitude!

His rule of justice, order, peace,
Made possible the world's release;
Taught prince and serf that power is but a trust,
And rule alone, which serves the ruled, is just;

That Freedom generous is, but strong
In hate of fraud and selfish wrong,
Pretence that turns her holy truth to lies,
And lawless license masking in her guise.

Land of his love! with one glad voice
Let thy great sisterhood rejoice;
A century's suns o'er thee have risen and set,
And, God be praised, we are one nation yet.

And still we trust the years to be
Shall prove his hope was destiny,
Leaving our flag, with all its added stars,
Unrent by faction and unstained by wars.

Lo! where with patient toil he nursed
And trained the new-set plant at first,
The widening branches of a stately tree
Stretch from the sunrise to the sunset sea.

And in its broad and sheltering shade,
Sitting with none to make afraid,
Were we now silent, through each mighty limb,
The winds of heaven would sing the praise of him....

JOHN GREENLEAF WHITTIER

ON NOVEMBER 6, 1792, Washington was again unanimously chosen President, and was inaugurated March 4, 1793. Three years later he issued a "farewell address," firmly declining a third term, and on March 4, 1797, when his second term ended, he returned once again to the quiet of his beloved Virginia estate.

WASHINGTON

[*From* "Ode to Napoleon Bonaparte"]

WHERE may the wearied eye repose
   When gazing on the great;
Where neither guilty glory glows,
   Nor despicable state?
Yes — one — the first — the last — the best —
The Cincinnatus of the West,
   Whom envy dared not hate,
Bequeathed the name of Washington,
To make man blush there was but one!

GEORGE GORDON BYRON

His life was nearing its close, and the end came December 14, 1799, after an illness lasting only a few days. No happier characterization of him has ever been made than that of Richard Henry Lee in the resolutions adopted by Congress a few days later: "First in war, first in peace, and first in the hearts of his countrymen."

WASHINGTON

[*From* "Under the Old Elm"]

SOLDIER and statesman, rarest unison;
High-poised example of great duties done
Simply as breathing, a world's honors worn
As life's indifferent gifts to all men born;
Dumb for himself, unless it were to God,
But for his barefoot soldiers eloquent,
Tramping the snow to coral where they trod,
Held by his awe in hollow-eyed content;
Modest, yet firm as Nature's self; unblamed
Save by the men his nobler temper shamed;
Never seduced through show of present good
By other than unsetting lights to steer,
New-trimmed in Heaven, nor than his steadfast mood
More steadfast, far from rashness as from fear;
Rigid, but with himself first, grasping still
In swerveless poise the wave-beat helm of will;
Not honored then or now because he wooed
The popular voice, but that he still withstood;
Broad-minded, higher-souled, there is but one
Who was all this and ours, and all men's — Washington.

JAMES RUSSELL LOWELL

THE funeral took place on December 18 at Mount Vernon, where his body still rests in a modest and simple tomb which has become the great national shrine of the country he served so well.

AT THE TOMB OF WASHINGTON

HERE let the brows be bared
Before the land's great son,
He who undaunted dared,
Our Washington!

From dole, despair and doubt,
  Deceit and enmity,
He led us up and out
  To Victory.

A Pharos in the night,
  A pillar in the dawn,
By his inspiring light
  May we fare on!

Day upon hastening day
  Still let us reverence him;
Fame never, never may
  His laurels dim!

CLINTON SCOLLARD

HE REMAINS America's foremost soldier, statesman and patriot.
No greater name has ever been written on the scroll of history.

INSCRIPTION AT MOUNT VERNON

WASHINGTON, the brave, the wise, the good,
Supreme in war, in council, and in peace,
Valiant without ambition, discreet without fear,
Confident without presumption.
In disaster, calm; in success, moderate; in all, himself.
The hero, the patriot, the Christian.
The father of nations, the friend of mankind,
Who, when he had won all, renounced all,
And sought in the bosom of his family and of nature, retire-
    ment,
And in the hope of religion, immortality.

PART III
CONQUERING THE CONTINENT

O BEAUTIFUL, MY COUNTRY

"O BEAUTIFUL, my country!"
    Be thine a nobler care,
Than all thy wealth of commerce,
    Thy harvest waving fair;
Be it thy pride to lift up
    The manhood of the poor;
Be thou to the oppressèd
    Fair Freedom's open door.

For thee our fathers suffered,
    For thee they toiled and prayed;
Upon thy holy altar
    Their willing lives they laid.
Thou hast no common birthright;
    Grand memories on thee shine,
The blood of pilgrim nations,
    Commingled, flows in thine.

O beautiful, our country!
    Round thee in love we draw;
Thine is the grace of freedom,
    The majesty of law.
Be righteousness thy scepter,
    Justice thy diadem;
And on thy shining forehead
    Be peace the crowning gem.

FREDERICK L. HOSMER

CHAPTER I

THE BRITISH AGAIN

WHEN John Adams succeeded Washington as President on March 4, 1797, war was raging between France and England, and both were constantly violating American rights upon the sea. It seemed certain that the country would be drawn into a European war — as was to happen from the same cause in 1917! — and these circumstances gave birth in June, 1798, to one of the most popular political songs ever written.

ADAMS AND LIBERTY
[1798]

YE SONS of Columbia, who bravely have fought
    For those rights which unstained from your sires have
        descended,
May you long taste the blessings your valor has bought,
    And your sons reap the soil which their fathers defended.
      'Mid the reign of mild peace,
      May your nation increase,
With the glory of Rome and the wisdom of Greece;
    And ne'er shall the sons of Columbia be slaves,
    While the earth bears a plant, or the sea rolls its waves....

The fame of our arms, of our laws the mild sway,
    Had justly ennobled our nation in story,
Till the dark clouds of faction obscured our young day,
    And enveloped the sun of American glory.
      But let traitors be told,
      Who their country have sold,
And bartered their God for his image in gold,
    That ne'er will the sons of Columbia be slaves,
    While the earth bears a plant, or the sea rolls its waves....

'Tis the fire of the flint, each American warms:
    Let Rome's haughty victors beware of collision,

Let them bring all the vassals of Europe in arms,
  We're a world by ourselves, and disdain a division.
    While, with patriot pride,
    To our laws we're allied,
No foe can subdue us, no faction divide,
  For ne'er shall the sons of Columbia be slaves,
  While the earth bears a plant, or the sea rolls its waves.

Our mountains are crowned with imperial oak;
  Whose roots, like our liberties, ages have nourished;
But long ere our nation submits to the yoke,
  Not a tree shall be left on the field where it flourished.
    Should invasion impend,
    Every grove would descend,
From the hill-tops, they shaded, our shores to defend.
  For ne'er shall the sons of Columbia be slaves,
  While the earth bears a plant, or the sea rolls its waves...

Should the tempest of war overshadow our land,
  Its bolts could ne'er rend Freedom's temple asunder;
For, unmoved, at its portal, would Washington stand,
  And repulse, with his breast, the assaults of the thunder!
    His sword from the sleep
    Of its scabbard would leap,
And conduct, with its point, every flash to the deep!
  For ne'er shall the sons of Columbia be slaves,
  While the earth bears a plant, or the sea rolls its waves.

Let fame to the world sound America's voice;
  No intrigues can her sons from their government sever;
Her pride is her Adams; her laws are his choice,
  And shall flourish, till Liberty slumbers forever.
    Then unite heart and hand,
    Like Leonidas' band,
And swear to the God of the ocean and land,
  That ne'er shall the sons of Columbia be slaves,
  While the earth bears a plant, or the sea rolls its waves.
                                        ROBERT TREAT PAINE

In May, 1798, a young singer, who had been a schoolmate of Francis Hopkinson, was having a benefit at the Chestnut Street Theater in Philadelphia, and asked Hopkinson to write a patriotic song for him to sing upon this occasion. Hopkinson said he would try, and, with America's troubles with France and England in mind, sat down and wrote "Hail, Columbia!"

HAIL, COLUMBIA

Hail! Columbia, happy land!
Hail! ye heroes, heav'n-born band,
Who fought and bled in freedom's cause,
Who fought and bled in freedom's cause,
And when the storm of war was gone,
Enjoyed the peace your valor won;
Let independence be your boast,
Ever mindful what it cost,
Ever grateful for the prize,
Let its altar reach the skies.
 Chorus — Firm, united let us be,
    Rallying round our liberty,
    As a band of brothers joined,
    Peace and safety we shall find.

Immortal patriots, rise once more!
Defend your rights, defend your shore;
Let no rude foe with impious hand,
Let no rude foe with impious hand
Invade the shrine where sacred lies
Of toil and blood the well-earned prize;
While offering peace, sincere and just,
In heav'n we place a manly trust,
That truth and justice may prevail,
And ev'ry scheme of bondage fail.

Sound, sound the trump of fame!
Let Washington's great name
Ring thro' the world with loud applause!
Ring thro' the world with loud applause!

Let ev'ry clime to freedom dear
Listen with a joyful ear;
With equal skill, with steady pow'r,
He governs in the fearful hour
Of horrid war, or guides with ease
The happier time of honest peace.

Behold the chief, who now commands,
Once more to serve his country stands,
The rock on which the storm will beat!
The rock on which the storm will beat!
But armed in virtue, firm and true,
His hopes are fixed on heav'n and you.
When hope was sinking in dismay,
When gloom obscured Columbia's day,
His steady mind, from changes free,
Resolved on death or liberty.

JOSEPH HOPKINSON

THE controversy with France was finally adjusted, but that with England grew worse and worse, for she claimed the right to stop and search the ships of the United States and to seize any seamen who were alleged to be of British birth. American feeling grew steadily more bitter, various incidents fanned the flames, and on June 18, 1812, Congress declared war.

FAREWELL, PEACE

[June 18, 1812]

FAREWELL, Peace! another crisis
    Calls us to "the last appeal,"
Made when monarchs and their vices
    Leave no argument but *steel*.
When injustice and oppression
    Dare avow the tyrant's plea,

Who would recommend submission?
　Virtue bids us to be free.

History spreads her page before us,
　Time unrolls his ample scroll;
Truth unfolds them, to assure us,
　States, united, ne'er can fall.
See, in annals Greek and Roman,
　What immortal deeds we find;
When those gallant sons of woman
　In their country's cause combined.

Sons of Freedom! brave descendants
　From a race of heroes tried,
To preserve our independence
　Let all Europe be defied.
Let not all the world, united,
　Rob us of one sacred right:
Every patriot heart's delighted
　In his country's cause to fight.

Come then, War! with hearts elated
　To thy standard we will fly;
Every bosom animated
　Either to live free or die.
May the wretch that shrinks from duty,
　Or deserts the glorious strife,
Never know the smile of beauty,
　Nor the blessing of a wife.

UNKNOWN

ENGLAND won the first victory by capturing Detroit, but the fury
which the news of this disaster aroused was tempered by rejoicing
over a remarkable victory on the ocean. On August 19, Captain
Isaac Hull, in command of the Constitution, sighted the British
frigate Guerrière off Halifax, attacked at once and reduced the enemy

to a "perfect wreck." The Constitution sustained so little damage
to her hull that she was ever afterwards known as "Old Ironsides."

FIRST FRUITS IN 1812

[August 19, 1812]

WHAT *is that a-billowing there*
Like a thunderhead in air?
Why should such a sight be whitening the seas?
That's a Yankee man-o'-war,
And three things she's seeking for —
For a prize, and for a battle, and a breeze.

When the war blew o'er the sea
Out went Hull and out went we
In the Constitution, looking for the foe;
But five British ships came down —
And we got to Boston-town
By a mighty narrow margin, you must know!

Captain Hull can't fight their fleet,
But he fairly aches to meet
Quite the prettiest British ship of all there were;
So he stands again to sea
In the hope that on his lee
He'll catch Dacres and his pretty Guerrière.

'Tis an August afternoon
Not a day too late or soon,
When we raise a ship whose lettered mainsail reads:
All who meet me have a care,
I am England's Guerrière;
So Hull gayly clears for action as he speeds.

Cheery bells had chanted five
On the happiest day alive
When we Yankees dance to quarters at his call;

While the British bang away
With their broadsides' screech and **bray;**
But the Constitution never fires a ball.

We send up three times to ask
If we sha'n't begin our task?
Captain Hull sends back each time the answer *No;*
Till to half a pistol-shot
The two frigates he had brought,
Then he whispers, *Lay along!* — and we let go.

Twice our broadside lights and lifts,
And the Briton, crippled, drifts
With her mizzen dangling hopeless at her poop:
Laughs a Yankee, *She's a brig!*
Says our Captain, *That's too big;*
Try another, so we'll have her for a sloop!

We hurrah, and fire again,
Lay aboard of her like men,
And, like men, they beat us off, and try in turn;
But we drive bold Dacres back
With our muskets' snap and crack —
All the while our crashing broadsides boom and burn.

'Tis but half an hour, bare,
When that pretty Guerrière
Not a stick calls hers aloft or hers alow,
Save the mizzen's shattered mast,
Where her "meteor flag" 's nailed fast
Till, a fallen star, we quench its ruddy glow.

Dacres, injured, o'er our side
Slowly bears his sword of pride,
Holds it out, as Hull stands there in his renown:
No, no! says th' American,
Never, from so brave a man —
But I see you're wounded, let me help you down.

All that night we work in vain
Keeping her upon the main,
But we've hulled her far too often, and at last
In a blaze of fire there
Dies the pretty Guerrière;
While away we cheerly sail upon the blast.

Oh, the breeze that blows so free!
Oh, the prize beneath the sea!
Oh, the battle! — was there ever better won?
Still the happy Yankee cheers
Are a-ringing in our ears
From old Boston, glorying in what we've done.

What is that a-billowing there
Like a thunderhead in air?
Why should such a sight be whitening the seas?
That's Old Ir'nsides, trim and taut,
And she's found the things she sought —
Found a prize, a bully battle, and a breeze!

WALLACE RICE

ANOTHER victory was soon to be recorded. On the morning of
October 25, the British frigate Macedonian was overhauled near the
Canary Islands by the American 44, United States, and an hour
after the action began was reduced to a mass of wreckage. The
United States was commanded by Captain Stephen Decatur, and
just before she engaged the Macedonian an incident occurred which
showed his crew's unbounded confidence in him.

JACK CREAMER

[October 25, 1812]

THE boarding nettings are triced for fight;
Pike and cutlass are shining bright;
The boatswain's whistle pipes loud and shrill;
Gunner and topman work with a will;

Rough old sailor and reefer trim
Jest as they stand by the cannon grim;
There's a fighting glint in Decatur's eye,
And brave Old Glory floats out on high.

But many a heart beats fast below
The laughing lips as they near the foe;
For the pluckiest knows, though no man quails,
That the breath of death is filling the sails.
Only one little face is wan;
Only one childish mouth is drawn;
One little heart is sad and sore
To the watchful eye of the Commodore.
Little Jack Creamer, ten years old,
In no purser's book or watch enrolled,
Must mope or skulk while his shipmates fight, —
No wonder his little face is white!

"Why, Jack, old man, so blue and sad?
Afraid of the music?" The face of the lad
With mingled shame and anger burns.
Quick to the Commodore he turns:

"I'm not a coward, but I think if you —
Excuse me, Capt'n, I mean if you knew
(I s'pose it's because I'm young and small)
I'm not on the books! I'm no one at all!
And as soon as this fighting work is done,
And we get our prize-money, everyone
Has his share of the plunder — *I* get none."

"And you're sure we shall take her?" "Sure? Why, sir,
She's only a blessed Britisher!
We'll take her easy enough, I bet;
But glory's all that I'm going to get!"
"Glory! I doubt if I get more,
If I get so much," said the Commodore;

"But faith goes far in the race for fame,
And down on the books shall go your name."

Bravely the little seaman stood
To his post while the scuppers ran with blood,
While grizzled veterans looked and smiled
And gathered new courage from the child;
Till the enemy, crippled in pride and might,
Struck his crimson flag and gave up the fight.
Then little Jack Creamer stood once more
Face to face with the Commodore.

"You have got your glory," he said, "my lad,
And money to make your sweetheart glad.
Now, who may she be?"   "My mother, sir;
I want you to send the half to her."
"And the rest?"   Jack blushed and hung his head;
"I'll buy some schoolin' with that," he said.

Decatur laughed; then in graver mood:
'The first is the better, but both are good.
Your mother shall never know want while I
Have a ship to sail, or a flag to fly;
And schooling you'll have till all is blue,
But little the lubbers can teach to you."

Midshipman Creamer's story is told —
They did such things in the days of old,
When faith and courage won sure reward,
And the quarter-deck was not triply barred,
To the forecastle hero; for men were men,
And the Nation was close to its Maker then.

JAMES JEFFREY ROCHE

GENERAL WILLIAM HENRY HARRISON, meanwhile, at the head of the western army, was besieged in Fort Meigs, at the mouth of the

Maumee River, by a large force of Indians and British. On May 1, 1813, the British made a determined assault, but were beaten off, and a few days later raised the siege and retreated to Canada.

OLD FORT MEIGS

[April 28–May 9, 1813]

OH! LONELY is our old green fort,
  Where oft, in days of old,
Our gallant soldiers bravely fought
  'Gainst savage allies bold;
But with the change of years have passed
  That unrelenting foe,
Since we fought here with Harrison,
  A long time ago.

It seems but yesterday I heard,
  From yonder thicket nigh,
The unerring rifle's sharp report,
  The Indian's startling cry.
Yon brooklet flowing at our feet,
  With crimson gore did flow,
When we fought here with Harrison,
  A long time ago.

The river rolls between its banks,
  As when of old we came,
Each grassy path, each shady nook,
  Seems to me still the same;
But we are scattered now, whose faith
  Pledged here, through weal or woe,
With Harrison our soil to guard,
  A long time ago.

But many a soldier's lip is mute,
  And clouded many a brow,
And hearts that beat for honor then,
  Have ceased their throbbing now.

We ne'er shall meet again in life
  As then we met, I trow,
When we fought here with Harrison,
  A long time ago.

UNKNOWN

THE remarkable series of victories on the ocean was finally broken by a defeat, for on June 1, 1813, the 26-gun frigate Chesapeake was defeated and captured by the British 38-gun Shannon.

THE SHANNON AND THE CHESAPEAKE

[June 1, 1813]

THE captain of the Shannon came sailing up the bay,
A reeling wind flung out behind his pennons bright and gay;
His cannon crashed a challenge; the smoke that hid the sea
Was driven hard to windward and drifted back to lee.

The captain of the Shannon sent word into the town:
Was Lawrence there, and would he dare to sail his frigate
    down
And meet him at the harbor's mouth and fight him, gun to gun,
For honor's sake, with pride at stake, until the fight was won?

Now, long the gallant Lawrence had scoured the bitter main;
With many a scar and wound of war his ship was home again;
His crew, relieved from service, were scattered far and wide,
And scarcely one, his duty done, had lingered by his side.

But to refuse the challenge? Could he outlive the shame?
Brave men and true, but deadly few, he gathered to his fame,
Once more the great ship Chesapeake prepared her for the
    fight —
"I'll bring the foe to town in tow," he said, "before tonight!"

High on the hills of Hingham that overlooked the shore,
To watch the fray and hope and pray, for they could do no
    more,

The children of the country watched the children of the sea
When the smoke drove hard to windward and drifted back
to lee.

"How can he fight," they whispered, "with only half a crew,
Though they be rare to do and dare, yet what can brave men
do?"
But when the Chesapeake came down, the Stars and Stripes
on high,
Stilled was each fear, and cheer on cheer resounded to the sky.

The Captain of the Shannon, he swore both long and loud:
"This victory, where'er it be, shall make two nations proud!
Now onward to this victory or downward to defeat!
A sailor's life is sweet with strife, a sailor's death as sweet."

And as when lightnings rend the sky and gloomy thunders
roar,
And crashing surge plays devil's dirge upon the stricken shore,
With thunder and with sheets of flame the two ships rang
with shot,
And every gun burst forth a sun of iron crimson-hot.

And twice they lashed together and twice they tore apart,
And iron balls burst wooden walls and pierced each oaken
heart.
Still from the hills of Hingham men watched with hopes and
fears,
While all the bay was torn that day with shot that rained
like tears.

The tall masts of the Chesapeake went groaning by the board;
The Shannon's spars were weak with scars when Broke cast
down his sword;
"Now woe," he cried, "to England, and shame and woe
to me!"
The smoke drove hard to windward and drifted back to lee.

"Give them one breaking broadside more," he cried, "before
    we strike!"
But one grim ball that ruined all for hope and home alike
Laid Lawrence low in glory, yet from his pallid lip
Rang to the land his last command: "Boys, don't give up
    the ship!"...

The wounded wept like women when they hauled her ensign
    down.
Men's cheeks were pale as with the tale from Hingham to
    the town
They hurried in swift silence, while toward the eastern night
The victor bore away from shore and vanished out of sight.

Hail to the great ship Chesapeake! Hail to the hero brave
Who fought her fast, and loved her last, and shared her
    sudden grave!
And glory be to those that died for all eternity;
They lie apart at the mother-heart of God's eternal sea.

THOMAS TRACY BOUVÉ

CAPTAIN JAMES LAWRENCE, commander of the Chesapeake, was
fatally wounded early in the action, but until the last he kept crying
from the cockpit, "Keep the guns going! Fight her till she strikes or
sinks!" His last words are said to have been the famous "Don't
give up the ship!"

DEFEAT AND VICTORY

[June 1, 1813]

THROUGH the clangor of the cannon,
    Through the combat's wreck and reek,
Answer to th' o'ermastering Shannon
    Thunders from the Chesapeake:
Gallant Lawrence, wounded, dying,
    Speaks with still unconquered lip
Ere the bitter draught he drinks:

Keep the Flag flying!
  Fight her till she strikes or sinks!
  Don't give up the ship!

Still that voice is sounding o'er us,
  So bold Perry heard it call;
Farragut has joined its chorus;
  Porter, Dewey, Wainwright — all
Heard the voice of duty crying;
  Deathless word from dauntless lip
That our past and future links:
Keep the Flag flying!
  Fight her till she strikes or sinks!
  Don't give up the ship!

                              WALLACE RICE

NAPOLEON's abdication enabled England to turn her whole atten-
tion to the task of crushing America, thousands of troops were
shipped into Montreal, and early in August, 1814, a force of twelve
thousand regulars started to invade New York, while a British fleet
of nineteen vessels appeared on Lake Champlain. The American
commander on the lake was Thomas Macdonough, and by herculean
efforts he managed to get together a fleet of fourteen small vessels.
On September 11, the British fleet attacked him in Plattsburg Bay,
certain of victory, but was ignominiously defeated, and the land
force was compelled to retreat to Canada.

THE BATTLE OF PLATTSBURG BAY

[September 11, 1814]

Plattsburg Bay!   Plattsburg Bay!
Blue and gold in the dawning ray,
Crimson under the high noonday
With the reek of the fray!

It was Thomas Macdonough, as gallant a sailor
  As ever went scurrying over the main;
And he cried from his deck, *If they think I'm a quailer,*

And deem they can capture this Lake of Champlain,
We'll show them they're not fighting France, sir, nor Spain!

So from Cumberland Head to the little Crab Island
    He scattered his squadron in trim battleline;
And when he saw Downie come rounding the highland,
    He knelt him, beseeching for guidance divine,
    Imploring that Heaven would crown his design.

Then thundered the Eagle her lusty defiance;
    The stout Saratoga aroused with a roar;
Soon gunboat and galley in hearty alliance
    Their resonant volley of compliments pour;
    And ever Macdonough's the man to the fore!

And lo, when the fight toward its fiercest was swirling,
    A game-cock, released by a splintering ball,
Flew high in the ratlines, the smoke round him curling,
    And over the din gave his trumpeting call,
    An omen of ultimate triumph to all!

Then a valianter light touched the powder-grimed faces;
    Then faster the shot seemed to plunge from the gun;
And we shattered their yards and we sundered their braces,
    And the fume of our cannon — it shrouded the sun;
    Cried Macdonough — *Once more, and the battle is won!*

Now, the flag of the haughty Confiance is trailing;
    The Linnet in woe staggers in toward the shore;
The Finch is a wreck from her keel to her railing;
    The galleys flee fast to the strain of the oar;
    Macdonough! 'tis he is the man to the fore!

Oh, our main decks were grim and our gun decks were gory,
    And many a brave brow was pallid with pain;
And while some won to death, yet we all won to glory
    Who fought with Macdonough that day on Champlain,
    And humbled her pride who is queen of the main!
                                    CLINTON SCOLLARD

THE blow at New York had failed, but another aimed at the Nation's Capital fell with deadly effect. On August 14, 1814, a strong British force landed in Chesapeake Bay, entered Washington and burned the Capitol, the White House, and many other public buildings. Then Baltimore was attacked, and on September 13, the British fleet opened a terrific bombardment against Fort McHenry, two miles above the city. The fort held out all night and in the morning the British withdrew.

FORT McHENRY

[September 13, 1814]

THY blue waves, Patapsco, flowed soft and serene,
    Thy hills and thy valleys were cheerful and gay,
While the day-star of Peace shed its beams on the scene,
    And youth, love, and beauty reflected its ray.

Where white-bosomed commerce late reigned o'er thy tide,
    And zephyrs of gladness expanded each sail,
I saw hostile squadrons in dread array ride,
    While their thunders reëchoed o'er hill and o'er vale.

But our heroes, thy sons, proud in panoply rose,
    For their homes, — for their altars, — to conquer or die;
With the lightning of freedom encountered their foes;
    Taught the veteran to tremble, the valiant to fly.

Now, how tranquil thy scenes where the clangors of war
    Late broke the soft dreams of the fair and the young!
To the tombs of thy heroes shall beauty repair,
    And their deeds by our bards shall forever be sung.

UNKNOWN

JUST before the bombardment began, Francis Scott Key, District Attorney of Washington, had put out to the British flagship to arrange for an exchange of prisoners, and was directed to stay until the attack was over. All through the night he watched the flaming shells, and when, by the first rays of the rising sun, he saw his country's flag still waving above the fort, he hastily wrote on the back of a letter the verses which have since become America's national anthem, and which gave the flag the name of "The Star-Spangled Banner." No song was ever inspired by more thrilling circumstances.

THE STAR-SPANGLED BANNER

[September 13, 1814]

O SAY, can you see, by the dawn's early light,
    What so proudly we hailed at the twilight's last gleaming?
Whose broad stripes and bright stars, through the perilous
      fight,
    O'er the ramparts we watched were so gallantly streaming!
And the rocket's red glare, the bombs bursting in air,
Gave proof through the night that our flag was still there:
    O say, does that star-spangled banner yet wave
    O'er the land of the free and the home of the brave?

On the shore, dimly seen through the mists of the deep,
    Where the foe's haughty host in dread silence reposes,
What is that which the breeze, o'er the towering steep,
    As it fitfully blows, now conceals, now discloses?
Now it catches the gleam of the morning's first beam,
In full glory reflected now shines on the stream:
    'Tis the star-spangled banner! O long may it wave
    O'er the land of the free and the home of the brave!

And where is that band who so vauntingly swore
    That the havoc of war and the battle's confusion
A home and a country should leave us no more?
    Their blood has washed out their foul footsteps' pollution.
No refuge could save the hireling and slave
From the terror of flight, or the gloom of the grave:
    And the star-spangled banner in triumph doth wave
    O'er the land of the free and the home of the brave!

Oh! thus be it ever, when freemen shall stand
    Between their loved homes and the war's desolation!

Blest with victory and peace, may the heaven-rescued land
  Praise the Power that hath made and preserved us a nation.
Then conquer we must, for our cause it is just,
And this be our motto: "In God is our trust."
  And the star-spangled banner in triumph shall wave
  O'er the land of the free and the home of the brave.

FRANCIS SCOTT KEY

THE destruction of Washington was one of the most brutal acts of vandalism ever committed by a Christian army, and it gave added strength to an anti-war party which had been formed in England.

THE BOWER OF PEACE

[From "Ode Written during the War with America, 1814"]

WHEN shall the Island Queen of Ocean lay
    The thunderbolt aside,
And, twining olives with her laurel crown,
    Rest in the Bower of Peace?

Not long may this unnatural strife endure
    Beyond the Atlantic deep;
Not long may men, with vain ambition drunk,
    And insolent in wrong,
  Afflict with their misrule the indignant land
    Where Washington hath left
    His awful memory
    A light for after-times!
  Vile instruments of fallen Tyranny
In their own annals, by their countrymen,
For lasting shame shall they be written down.
  Soon may the better Genius there prevail!
  Then will the Island Queen of Ocean lay
    The thunderbolt aside,
And, twining olives with her laurel crown,
    Rest in the Bower of Peace.

ROBERT SOUTHEY

In December, 1814, British and American commissioners met at Ghent, Belgium, and agreed upon terms of peace.　But this was long before the days of the telegraph, and General Andrew Jackson, who had been sent to defend New Orleans, knew nothing about it.　Neither did the commander of a great British fleet which appeared before the city just as Jackson reached it.　Jackson intrenched his little army, and on January 8, 1815, was attacked by the full British force, seven thousand strong.　Jackson's troops were largely frontiersmen, cool-headed, expert riflemen, and their fire was so deadly that the enemy, after several desperate attacks, was routed with a loss of over two thousand.　The American loss was only eight killed and fourteen wounded.

THE BATTLE OF NEW ORLEANS

[January 8, 1815]

Here, in my rude log cabin,
　　Few poorer men there be
Among the mountain ranges
　　Of Eastern Tennessee.
My limbs are weak and shrunken,
　　White hairs upon my brow,
My dog — lie still old fellow! —
　　My sole companion now.
Yet I, when young and lusty,
　　Have gone through stirring scenes,
For I went down with Carroll
　　To fight at New Orleans.

You say you'd like to hear me
　　The stirring story tell,
Of those who stood the battle
　　And those who fighting fell.
Short work to count our losses —
　　We stood and dropped the foe
As easily as by firelight
　　Men shoot the buck or doe.
And while they fell by hundreds
　　Upon the bloody plain,

Of us, fourteen were wounded
    And only eight were slain.

The eighth of January,
    Before the break of day,
Our raw and hasty levies
    Were brought into array.
No cotton-bales before us —
    Some fool that falsehood told;
Before us was an earthwork
    Built from the swampy mold
And there we stood in silence,
    And waited with a frown.
To greet with bloody welcome
    The bull-dogs of the Crown.

The heavy fog of morning
    Still hid the plain from sight,
When came a thread of scarlet
    Marked faintly in the white.
We fired a single cannon,
    And as its thunders rolled,
The mist before us lifted
    In many a heavy fold —
The mist before us lifted
    And in their bravery fine
Came rushing to their ruin
    The fearless British line....

Our rifles firmly grasping,
    And heedless of the din,
We stood in silence waiting
    For orders to begin.
Our fingers on the triggers,
    Our hearts, with anger stirred,
Grew still more fierce and eager
    As Jackson's voice was heard:

"Stand steady!   Waste no powder!
    Wait till your shots will tell!
Today the work you finish —
    See that you do it well!"

Their columns drawing nearer,
    We felt our patience tire,
When came the voice of Carroll,
    Distinct and measured, "Fire!"
Oh! then you should have marked us
    Our volleys on them pour —
Have heard our joyous rifles
    Ring sharply through the roar,
And seen their foremost columns
    Melt hastily away
As snow in mountain gorges
    Before the floods of May.

They soon re-formed their columns,
    And, mid the fatal rain
We never ceased to hurtle,
    Came to their work again.
The Forty-fourth is with them,
    That first its laurels won
With stout old Abercrombie
    Beneath an eastern sun.
It rushes to the battle,
    And, though within the rear
Its leader is a laggard,
    It shows no signs of fear.

It did not need its colonel,
    For soon there came instead
An eagle-eyed commander,
    And on its march he led.
'Twas Pakenham in person,
    The leader of the field;

I knew it by the cheering
  That loudly round him pealed;
And by his quick, sharp movement
  We felt his heart was stirred,
As when at Salamanca
  He led the fighting Third.

I raised my rifle quickly,
  I sighted at his breast,
God save the gallant leader
  And take him to his rest!
I did not draw the trigger,
  I could not for my life.
So calm he sat his charger
  Amid the deadly strife,
That in my fiercest moment
  A prayer arose from me —
God save that gallant leader,
  Our foeman though he be!

Sir Edward's charger staggers;
  He leaps at once to ground.
And ere the beast falls bleeding
  Another horse is found.
His right arm falls — 'tis wounded;
  He waves on high his left;
In vain he leads the movement,
  The ranks in twain are cleft.
The men in scarlet waver
  Before the men in brown,
And fly in utter panic —
  The soldiers of the Crown!

I thought the work was over,
  But nearer shouts were heard,
And came, with Gibbs to head it,
  The gallant Ninety-third.

Then Pakenham, exulting,
   With proud and joyous glance,
Cried, "Children of the tartan —
   Bold Highlanders — advance!
Advance to scale the breastworks,
   And drive them from their hold,
And show the stainless courage
   That marked your sires of old!"

His voice as yet was ringing,
   When, quick as light, there came
The roaring of a cannon,
   And earth seemed all aflame.
Who causes thus the thunder
   The doom of men to speak?
It is the Baratarian,
   The fearless Dominique.
Down through the marshaled Scotsmen
   The step of death is heard,
And by the fierce tornado
   Falls half the Ninety-third.

The smoke passed slowly upward
   And, as it soared on high,
I saw the brave commander
   In dying anguish lie.
They bear him from the battle
   Who never fled the foe;
Unmoved by death around them
   His bearers softly go.
In vain their care, so gentle,
   Fades earth and all its scenes;
The man of Salamanca
   Lies dead at New Orleans....

The stormers had retreated,
   The bloody work was o'er;
The feet of the invaders
   Were soon to leave our shore.

We rested on our rifles
 And talked about the fight,
When came a sudden murmur
 Like fire from left to right;
We turned and saw our chieftain,
 And then, good friend of mine,
You should have heard the cheering
 That rang along the line....

In answer to our shouting
 Fire lit his eye of gray;
Erect, but thin and pallid,
 He passed upon his bay.
Weak from the baffled fever,
 And shrunken in each limb,
The swamps of Alabama
 Had done their work on him;
But spite of that and fasting,
 And hours of sleepless care,
The soul of Andrew Jackson
 Shone forth in glory there.

THOMAS DUNN ENGLISH

Nor was there any wireless in 1815, and on the afternoon of February 20, the famous old Constitution was sailing along near Madeira, when she sighted two British warships. They were the Cyane and the Levant. The Constitution overhauled them, attacked them simultaneously, and after a fierce fight compelled them both to surrender.

THE CONSTITUTION'S LAST FIGHT

[February 20, 1815]

A Yankee ship and a Yankee crew —
 Constitution, where ye bound for?
Wherever, my lad, there's fight to be had
 Acrost the Western ocean.

Our captain was married in Boston town
    And sailed next day to sea;
For all must go when the State says so;
    Blow high, blow low, sailed we.

"Now, what shall I bring for a bridal gift
    When my home-bound pennant flies?
The rarest that be on land or sea
    It shall be my lady's prize."

"There's never a prize on sea or land
    Could bring such joy to me
As my true love sound and homeward bound
    With a king's ship under his lee."

The Western ocean is wide and deep,
    And wild its tempests blow,
But bravely rides "Old Ironsides,"
    A-cruising to and fro.

We cruised to the east and we cruised to north,
    And southing far went we,
And at last off Cape de Verd we raised
    Two frigates sailing free.

Oh, God made man, and man made ships,
    But God makes very few
Like him who sailed our ship that day,
    And fought her, one to two.

He gained the weather-gage of both,
    He held them both a-lee;
And gun for gun, till set of sun,
    He spoke them fair and free;

Till the night-fog fell on spar and sail,
    And ship, and sea, and shore,

And our only aim was the bursting flame
  And the hidden cannon's roar.

Then a long rift in the mist showed up
  The stout Cyane, close-hauled
To swing in our wake and our quarter rake,
  And a boasting Briton bawled:

'Starboard and larboard, we've got him fast
  Where his heels won't take him through;
Let him luff or wear, he'll find us there —
  Ho, Yankee, which will you do?"

We did not luff and we did not wear,
  But braced our topsails back,
Till the sternway drew us fair and true
  Broadsides athwart her track.

Athwart her track and across her bows
  We raked her fore and aft,
And out of the fight and into the night
  Drifted the beaten craft.

The slow Levant came up too late;
  No need had we to stir;
Her decks we swept with fire, and kept
  The flies from troubling her.

We raked her again, and her flag came down —
  The haughtiest flag that floats —
And the lime-juice dogs lay there like logs,
  With never a bark in their throats.

With never a bark and never a bite,
  But only an oath to break,
As we squared away for Praya Bay
  With our prizes in our wake.

Parole they gave and parole they broke,
  What matters the cowardly cheat,
If the captain's bride was satisfied
  With the one prize laid at her feet?

A Yankee ship and a Yankee crew —
  Constitution, where ye bound for?
Wherever the British prizes be,
Though it's one to two, or one to three —
"Old Ironsides" means victory,
  Acrost the Western ocean.

                    JAMES JEFFREY ROCHE

ON SEPTEMBER 12, 1830, the Boston *Advertiser* printed a paragraph
stating that the Secretary of the Navy had recommended that "Old
Ironsides" be sold to be broken up. Two days later, in the same
paper, appeared the famous poem by Oliver Wendell Holmes, which
instantly became a sort of national battle-cry. Instead of being
broken up, the Constitution was rebuilt, and is still maintained in
perfect condition.

OLD IRONSIDES

[September 14, 1830]

AYE, tear her tattered ensign down!
  Long has it waved on high,
And many an eye has danced to see
  That banner in the sky;
Beneath it rung the battle shout,
  And burst the cannon's roar; —
The meteor of the ocean air
  Shall sweep the clouds no more.

Her deck, once red with heroes' blood,
  Where knelt the vanquished foe,
When winds were hurrying o'er the flood,
  And waves were white below,

No more shall feel the victor's tread,
  Or know the conquered knee; —
The harpies of the shore shall pluck
  The eagle of the sea!

Oh, better that her shattered hulk
  Should sink beneath the wave;
Her thunders shook the mighty deep,
  And there should be her grave;
Nail to the mast her holy flag,
  Set every threadbare sail,
And give her to the god of storms,
  The lightning and the gale!

OLIVER WENDELL HOLMES

CHAPTER II

TEXAS AND CALIFORNIA

AT THE close of the Revolution, the country west of the Alleghany Mountains was still an unbroken wilderness, save for a few settlements in Kentucky, which Daniel Boone had explored, and a handful of trading-posts in the Illinois country, where pelts were purchased from the Indians. But these were mere pin-points in the great stretches of virgin forest, amid which the first settlers hewed out their homes.

THE SETTLER

His echoing axe the settler swung
   Amid the sea-like solitude,
And, rushing, thundering, down were flung
   The Titans of the wood;
Loud shrieked the eagle, as he dashed
From out his mossy nest, which crashed
   With its supporting bough,
And the first sunlight, leaping, flashed
   On the wolf's haunt below.

Rude was the garb and strong the frame
   Of him who plied his ceaseless toil:
To form that garb the wildwood game
   Contributed their spoil;
The soul that warmed that frame disdained
The tinsel, gaud, and glare that reigned
   Where men their crowds collect;
The simple fur, untrimmed, unstained,
   This forest-tamer decked.

The paths which wound 'mid gorgeous trees,
   The stream whose bright lips kissed their flowers,
The winds that swelled their harmonies
   Through those sun-hiding bowers,

The temple vast, the green arcade,
The nestling vale, the grassy glade,
   Dark cave, and swampy lair;
These scenes and sounds majestic made
   His world, his pleasures, there.

His roof adorned a pleasant spot;
   Mid the black logs green glowed the grain,
And herbs and plants the woods knew not
   Throve in the sun and rain.
The smoke-wreath curling o'er the dell,
The low, the bleat, the tinkling bell,
   All made a landscape strange,
Which was the living chronicle
   Of deeds that wrought the change.

The violet sprung at spring's first tinge,
   The rose of summer spread its glow,
The maize hung out its autumn fringe,
   Rude winter brought his snow;
And still the lone one labored there,
His shout and whistle broke the air,
   As cheerily he plied
His garden-spade, or drove his share
   Along the hillock's side....

Humble the lot, yet his the race,
   When Liberty sent forth her cry,
Who thronged in conflict's deadliest place,
   To fight — to bleed — to die!
Who cumbered Bunker's height of red,
By hope through weary years were led,
   And witnessed Yorktown's sun
Blaze on a nation's banner spread,
   A nation's freedom won.

                     ALFRED B. STREET

DEATH was ever present, and in its most hideous form, for north-west of the Ohio dwelt the powerful Delaware and Shawanese Indi-ans, ready at any moment to march against the border settlements and to surprise isolated dwellings.   In this incessant warfare, the frontier women played no little part.

THE MOTHERS OF THE WEST

THE Mothers of our Forest-Land!
    Stout-hearted dames were they;
With nerve to wield the battle-brand,
    And join the border-fray.
Our rough land had no braver,
    In its days of blood and strife —
Aye ready for severest toil,
    Aye free to peril life.

The Mothers of our Forest-Land!
    On old Kan-tuc-kee's soil,
How shared they, with each dauntless band,
    War's tempest and Life's toil!
They shrank not from the foeman —
    They quailed not in the fight —
But cheered their husbands through the day,
    And soothed them through the night.

The Mothers of our Forest-Land!
    Their bosoms pillowed *men!*
And proud were they by such to stand,
    In hammock, fort, or glen.
To load the sure old rifle —
    To run the leaden ball —
To watch a battling husband's place,
    And fill it should he fall.

The Mothers of our Forest-Land!
    Such were their daily deeds.
Their monument! — where does it stand?
    Their epitaph! — who reads?

No braver dames had Sparta,
    No nobler matrons Rome —
Yet who or lauds or honors them,
    E'en in their own green home!

The Mothers of our Forest-Land!
    They sleep in unknown graves:
And had they borne and nursed a band
    Of ingrates, or of slaves,
They had not been more neglected!
    But their graves shall yet be found,
And their monuments dot here and there
    "The Dark and Bloody Ground."
                    WILLIAM D. GALLAGHER

THE land northwest of the Ohio was very fertile, but it was the favorite hunting-ground of these savage tribes, and the man who attempted to settle there took his life in his hands. Finally, on August 20, 1794, General Anthony Wayne defeated the Indians in a great battle on the Maumee and compelled them to sue for peace. They ceded twenty-five thousand square miles of territory to the Americans, and settlers flocked into the country.

THE FOUNDERS OF OHIO

THE footsteps of a hundred years
    Have echoed, since o'er Braddock's Road
Bold Putnam and the Pioneers
    Led History the way they strode.

On wild Monongahela stream
    They launched the Mayflower of the West,
A perfect State their civic dream,
    A new New World their pilgrim quest.

When April robed the Buckeye trees
    Muskingum's bosky shore they trod;
They pitched their tents, and to the breeze
    Flung freedom's star-flag, thanking God.

As glides the Oyo's solemn flood,
　　So fleeted their eventful years;
Resurgent in their children's blood,
　　They still live on — the Pioneers.

Their fame shrinks not to names and dates
　　On votive stone, the prey of time; —
Behold where monumental States
　　Immortalize their lives sublime!
　　　　　　　　WILLIAM HENRY VENABLE

In 1804, two daring explorers, Captain Meriwether Lewis and Lieutenant William Clark, of the First United States Infantry, were appointed by the Government to seek water communication with the Pacific Coast, and started westward on May 14. They ascended the Missouri, crossed the mountains and descended the Columbia, reaching its mouth November 15, 1805. On January 14, 1807, they were back in Washington, and the following poem was read at a dinner given in their honor.

ON THE DISCOVERIES OF CAPTAIN LEWIS

[January 14, 1807]

Let the Nile cloak his head in the clouds, and defy
　　The researches of science and time;
Let the Niger escape the keen traveler's eye,
　　By plunging or changing his clime.

Columbus! not so shall thy boundless domain
　　Defraud thy brave sons of their right;
Streams, midlands, and shorelands elude us in vain.
　　We shall drag their dark regions to light.

Look down, sainted sage, from thy synod of Gods;
　　See, inspired by thy venturous soul,
Mackenzie roll northward his earth-draining floods,
　　And surge the broad waves to the pole.

With the same soaring genius thy Lewis ascends,
    And, seizing the car of the sun,
O'er the sky-propping hills and high waters he bends,
    And gives the proud earth a new zone.

Potowmak, Ohio, Missouri had felt
    Half her globe in their cincture comprest;
His long curving course has completed the belt,
    And tamed the last tide of the west.

Then hear the loud voice of the nation proclaim,
    And all ages resound the decree:
Let our occident stream bear the young hero's name,
    Who taught him his path to the sea.

These four brother floods, like a garland of flowers,
    Shall entwine all our states in a band
Conform and confederate their wide-spreading powers,
    And their wealth and their wisdom expand.

From Darien to Davis one garden shall bloom,
    Where war's weary banners are furl'd,
And the far scenting breezes that waft its perfume,
    Shall settle the storms of the world.

Then hear the loud voice of the nation proclaim
    And all ages resound the decree:
Let our occident stream bear the young hero's name,
    Who taught him his path to the sea.

                    JOEL BARLOW

A FEW years later, another great territory away to the south was claiming attention. Texas, the northernmost province of Mexico, had drawn many settlers from the United States, and when, in 1834, General Santa Anna abolished the Mexican constitution and established a military despotism, the citizens of Texas revolted and de clared their independence. General Cos, the military governor, was besieged at Bejar, and captured after a desperate assault led by Benjamin R. Milam.

THE VALOR OF BEN MILAM

December 5–11, 1835]

OH, *who will follow old Ben Milam into San Antonio?*
Such was the thrilling word we heard in the chill December glow;
Such was the thrilling word we heard, and a ringing, answering cry
Went up from the dun adobe walls to the cloudless Texas sky.

He had won from the reek of a Mexique jail back without map or chart,
With his mother-wit and his hero-grit and his stanch Kentucky heart;
He had trudged by vale and by mountain trail, and by thorny and thirsty plain,
And now, with joy on his grizzled brow he had come to his own again.

They're the spawn of Hell! we heard him tell; *they will knife and lie and cheat;*
At the board of none of the swarthy horde would I deign to sit at meat;
They hold it naught that I bled and fought when Spain was their ruthless foe:
Oh, who will follow old Ben Milam into San Antonio?

It was four to one, not gun for gun, but never a curse cared we,
Three hundred faithful and fearless men who had sworn to make Texas free.
It was mighty odds, by all the gods, this brute of the Mexique dam,
But it was not much for heroes such as followed old Ben Milam!

With rifle-crack and sabre-hack we drove them back in the
    street;
From house to house in the red carouse we hastened their
    flying feet;
And ever that shout kept pealing out with a swift and sure
    death-blow:
Oh, who will follow old Ben Milam into San Antonio?

Behind the walls from the hurtling balls Cos cowered and
    swore in his beard,
While we slashed and slew from dawn till dew, and, Bexar,
    how we cheered!
But ere failed each ruse, and the white of truce on the failing
    day was thrown,
Our fearless soul had gone to the goal, the Land of the Great
    Unknown.

Death brought the darksome boon too soon to this truest
    one of the true,
Or, men of the fated Alamo, Milam had died with you!
So when their names that now are Fame's — the scorner of
    braggart sham; —
In song be praised, let a rouse be raised for the name of
    Ben Milam!

CLINTON SCOLLARD

On February 23, 1836, Santa Anna appeared at the head of two
thousand men before San Antonio. The town was guarded by a fort
called the Alamo, held by Colonel William Travis and one hundred
and fifty Texans. After a terrific struggle, the Mexicans carried the
fort on March 6. Six of the Texans, including Travis, Bowie, and
Crockett, were taken alive, but were immediately put to death.

THE DEFENSE OF THE ALAMO

[March 6, 1835]

Santa Anna came storming, as a storm might come;
    There was rumble of cannon; there was rattle of blade;

There was cavalry, infantry, bugle and drum —
    Full seven proud thousand in pomp and parade.
The chivalry, flower of all Mexico;
And a gaunt two hundred in the Alamo!

And thirty lay sick, and some were shot through;
    For the siege had been bitter, and bloody, and long.
"Surrender, or die!" — "Men, what will *you* do?"
    And Travis, great Travis, drew sword, quick and strong;
Drew a line at his feet...."Will you come?   Will you go?
I die with my wounded, in the Alamo."

Then Bowie gasped, "Lead me over that line!"
    Then Crockett, one hand to the sick, one hand to his gun,
Crossed with him; then never a word or a sign
    Till all, sick or well, all, all save but one,
One man.   Then a woman stepped, praying, and slow
Across, to die with the heroes of the Alamo.

Then that one coward fled, in the night, in that night
    When all men silently prayed and thought
Of home; of tomorrow; of God and the right,
    Till dawn; then Travis sent his single last cannon-shot,
In answer to insolent Mexico,
From the old bell-tower of the Alamo.

Then came Santa Anna; a crescent of flame!
    Then the red escalade; then the fight hand to hand;
Such an unequal fight as never had name
    Since the Persian hordes butchered that doomed Spartan
        band.
All day — all day and all night; and the morning? so slow,
Through the battle smoke mantling the Alamo.

Then silence!   Such silence!   Two thousand lay dead
    In a crescent outside!   And within?   Not a breath
Save the gasp of a woman, with gory gashed head,
    All alone, all alone there, waiting for death;

And she but a nurse. Yet when shall we know
Another like this of the Alamo?

Shout "Victory, victory, victory ho!"
    I say, 'tis not always with the hosts that win!
I say that the victory, high or low,
    Is given the hero who grapples with sin,
Or legion or single; just asking to know
When duty fronts death in his Alamo.

JOAQUIN MILLER

A FEW days later, at Goliad, Colonel Fannin and four hundred Texans surrendered to the Mexicans under solemn assurance that their lives would be spared. On March 27, the prisoners, who had, of course, been disarmed, were marched out under guard and shot down to the last man. This brutal massacre aroused the wildest indignation, recruits flocked to the army under Sam Houston, and on April 21 surprised Santa Anna at San Jacinto and exacted terrible vengeance.

THE FIGHT AT SAN JACINTO

[April 21, 1836]

"Now for a brisk and cheerful fight!"
    Said Harman, big and droll,
As he coaxed his flint and steel for a light,
    And puffed at his cold clay bowl;
"For we are a skulking lot," says he,
    "Of land-thieves hereabout,
And the bold señores, two to one,
    Have come to smoke us out."

Santa Anna and Castrillon,
    Almonte brave and gay,
Portilla red from Goliad,
    And Cos with his smart array.

Dulces and cigaritos,
   And the light guitar, ting-tum!
Sant' Anna courts siesta —
   And Sam Houston taps his drum.

The buck stands still in the timber —
   "Is't the patter of nuts that fall?"
The foal of the wild mare whinnies —
   "Did he hear the Commanche call?"
In the brake by the crawling bayou
   The slinking she-wolves howl,
And the mustang's snort in the river sedge
   Has startled the paddling fowl.

A soft low tap, and a muffled tap,
   And a roll not loud nor long —
We would not break Sant' Anna's nap,
   Nor spoil Almonte's song.
Saddles and knives and rifles!
   Lord! but the men were glad
When Deaf Smith muttered "Alamo!"
   And Karnes hissed "Goliad!"

The drummer tucked his sticks in his belt,
   And the fifer gripped his gun.
Oh, for one free, wild Texan yell,
   And we took the slope in a run!
But never a shout nor a shot we spent,
   Nor an oath nor a prayer that day,
Till we faced the bravos, eye to eye,
   And then we blazed away.

Then we knew the rapture of Ben Milam,
   And the glory that Travis made,
With Bowie's lunge and Crockett's shot,
   And Fannin's dancing blade;
And the heart of the fighter, bounding free
   In his joy so hot and mad —
When Millard charged for Alamo,
   Lamar for Goliad.

Deaf Smith rode straight, with reeking spur,
    Into the shock and rout:
"I've hacked and burned the bayou bridge,
    There's no sneak's back-way out!"
Muzzle or butt for Goliad,
    Pistol and blade and fist!
Oh, for the knife that never glanced,
    And the gun that never missed!

Dulces and cigaritos,
    Song and the mandolin!
That gory swamp was a gruesome grove
    To dance fandangos in.
We bridged the bog with the sprawling herd
    That fell in that frantic rout;
We slew and slew till the sun set red,
    And the Texan star flashed out.

JOHN WILLIAMSON PALMER

THE victory at San Jacinto ended the war. Santa Anna signed a treaty recognizing the Republic of Texas, which at once sent commissioners to Washington to ask for admission to the Union. Mexico warned the United States that she would consider this an act of war, but on December 29, 1845, Texas was admitted, and an American army under General Zachary Taylor was hurried southward to meet the Mexican army assembled along the Rio Grande. On May 8, the two armies met at Palo Alto, and the Mexicans were defeated.

THE GUNS IN THE GRASS

[May 8, 1846]

As HANG two mighty thunderclouds
    Ere lightnings link the twain,
So lie we and the Mexican
    On Palo Alto plain;
And silence, solemn, dread, profound,
Broods o'er the waiting battle-ground.

We see the foeman's musketeers
    Deployed upon his right,
And on his left the cavalry
    Stand, hungry for the fight;
But that blank center — what? Alas,
'Tis hidden by the prairie grass!

Old Rough-and-Ready scans the foe;
    "I would I knew," says he,
"Whether or no that lofty grass
    Conceals artillery.
Could I but bring that spot in ken,
'Twere worth to me five thousand men!"

Then forward steps Lieutenant Blake,
    Touches his hat, and says,
"I wait command to ride and see
    What 'neath that prairie lays."
We stand amazed: no cowards, we:
But this is more than bravery!

"'Command!'" cries Taylor; "nay, I ne'er
    To such a deed 'command!'"
Then bends he o'er his horse's neck
    And takes as brave a hand
As e'er a loyal saber bore:
"God bless you, Blake," he says — no more.

The soldier to his saddle springs
    And gayly waves good-bye,
Determination on his lips,
    A proud light in his eye:
And then, as pity holds our breath,
We see him dare that road of death.

To utmost pace his steed he spurs.
    Save that his sword hangs free,
It were as though a madman charged
    A nation's chivalry!

On, on, he flies, his steed unreined
Till yonder hillock's crest is gained.

And now he checks his horse, dismounts,
    And coolly through his glass
Surveys the phalanx of the foe
    That lies beyond the grass.
A musket-flash! They move! Advance!
Halt! — 'twas the sunlight on a lance!

He turns, remounts, and speeds him back.
    Hark! what is that we hear?
Across the rolling prairie rings —
    A gun? ah, no — a cheer!
A noble tribute sweeps the plain:
A thousand throats take up the strain.

Safe!   But the secret to unveil
    Taylor no longer seeks;
For with a roar that shakes the earth
    That unmasked center speaks!
'Gainst fearful odds, till set of sun,
We battle — and the field is won!

THOMAS FROST

IN AUGUST, General Taylor advanced on Monterey, a town believed
to be impregnable, where General Arista had collected an army of
ten thousand men.   The American forces reached the town on Sep-
tember 19, and after two days' desperate fighting, compelled its sur-
render.

MONTEREY

[September 23, 1846]

WE WERE not many, we who stood
    Before the iron sleet that day:
Yet many a gallant spirit would
Give half his years if but he could
    Have been with us at Monterey.

Now here, now there, the shot is hailed
  In deadly drifts of fiery spray,
Yet not a single soldier quailed
When wounded comrades round them wailed
  Their dying shout at Monterey.

And on — still on our column kept
  Through walls of flame its withering way;
Where fell the dead, the living stept,
Still charging on the guns which swept
  The slippery streets of Monterey.

The foe himself recoiled aghast,
  When, striking where he strongest lay,
We swooped his flanking batteries past,
And braving full their murderous blast,
  Stormed home the towers of Monterey.

Our banners on those turrets wave,
  And there our evening bugles play:
Where orange-boughs above their grave
Keep green the memory of the brave
  Who fought and fell at Monterey.

We are not many — we who pressed
  Beside the brave who fell that day —
But who of us has not confessed
He'd rather share their warrior rest
  Than not have been at Monterey?
                CHARLES FENNO HOFFMAN

SANTA ANNA meanwhile had collected a great army, and General
Taylor fell back on the village of Buena Vista. There, on February
22, 1847, Santa Anna summoned him to surrender, warning him that
he was surrounded by twenty thousand men. "General Taylor
never surrenders!" was the reply, and the Mexicans advanced to
the attack, only to be completely routed after a two days' struggle.
In this remarkable battle, the American forces numbered 4600, the

Mexicans over 23,000. The Mexican losses exceeded 2500, while 264 Americans were killed. Many of them were from Kentucky, and Theodore O'Hara's famous poem was written to commemorate them.

THE BIVOUAC OF THE DEAD

THE muffled drum's sad roll has beat
    The soldier's last tattoo;
No more on Life's parade shall meet
    That brave and fallen few.
On Fame's eternal camping-ground
    Their silent tents are spread,
And Glory guards, with solemn round,
    The bivouac of the dead.

No rumor of the foe's advance
    Now swells upon the wind;
No troubled thought at midnight haunts
    Of loved ones left behind;
No vision of the morrow's strife
    The warrior's dream alarms;
No braying horn nor screaming fife
    At dawn shall call to arms.

Their shivered swords are red with rust;
    Their plumèd heads are bowed;
Their haughty banner, trailed in dust,
    Is now their martial shroud.
And plenteous funeral tears have washed
    The red stains from each brow,
And the proud forms, by battle gashed,
    Are free from anguish now.

The neighing troop, the flashing blade,
    The bugle's stirring blast,
The charge, the dreadful cannonade,
    The din and shout are past;

Nor war's wild note, nor glory's peal,
　　Shall thrill with fierce delight
Those breasts that nevermore may feel
　　The rapture of the fight....

Rest on, embalmed and sainted dead!
　　Dear as the blood ye gave,
No impious footstep here shall tread
　　The herbage of your grave;
Nor shall your story be forgot,
　　While Fame her record keeps,
Or Honor points the hallowed spot
　　Where Valor proudly sleeps.

Theodore O'Hara

On March 9, 1847, General Winfield Scott arrived off Vera Cruz, with twelve thousand men, to march against Mexico City. He reached it August 20, and advanced to the attack on September 8, choosing the approach guarded by the formidable works of Chapultepec and Molino del Rey, or the King's Mill. The latter was carried by assault, after a fierce hand-to-hand struggle.

BATTLE OF THE KING'S MILL

[September 8, 1847]

Said my landlord, white-headed Gil Gomez,
　　With newspaper held in his hand —
"So they've built from El Paso a railway
　　That Yankees may visit our land.
As guests let them come and be welcome,
　　But not as they came here before;
They are rather rough fellows to handle
　　In the rush of the battle and roar.

"They took Vera Cruz and its castle;
　　In triumph they marched through the land;
We fought them with desperate daring,
　　But lacked the right man to command.

They stormed, at a loss, Cerro Gordo —
    Every mile in their movement it cost;
And when they arrived at Puebla,
    Some thousands of men they had lost.

"Ere our capital fell, and the city
    By foreign invaders was won,
We called out among its defenders
    Each man who could handle a gun.
Chapultepec stood in their pathway;
    Churubusco they had to attack;
The mill of the King — well, I fought there,
    And they were a hard nut to crack.

"While their right was assailing the ramparts,
    Our force struck their left on the field,
Where our colonel, in language that stirred us
    To love of our country appealed.
And we swore that we never would falter
    Before either saber or ball;
We would beat back the foeman before us,
    Or dead on the battle-field fall.

"Fine words, you may say, but we meant them;
    And so when they came up the hill,
We poured on them volley on volley,
    And riddled their ranks with a will.
Their line in a moment was broken;
    They closed it, and came with a cheer;
But still we fired quickly and deadly,
    And felt neither pity nor fear.

"We smote the blue column with grapeshot,
    But it rushed as the wild torrent runs;
At the pieces they slew our best gunners,
    And took in the struggle our guns.
We sprang in a rage to retake them,
    And lost nearly half of our men;

Then, baffled and beaten, retreated,
　And gained our position again.

"Ceased their yell, and in spite of our firing
　They dressed like an arrow in line,
Then, standing there moveless a moment,
　Their eyes flashed with purpose malign,
All still as the twilight in summer,
　No cloud on the sky to deform,
Like the lull in the voices of nature
　Ere wakens the whirlwind and storm.

"We had fought them with death-daring spirit
　And courage unyielding till then;
No man could have forced us to falter,
　But these were more demons than men.
Our ranks had been torn by their bullets,
　We filled all the gaps they had made;
But the pall of that terrible silence
　The hearts of our boldest dismayed.

"Before us no roaring of cannon,
　Rifle-rattle, or musketry peal;
But there on the ocean of battle
　Surged steady the billow of steel.
Fierce we opened our fire on the column,
　We pierced it with ball here and there;
But it swept on in pitiless sternness
　Till we faltered and fled in despair.

"After that all their movements were easy;
　At their storming Chapultepec fell,
And that ended the war — we were beaten:
　No story is left me to tell.
And now they come back to invade us,
　Though not with the bullet and blade;
They are here with their goods on a railway,
　To conquer the country by trade."
THOMAS DUNN ENGLISH

CHAPULTEPEC, the stronger of the two, still remained, and on the morning of September 13, two storming parties rushed it, swarmed over the walls, swept back the garrison, and planted the American flag on the ramparts. The Mexican army hastened to evacuate the city, and on September 14, the Stars and Stripes floated over the capital of Mexico.

THE SIEGE OF CHAPULTEPEC

[September 13, 1847]

WIDE o'er the valley the pennons are fluttering,
War's sullen story the deep guns are muttering,
Forward! blue-jackets, in good steady order,
Strike for the fame of your good northern border;
Forever shall history tell of the bloody check
Waiting the foe at the siege of Chapultepec.

Let the proud deeds of your fathers inspire ye still,
Think ye of Monmouth, and Princeton, and Bunker Hill,
Come from your hallowed graves, famous in story,
Shades of our heroes, and lead us to glory.
Side by side, son and father with hoary head
Struggle for triumph, or death on a gory bed.

Hark! to the charge! the war-hail is pattering,
The foe through our ranks red rain is scattering;
Huzza! forward! no halting or flagging till
Proudly the red stripes float o'er yon rocky hill.
Northern and Southerner, let your feuds smolder;
Charge! for our banner's fame, shoulder to shoulder!

Flash the fort guns, and thunders their stunning swell
Far o'er the valley to white Popocatapetl,
Death revels high in the midst of the bloody sport,
Bursting in flame from each black-throated castle-port,
Press on the line with keen sabers dripping wet,
Cheer, as ye smite with the death-dealing bayonet!

Our bold Northern eagle, king of the firmament,
Shares with no rival the skies of the continent.
Yields the fierce foeman; down let his flag be hurled,
Shout, as our own from the turret is wide unfurled!
Shout! for long shall Mexico mourn the wreck
Of her proud state at the siege of Chapultepec.

WILLIAM HAINES LYTLE

MEANWHILE, General Stephen Kearny, at the head of the Army of
the West, had seized New Mexico and then pressed on to California,
defeated the Mexicans at Sacramento, and took possession of the
province.   Mexico sued for peace, accepted the Rio Grande as her
northern boundary, and ceded New Mexico and California to the
United States, in return for a payment of $15,000,000.   On June 12,
1848, the last of the United States troops left the City of Mexico.
They were received at home with the wildest enthusiasm.

THE VOLUNTEERS

THE Volunteers! the Volunteers!
I dream, as in the bygone years,
I hear again their stirring cheers,
    And see their banners shine,
What time the yet unconquered North
Pours to the wars her legions forth,
For many a wrong to strike a blow
With mailèd hand at Mexico....

Blent with the roar of guns and bombs,
How grandly from the dim past comes
The roll of their victorious drums,
    Their bugles' joyous notes,
When over Mexico's proud towers,
And the fair valley's storied bowers,
Fit recompense of toil and scars,
In triumph waved their flag of stars.

Ah, comrades, of your own tried troop,
Whose honor ne'er to shame might stoop,

Of lion heart and eagle swoop,
  But you alone remain;
On all the rest has fallen the hush
Of death; the men whose battle-rush
Was wild as sun-loosed torrent's flow
From Orizaba's crest of snow.

The Volunteers! the Volunteers!
God send us peace through all our years,
But if the cloud of war appears,
  We'll see them once again.
From broad Ohio's peaceful side,
From where the Maumee pours its tide,
From storm-lashed Erie's wintry shore,
Shall spring the Volunteers once more.

WILLIAM HAINES LYTLE

As a province of Mexico, California had been little more than a myth
to most Americans, but scarcely had it been acquired for the Union,
when the whole country was electrified by the news that gold had
been discovered there. Within a few months, thousands of men had
started to seek their fortunes in this new El Dorado.

THE GOLD-SEEKERS

I saw these dreamers of dreams go by,
  I trod in their footsteps a space;
Each marched with his eyes on the sky,
  Each passed with a light on his face.

They came from the hopeless and sad,
  They faced the future and gold;
Some the tooth of want's wolf had made mad,
  And some at the forge had grown old.

Behind them these serfs of the tool
  The rags of their service had flung;
No longer of fortune the fool,
  This word from each bearded lip rung:

"Once more I'm a man, I am free!
    No man is my master, I say;
Tomorrow I fail, it may be —
    No matter, I'm freeman today."

They go to a toil that is sure,
    To despair and hunger and cold;
Their sickness no warning can cure,
    They are mad with a longing for gold.

The light will fade from each eye,
    The smile from each face;
They will curse the impassable sky,
    And the earth when the snow torrents race

Some will sink by the way and be laid
    In the frost of the desolate earth;
And some will return to a maid,
    Empty of hand as at birth.

But this out of all will remain,
    They have lived and have tossed;
So much in the game will be gain,
    Though the gold of the dice has been lost.
                   HAMLIN GARLAND

MOST of the gold-seekers crossed the plains, and the trails were soon marked by the skeletons of horses and oxen, and by the graves of the hundreds who had perished from hardship or been butchered by the Indians. Very few of those who reached California ever discovered any gold.

THE DAYS OF 'FORTY-NINE

YOU are looking now on old Tom Moore,
    A relic of bygone days;
A Bummer, too, they call me now,
    But what care I for praise?

For my heart is filled with the days of yore,
    And oft I do repine
For the Days of Old and the Days of Gold,
    And the Days of 'Forty-nine!

I had comrades then who loved me well,
    A jovial, saucy crew:
There were some hard cases, I must confess,
    But they all were brave and true;
Who would never flinch, whate'er the pinch,
    Who would never fret nor whine,
But like good old Bricks they stood the kicks
    In the Days of 'Forty-nine....

But now my comrades all are gone,
    Not one remains to toast;
They have left me here in my misery,
    Like some poor, wandering ghost.
And as I go from place to place,
    Folks call me a "Traveling Sign,"
Saying, "There goes Tom Moore, a Bummer, sure,
    From the Days of 'Forty-nine."

                  UNKNOWN

ON SEPTEMBER 9, 1850, California was admitted to the Union, the thirty-first State. The United States of America stretched from the Atlantic to the Pacific, and from the St. Lawrence to the Gulf of Mexico.

CALIFORNIA

[September 9, 1850]

LAND of gold! — thy sisters greet thee,
    O'er the mountain and the main;
See — they stretch the hand to meet thee,
    Youngest of our household train.

Many a form their love hath fostered
    Lingers 'neath thy sunny sky,
And their spirit-tokens brighten
    Every link of sympathy.

We 'mid storms of war were cradled,
    'Mid the shock of angry foes;
Thou, with sudden, dreamlike splendor —
    Pallas-born — in vigor rose.

Children of one common country,
    Strong in friendship let us stand,
With united ardor earning
    Glory for our Mother Land.

They of gold and they of iron,
    They who reap the bearded wheat,
They who rear the snowy cotton,
    Pour their treasures at her feet;

While with smiling exultation,
    She, who marks their filial part,
Like the mother of the Gracchi,
    Folds her jewels to her heart.
                    LYDIA HUNTLEY SIGOURNEY

PART IV
THE STRUGGLE FOR THE UNION

BATTLE HYMN OF THE REPUBLIC

MINE eyes have seen the glory of the coming of the Lord:
He is trampling out the vintage where the grapes of wrath are
      stored;
He hath loosed the fateful lightning of his terrible swift sword:
           His truth is marching on.

I have seen Him in the watch-fires of a hundred circling
      camps;
They have builded Him an altar in the evening dews and
      damps;
I can read his righteous sentence by the dim and flaring
      lamps.
          His day is marching on.

I have read a fiery gospel, writ in burnished rows of steel:
"As ye deal with my contemners, so with you my grace shall
      deal;
Let the Hero, born of woman, crush the serpent with his heel,
          Since God is marching on."

He has sounded forth the trumpet that shall never call re-
      treat;
He is sifting out the hearts of men before his judgment-seat:
Oh! be swift, my soul, to answer Him! be jubilant, my feet!
          Our God is marching on.

In the beauty of the lilies Christ was born across the sea,
With a glory in his bosom that transfigures you and me:
As He died to make men holy, let us die to make men free,
          While God is marching on.
                    JULIA WARD HOWE

CHAPTER I

CIVIL WAR

NEGRO slavery in the United States began in 1619, when a cargo of Africans was sold in Virginia. It gradually spread to all the states, but by 1800 had been abolished in most of the northern ones. The South, however, considered slave labor essential to the cotton and tobacco industries. In 1854, a new territory, called Kansas, was formed, and the fight for it began at once, slave-holders pouring into it from Missouri, and large parties of "Free-Soilers" starting from New England. The first party set out in July, 1854, and John G. Whittier sent them a hymn, which was sung over and over during the long journey.

THE KANSAS EMIGRANTS

[July, 1854]

WE CROSS the prairie as of old
    The pilgrims crossed the sea,
To make the West, as they the East,
    The homestead of the free!

We go to rear a wall of men
    On Freedom's southern line,
And plant beside the cotton-tree
    The rugged Northern pine!

We're flowing from our native hills
    As our free rivers flow:
The blessing of our Mother-land
    Is on us as we go.

We go to plant her common schools
    On distant prairie swells,
And give the Sabbaths of the wild
    The music of her bells.

Upbearing, like the Ark of old,
  The Bible in our van,
We go to test the truth of God
  Against the fraud of man.

No pause, nor rest, save where the streams
  That feed the Kansas run,
Save where our Pilgrim gonfalon
  Shall flout the setting sun!

We'll tread the prairie as of old
  Our fathers sailed the sea,
And make the West, as they the East,
  The homestead of the free!
                    JOHN GREENLEAF WHITTIER

SUCH disorder followed in Kansas that in 1856, the governor pro-claimed the territory in a state of insurrection. One of the strong-holds of the Free Soil party was the town of Lawrence, and on Sep-tember 14, it was attacked by a force of twenty-five hundred Mis-sourians, but after a hot fight they were beaten off.

THE DEFENSE OF LAWRENCE

[September 14, 1856]

ALL night upon the guarded hill,
  Until the stars were low,
Wrapped round as with Jehovah's will,
  We waited for the foe;
All night the silent sentinels
  Moved by like gliding ghosts;
All night the fancied warning bells
  Held all men to their posts.

We heard the sleeping prairies breathe,
  The forest's human moans,
The hungry gnashing of the teeth
  Of wolves on bleaching bones;

We marked the roar of rushing fires,
  The neigh of frightened steeds,
The voices as of far-off lyres
  Among the river reeds.

We were but thirty-nine who lay
  Beside our rifles then;
We were but thirty-nine, and they
  Were twenty hundred men.
Our lean limbs shook and reeled about,
  Our feet were gashed and bare,
And all the breezes shredded out
  Our garments in the air....

They came: the blessed Sabbath day,
  That soothed our swollen veins,
Like God's sweet benediction, lay
  On all the singing plains;
The valleys shouted to the sun,
  The great woods clapped their hands,
And joy and glory seemed to run
  Like rivers through the lands.

And then our daughters and our wives,
  And men whose heads were white,
Rose sudden into kingly lives
  And walked forth to the fight;
And we drew aim along our guns
  And calmed our quickening breath,
Then, as is meet for Freedom's sons,
  Shook loving hands with Death.

And when three hundred of the foe
  Rode up in scorn and pride,
Whoso had watched us then might know
  That God was on our side;
For all at once a mighty thrill
  Of grandeur through us swept,

And strong and swiftly down the hill
    Like Gideons we leapt.

And all throughout that Sabbath day
    A wall of fire we stood,
And held the baffled foe at bay,
    And streaked the ground with blood,
And when the sun was very low
    They wheeled their stricken flanks,
And passed on, wearily and slow,
    Beyond the river banks.

Beneath the everlasting stars
    We bended childlike knees,
And thanked God for the shining scars
    Of His large victories.
And some, who lingered, said they heard
    Such wondrous music pass
As though a seraph's voice had stirred
    The pulses of the grass.

RICHARD REALF

GOVERNMENT troops were finally thrown into the territory to pre-
serve peace, and John Brown, one of the leaders of the Free-Soilers,
decided to strike a blow in Virginia.   On the night of October 16,
1859, at the head of a little band of eighteen men, including two
of his sons, he surprised and captured the United States Arsenal at
Harper's Ferry.   He was attacked next day by an overwhelming
force of marines and militia, most of his men were killed, and he
himself was taken prisoner.

HOW OLD BROWN TOOK HARPER'S FERRY

[October 16, 1859]

JOHN BROWN in Kansas settled, like a steadfast Yankee
    farmer,
Brave and godly, with four sons, all stalwart men of might.

There he spoke aloud for freedom, and the Border-strife
  grew warmer,
  Till the Rangers fired his dwelling, in his absence, in the
    night;
         And Old Brown,
         Osawatomie Brown,
Came homeward in the morning — to find his house burned
  down.

Then he grasped his trusty rifle and boldly fought for freedom;
  Smote from border unto border the fierce, invading band;
And he and his brave boys vowed — so might Heaven help
  and speed 'em! —
  They would save those grand old prairies from the curse
    that blights the land;
         And Old Brown,
         Osawatomie Brown,
Said, "Boys, the Lord will aid us!" and he shoved his ramrod
  down.

And the Lord *did* aid these men, and they labored day and
  even,
  Saving Kansas from its peril; and their very lives seemed
    charmed,
Till the ruffians killed one son, in the blessed light of Heaven—
  In cold blood the fellows slew him, as he journeyed all
    unarmed;
         Then Old Brown,
         Osawatomie Brown,
Shed not a tear, but shut his teeth, and frowned a terrible
  frown!

Then they seized another brave boy — not amid the heat of
  battle,
  But in peace, behind his plowshare — and they loaded
    him with chains,
And with pikes, before their horses, even as they goad their
  cattle,

Drove him cruelly, for their sport, and at last blew out
  his brains;
      Then Old Brown,
      Osawatomie Brown,
Raised his right hand up to Heaven, calling Heaven's ven-
  geance down.

And he swore a fearful oath, by the name of the Almighty,
  He would hunt this ravening evil that had scathed and
    torn him so;
He would seize it by the vitals; he would crush it day and
    night; he
  Would so pursue its footsteps, so return it blow for blow,
      That Old Brown,
      Osawatomie Brown,
Should be a name to swear by, in backwoods or in town!

Then his beard became more grizzled, and his wild blue eye
    grew wilder,
  And more sharply curved his hawk's-nose, snuffing battle
    from afar;
And he and the two boys left, though the Kansas strife
    waxed milder,
  Grew more sullen, till was over the bloody Border War,
      And Old Brown,
      Osawatomie Brown,
Had gone crazy, as they reckoned by his fearful glare and
    frown.

So he left the plains of Kansas and their bitter woes behind
    him,
  Slipt off into Virginia, where the statesmen all are born,
Hired a farm by Harper's Ferry, and no one knew where to
    find him,
  Or whether he'd turned parson, or was jacketed and shorn;
      For Old Brown,
      Osawatomie Brown,
Mad as he was, knew texts enough to wear a parson's gown.

He bought no plows and harrows, spades and shovels, and
    such trifles;
  But quietly to his rancho there came, by every train,
Boxes full of pikes and pistols, and his well-beloved Sharp's
    rifles;
  And eighteen other madmen joined their leader there again.
              Says Old Brown,
              Osawatomie Brown,
"Boys, we've got an army large enough to march and take
    the town!

"Take the town, and seize the muskets, free the negroes and
    then arm them;
  Carry the county and the state, aye, and all the potent
    South.
On their own heads be the slaughter, if their victims rise to
    harm them —
  These Virginians! who believed not, nor would heed the
    warning mouth."
              Says Old Brown,
              Osawatomie Brown,
"The world shall see a Republic, or my name is not John
    Brown."

'Twas the sixteenth of October, on the evening of a Sunday:
  "This good work," declared the captain, "shall be on a holy
    night!"
It was on a Sunday evening, and before the noon of Monday,
  With two sons, and Captain Stephens, fifteen privates —
    black and white,
              Captain Brown,
              Osawatomie Brown,
Marched across the bridged Potomac, and knocked the
    sentry down;

Took the guarded armory-building, and the muskets and the
    cannon;
  Captured all the county majors and the colonels, one by one;

Scared to death each gallant scion of Virginia they ran on,
  And before the noon of Monday, I say, the deed was done.
          Mad Old Brown,
          Osawatomie Brown,
With his eighteen other crazy men, went in and took the town.

Very little noise and bluster, little smell of powder made he;
  It was all done in the midnight, like the Emperor's *coup
    d'état.*
"Cut the wires! Stop the rail-cars! Hold the streets and
    bridges!" said he,
  Then declared the new Republic, with himself for guiding
    star —
          This Old Brown,
          Osawatomie Brown;
And the bold two thousand citizens ran off and left the town.

Then was riding and railroading and expressing here and
    thither;
  And the Martinsburg Sharpshooters and the Charlestown
    Volunteers,
And the Shepherdstown and Winchester Militia hastened
    whither
  Old Brown was said to muster his ten thousand grenadiers.
          General Brown!
          Osawatomie Brown!
Behind whose rampant banner all the North was pouring down.

But at last, 'tis said, some prisoners escaped from Old Brown's
    durance,
  And the effervescent valor of the Chivalry broke out,
When they learned that nineteen madmen had the marvelous
    assurance —
  Only nineteen — thus to seize the place and drive them
    straight about;
          And Old Brown,
          Osawatomie Brown,
Found an army come to take him, encamped around the town.

But to storm, with all the forces I have mentioned, was too
    risky;
  So they hurried off to Richmond for the Government
    Marines,
Tore them from their weeping matrons, fired their souls with
    Bourbon whiskey,
  Till they battered down Brown's castle with their ladders
    and machines;
        And Old Brown,
        Osawatomie Brown,
Received three bayonet stabs, and a cut on his brave old
    crown.

Tallyho! the old Virginia gentry gather to the baying!
  In they rushed and killed the game, shooting lustily away;
And whene'er they slew a rebel, those who came too late for
    slaying,
  Not to lose a share of glory, fired their bullets in his clay;
        And Old Brown,
        Osawatomie Brown,
Saw his sons fall dead beside him, and between them laid
    him down.

How the conquerors wore their laurels; how they hastened on
    the trial;
  How Old Brown was placed, half dying, on the Charlestown
    court-house floor;
How he spoke his grand oration, in the scorn of all denial;
  What the brave old madman told them — these are known
    the country o'er.
        "Hang Old Brown,
        Osawatomie Brown,"
Said the judge, "and all such rebels!" with his most judicial
    frown.

But, Virginians, don't do it! for I tell you that the flagon,
  Filled with blood of Old Brown's offspring, was first poured
    by Southern hands;

And each drop from Old Brown's life-veins, like the red gore
    of the dragon,
  May spring up a vengeful Fury, hissing through your
    slave-worn lands!
              And Old Brown,
             Osawatomie Brown,
May trouble you more than ever, when you've nailed his
    coffin down!

EDMUND CLARENCE STEDMAN

THE excitement and rage of the South is easy to understand, for the
one thing it had always feared was a slave insurrection, and here, it
was alleged, was a man proposing to seize arms and ammunition for
that very purpose.   He was quickly brought to trial charged with
treason and murder in the first degree, was found guilty, and hanged
December 2, 1859.

BROWN OF OSAWATOMIE

[December 2, 1859]

JOHN BROWN of Osawatomie spake on his dying day:
"I will not have to shrive my soul a priest in Slavery's pay.
But let some poor slave-mother whom I have striven to free,
With her children, from the gallows-stair put up a prayer for
    me!"

John Brown of Osawatomie, they led him out to die;
And lo! a poor slave-mother with her little child pressed nigh.
Then the bold, blue eye grew tender, and the old harsh face
    grew mild,
As he stooped between the jeering ranks and kissed the
    negro's child!

The shadows of his stormy life that moment fell apart;
And they who blamed the bloody hand forgave the loving heart.
That kiss from all its guilty means redeemed the good intent,
And round the grisly fighter's hair the martyr's aureole bent!

Perish with him the folly that seeks through evil good!
Long live the generous purpose unstained with human blood!
Not the raid of midnight terror, but the thought which
   underlies;
Not the borderer's pride of daring, but the Christian's
   sacrifice.

Nevermore may yon Blue Ridges the Northern rifle hear,
Nor see the light of blazing homes flash on the negro's spear.
But let the free-winged angel Truth their guarded passes scale,
To teach that right is more than might, and justice more than
   mail!

So vainly shall Virginia set her battle in array;
In vain her trampling squadrons knead the winter snow with
   clay.
She may strike the pouncing eagle, but she dares not harm
   the dove;
And every gate she bars to Hate shall open wide to Love!

JOHN GREENLEAF WHITTIER

EDMUND CLARENCE STEDMAN had prophesied that "Old Brown,
Osawatomie Brown, may trouble you more than ever, when you've
nailed his coffin down," and this prophecy came true, for he became a
sort of symbol to the North, and "John Brown's Body" was the
most popular marching song in the war which was to follow.

JOHN BROWN'S BODY

JOHN BROWN'S body lies a-mold'ring in the grave,
John Brown's body lies a-mold'ring in the grave,
John Brown's body lies a-mold'ring in the grave —
   His soul is marching on!

Chorus: Glory! Glory Hallelujah!
   Glory! Glory Hallelujah!
   Glory! Glory Hallelujah!
   His soul is marching on!

John Brown died on the scaffold for the slave —
  His soul is marching on!

He has gone to be a soldier in the army of the Lord —
  His soul is marching on!

John Brown's knapsack is strapped upon his back —
  His soul is marching on!

We'll hang Jeff Davis to a sour apple tree,
  As we go marching on!
                              CHARLES SPRAGUE HALL (?)

IN THE midst of this excitement, the summer of 1860 swung around
and the Presidential nominations.   After a week of bitter debate,
the Southern delegates withdrew from the Democratic National
Convention, and the Northern delegates nominated Stephen A.
Douglas.   The Republicans met at Chicago, adopted a platform
protesting against the extension of slavery, and nominated for Presi-
dent an obscure Illinois lawyer named Abraham Lincoln.

THE MAUL

I SAW a boy in a black-jack wood,
  With a tall, lank, awkward "figger,"
Striking away with his heavy maul,
  By the side of a young slave "nigger."
And he said to himself, "I'll maul away,
  And cleave a path before me:
I'll hew all black-jacks out of my way,
  Till the Star of Fame shines o'er me."

I saw him again on a broad, swift stream,
  But the maul this time was a paddle;
And I watched the tiny rainbows gleam
  As he made the waves skedaddle.
And he said, "I'll paddle away, away,
  Till space shall flee before me:

And yet shall I live to see the day
   When the Star of Fame shines o'er me."

I saw him again with his musty books,
   A-pondering Coke and Story:
And little there was in his homely looks
   To tell of his future glory.
But he said, "I'll master, I know I will,
   The difficult task before me:
I'll maul away through the hard world still,
   Till the Star of Fame shines o'er me."

I saw him again, when he rose to cope,
   Hand to hand, with the "Western Giant":
His eye lit up with a beam of hope,
   On his sinewy strength reliant.
"I'll fight him," he said, "with the maul of Truth,
   Till he shrink and quail before me;
Till he stand abashed in astonished ruth,
   While the Star of Fame shines o'er me."

I saw him again in the White House chair,
   A-writing the Proclamation:
And the pen he used was the heaviest maul
   In this rail-mauling nation.
And he said, "'Tis the only way to make
   The traitors flee before us:
While the light it sheds will leave a wake
   That will shine when the sod grows o'er us."

I saw him again but the other night,
   And he shook my hand in greeting:
And little he thought how soon I'd write
   And tell the world of our meeting.
The hand I clasped has swung the maul,
   And my own has written its story.
But never, I ween, could any hand
   Write half of its toil and glory.

MARY E. NEALY

THE campaign was one of the most bitter ever waged in the United States, but the division among the Democrats gave Lincoln an immense advantage, and on November 6, 1860, he was elected President, receiving one hundred and eighty electoral votes.

LINCOLN, THE MAN OF THE PEOPLE

WHEN the Norn-Mother saw the Whirlwind Hour,
Greatening and darkening as it hurried on,
She left the strenuous heavens and came down
To make a man to meet the mortal need.
She took the tried clay of the common road —
Clay warm yet with the genial heat of Earth,
Dashed through it all a strain of prophecy;
Then mixed a laughter with the serious stuff.
It was a stuff to wear for centuries,
A man that matched the mountains, and compelled
The stars to look our way and honor us.

The color of the ground was in him, the red earth;
The tang and odor of the primal things —
The rectitude and patience of the rocks;
The gladness of the wind that shakes the corn;
The courage of the bird that dares the sea;
The justice of the rain that loves all leaves;
The pity of the snow that hides all scars;
The loving-kindness of the wayside well;
The tolerance and equity of light
That gives as freely to the shrinking weed
As to the great oak flaring to the wind —
To the grove's low hill as to the Matterhorn
That shoulders out the sky.

                                    And so he came,
From prairie cabin up to Capitol,
One fair Ideal led our chieftain on.
Forevermore he burned to do his deed
With the fine stroke and gesture of a king.

He built the rail-pile as he built the State,
Pouring his splendid strength through every blow,
The conscience of him testing every stroke,
To make his deed the measure of a man.

So came the Captain with a mighty heart:
And when the step of Earthquake shook the house,
Wrenching the rafters from their ancient hold,
He held the ridgepole up, and spiked again
The rafters of the Home.   He held his place —
Held the long purpose like a growing tree —
Held on through blame and faltered not at praise.
And when he fell in whirlwind, he went down
As when a kingly cedar green with boughs
Goes down with a great shout upon the hills,
And leaves a lonesome place against the sky.

Edwin Markham

Lincoln's election was the signal the South had been awaiting. On December 20, 1860, the State of South Carolina seceded from the Union, and a week later, the state troops seized Fort Moultrie, in Charleston Harbor, and took possession of the United States Arsenal at Charleston, with seventy-five thousand stands of arms. Georgia, Alabama, Florida, North Carolina, Mississippi, and Louisiana quickly followed South Carolina's example.

BROTHER JONATHAN'S LAMENT FOR SISTER CAROLINE

[December 20, 1860]

She has gone — she has left us in passion and pride —
Our stormy-browed sister, so long at our side!
She has torn her own star from our firmament's glow,
And turned on her brother the face of a foe!

O Caroline, Caroline, child of the sun,
We can never forget that our hearts have been one —
Our foreheads both sprinkled in Liberty's name,
From the fountain of blood with the finger of flame!

You were always too ready to fire at a touch;
But we said: "She is hasty,—she does not mean much."
We have scowled when you uttered some turbulent threat;
But Friendship still whispered: "Forgive and forget."

Has our love all died out?   Have its altars grown cold?
Has the curse come at last which the fathers foretold?
Then Nature must teach us the strength of the chain
That her petulant children would sever in vain.

They may fight till the buzzards are gorged with their spoil —
Till the harvest grows black as it rots in the soil,
Till the wolves and the catamounts troop from their caves,
And the shark tracks the pirate, the lord of the waves:

In vain is the strife!   When its fury is past,
Their fortunes must flow in one channel at last
As the torrents that rush from the mountains of snow
Roll mingled in peace through the valleys below.

Our Union is river, lake, ocean, and sky;
Man breaks not the medal, when God cuts the die!
Though darkened with sulphur, though cloven with steel,
The blue arch will brighten, the waters will heal!

O Caroline, Caroline, child of the sun,
There are battles with fate that can never be won!
The star-flowering banner must never be furled,
For its blossoms of light are the hope of the world!

Go, then, our rash sister, afar and aloof,
Run wild in the sunshine away from our roof;
But when your heart aches and your feet have grown sore,
Remember the pathway that leads to our door!

OLIVER WENDELL HOLMES

Fort Moultrie, in Charleston Harbor, had been held by a small garrison under Major Robert Anderson, and this was shifted to Fort Sumter, a stronger position, when Moultrie's capture became inevitable. Anderson remained in Sumter, despite the state's protests, and General Pierre T. Beauregard, in command of the Confederate forces, finally decided to bombard it.

ON FORT SUMTER

It was a noble Roman,
   In Rome's imperial day,
Who heard a coward croaker
   Before the battle say —
"They're safe in such a fortress;
   There is no way to shake it" —
"On, on!" exclaimed the hero,
   "I'll find a way, or make it!"

Is Fame your aspiration?
   Her path is steep and high;
In vain he seeks the temple,
   Content to gaze and sigh;
The crowded town is waiting,
   But he *alone* can take it
Who says, with "Southern firmness,"
   "I'll find a way, or make it!"

Is Glory your ambition?
   There is no royal road;
Alike we all must labor,
   Must climb to her abode;
Who feels the thirst for *glory*,
   In Helicon may slake it,
If he has but the "Southern will,"
   "To find a way, or make it!"

Is Sumter worth the getting?
   It must be bravely sought;

With wishing and with fretting
    The boon cannot be bought;
To *all* the prize is open,
    But only he can take it
Who says, with "SOUTHERN COURAGE,"
    "I'LL FIND A WAY, OR MAKE IT!"

In all impassioned warfare,
    The tale has ever been,
That victory crowns the valiant,
    The brave are they who win.
Though strong is "*Sumter Fortress,*"
    A HERO still may take it,
Who says, with "SOUTHERN DARING,"
    "I'LL FIND A WAY, OR MAKE IT!"

                                    UNKNOWN
Charleston, S.C., *Mercury.*

ON APRIL 11, Beauregard summoned Anderson to surrender. Anderson curtly refused, and at four-thirty o'clock on the morning of April 12, 1861, the first shot of the Civil War was fired. The fort answered, and the bombardment continued all day. By the 13th, the fort's ammunition was exhausted, Major Anderson accepted the terms of evacuation offered by General Beauregard, and on the afternoon of Sunday, April 14, the little garrison marched out with colors flying and drums beating. Not a man had been killed on either side.

SUMTER

[April 12, 1861]

CAME the morning of that day
When the God to whom we pray
Gave the soul of Henry Clay
        To the land;
How we loved him, living, dying!
But his birthday banners flying
Saw us asking and replying
        Hand to hand.

For we knew that far away,
Round the fort in Charleston Bay,
Hung the dark impending fray,
 Soon to fall;
And that Sumter's brave defender
Had the summons to surrender
Seventy loyal hearts and tender —
 (Those were all!)

And we knew the April sun
Lit the length of many a gun —
Hosts of batteries to the one
 Island crag;
Guns and mortars grimly frowning,
Johnson, Moultrie, Pinckney, crowning,
And ten thousand men disowning
 The old flag.

Oh, the fury of the fight
Even then was at its height!
Yet no breath, from noon till night,
 Reached us here;
We had almost ceased to wonder,
And the day had faded under,
When the echo of the thunder
 Filled each ear!

Then our hearts more fiercely beat,
As we crowded on the street,
Hot to gather and repeat
 All the tale;
All the doubtful chances turning,
Till our souls with shame were burning,
As if twice our bitter yearning
 Could avail!

Who had fired the earliest gun?
Was the fort by traitors won?

Was there succor?   What was done
    Who could know?
And once more our thoughts would wander
To the gallant, lone commander,
On his battered ramparts grander
    Than the foe.

Not too long the brave shall wait:
On their own heads be their fate,
Who against the hallowed State
    Dare begin;
Flag defied and compact riven!
In the record of high Heaven
How shall Southern men be shriven
    For the sin!
                EDMUND CLARENCE STEDMAN

CHARLESTON gave itself up to joy, and Beauregard became a popular
hero. Very different was the reception of the news at the North.
At last war had begun!

SUMTER

So, THEY *will* have it!
    The Black Witch (curse on her)
    Always had won her
Greediest demand — for we gave it —
    All but our honor!

Thirty hours thundered
    Siege-guns and mortars —
    (Flames in the quarters!)
One to a hundred
    Stood our brave Forters!

No more of parties! —
    Let them all molder —
    Here's work that's bolder!

Forward, my hearties!
  Shoulder to shoulder.

Sight o'er the trunnion —
  Send home the rammer —
  Linstock and hammer!
Speak for the Union!
  Tones that won't stammer!

Men of Columbia,
  Leal hearts from Annan,
  Brave lads of Shannon!
We are all one today —
  On with the cannon!

HENRY HOWARD BROWNELL

NOR was there any hesitation as to what steps should be taken.
The very next day, Monday, April 15, 1861, President Lincoln issued
a call for seventy-five thousand volunteers. "At the darkest hour in
the history of the Republic," Emerson wrote, "when it looked as if
the nation would be dismembered, pulverized into its original ele-
ments, the attack on Fort Sumter crystallized the North into a unit,
and the hope of mankind was saved."

OUR COUNTRY'S CALL

LAY down the axe; fling by the spade;
  Leave in its track the toiling plow;
The rifle and the bayonet-blade
  For arms like yours were fitter now;
And let the hands that ply the pen
  Quit the light task, and learn to wield
The horseman's crooked brand, and rein
  The charger on the battle-field.

Our country calls; away! away!
  To where the blood-stream blots the green.
Strike to defend the gentlest sway
  That Time in all his course has seen.

See, from a thousand coverts — see,
  Spring the armed foes that haunt her track;
They rush to smite her down, and we
  Must beat the banded traitors back.

Ho! sturdy as the oaks ye cleave,
  And moved as soon to fear and flight,
Men of the glade and forest! leave
  Your woodcraft for the field of fight.
The arms that wield the axe must pour
  An iron tempest on the foe;
His serried ranks shall reel before
  The arm that lays the panther low.

And ye, who breast the mountain storm
  By grassy steep or highland lake,
Come, for the land ye love, to form
  A bulwark that no foe can break.
Stand, like your own gray cliffs that mock
  The whirlwind, stand in her defense;
The blast as soon shall move the rock
  As rushing squadrons bear ye thence....

And ye, who throng, beside the deep,
  Her ports and hamlets of the strand,
In number like the waves that leap
  On his long murmuring marge of sand,
Come, like that deep, when, o'er his brim,
  He rises, all his floods to pour,
And flings the proudest barks that swim,
  A helpless wreck, against his shore!

Few, few were they whose swords of old
  Won the fair land in which we dwell,
But we are many, we who hold
  The grim resolve to guard it well.
Strike, for that broad and goodly land,
  Blow after blow, till men shall see

That Might and Right move hand in hand,
And glorious must their triumph be!

WILLIAM CULLEN BRYANT

THE people of the South were even more wildly enthusiastic for the war. Prompted by the belief that they must defend their property and their liberty, they rose as one man. All hearts were in the cause.

DIXIE

SOUTHRONS, hear your country call you!
Up, lest worse than death befall you!
　　To arms! To arms! To arms, in Dixie!
Lo! all the beacon-fires are lighted —
Let all hearts be now united!

　　To arms! To arms! To arms, in Dixie!
　　　Advance the flag of Dixie!
　　　　Hurrah! hurrah!
For Dixie's land we take our stand,
　　And live and die for Dixie!
　　　To arms! To arms!
　And conquer peace for Dixie!
　　　To arms! To arms!
　And conquer peace for Dixie!

Hear the Northern thunders mutter!
Northern flags in South winds flutter!
Send them back your fierce defiance!
Stamp upon the accursed alliance!

Fear no danger! Shun no labor!
Lift up rifle, pike, and saber!
Shoulder pressing close to shoulder,
Let the odds make each heart bolder!

How the South's great heart rejoices
At your cannons' ringing voices!
For faith betrayed, and pledges broken,
Wrongs inflicted, insults spoken.

Strong as lions, swift as eagles,
Back to their kennels hunt these beagles!
Cut the unequal bonds asunder!
Let them hence each other plunder!

Swear upon your country's altar
Never to submit or falter,
Till the spoilers are defeated,
Till the Lord's work is completed!

Halt not till our Federation
Secures among earth's powers its station!
Then at peace, and crowned with glory,
Hear your children tell the story!

If the loved ones weep in sadness,
Victory soon shall bring them gladness, —
        To arms!
Exultant pride soon vanquish sorrow;
Smiles chase tears away tomorrow.

To arms!   To arms!   To arms, in Dixie!
    Advance the flag of Dixie!
        Hurrah! hurrah!
For Dixie's land we take our stand,
    And live or die for Dixie!
        To arms!   To arms!
    And conquer peace for Dixie!
        To arms!   To arms!
    And conquer peace for Dixie!

ALBERT PIKE

"WE CONQUER or die!" was the watchword. No one foresaw how many were to die, nor what suffering, privation and terrible sacrifice were to mark the next four years.

"WE CONQUER OR DIE"

THE war drum is beating, prepare for the fight,
The stern bigot Northman exults in his might;
Gird on your bright weapons, your foemen are nigh,
And this be our watchword, "We conquer or die."

The trumpet is sounding from mountain to shore,
Your swords and your lances must slumber no more,
Fling forth to the sunlight your banner on high,
Inscribed with the watchword, "We conquer or die."

March on the battle-field, there to do or dare,
With shoulder to shoulder, all danger to share,
And let your proud watchword ring up to the sky,
Till the blue arch reëchoes, "We conquer or die."

Press forward undaunted nor think of retreat,
The enemy's host on the threshold to meet;
Strike firm, till the foeman before you shall fly,
Appalled by the watchword, "We conquer or die."

Go forth in the pathway our forefathers trod;
We, too, fight for freedom — our Captain is God,
Their blood in our veins, with their honors we vie,
Theirs, too, was the watchword, "We conquer or die."

We strike for the South — Mountain, Valley, and Plain,
For the South we will conquer again and again;
Her day of salvation and triumph is nigh,
Ours, then, be the watchword, "We conquer or die."

JAMES PIERPONT

CHAPTER II

THE FIRST CAMPAIGN

HOSTILITIES began without delay. In fact, the first blood was shed on April 19, 1861, one week after the fall of Fort Sumter, — and eighty-sixth anniversary of the battle of Lexington! — when the Sixth Massachusetts Regiment, marching through Baltimore to entrain for Washington, was attacked by Southern sympathizers. A desperate fight followed, during which three soldiers were killed and twenty wounded. Nine citizens of Baltimore were killed, and many wounded — how many was never known.

THE NINETEENTH OF APRIL

[1861]

THIS year, till late in April, the snow fell thick and light:
Thy truce-flag, friendly Nature, in clinging drifts of white,
Hung over field and city: now everywhere is seen,
In place of that white quietness, a sudden glow of green.

The verdure climbs the Common, beneath the leafless trees,
To where the glorious Stars and Stripes are floating on the
    breeze.
There, suddenly as spring awoke from winter's snow-draped
    gloom,
The Passion-Flower of Seventy-Six is bursting into bloom.

Dear is the time of roses, when earth to joy is wed,
And garden-plat and meadow wear one generous flush of red;
But now in dearer beauty, to her ancient colors true,
Blooms the old town of Boston in red and white and blue.

Along the whole awakening North are those bright emblems
    spread;
A summer noon of patriotism is burning overhead:
No party badges flaunting now, no word of clique or clan;
But "Up for God and Union!" is the shout of every man.

Oh, peace is dear to Northern hearts; our hard-earned homes
    more dear;
But Freedom is beyond the price of any earthly cheer;
And Freedom's flag is sacred; he who would work it harm,
Let him, although a brother, beware our strong right arm!

A brother! ah, the sorrow, the anguish of that word!
The fratricidal strife begun, when will its end be heard?
Not this the boon that patriot hearts have prayed and waited
    for; —
We loved them, and we longed for peace: but they would
    have it war.

Yes; war! on this memorial day, the day of Lexington,
A lightning-thrill along the wires from heart to heart has run.
Brave men we gazed on yesterday, today for us have bled:
Again is Massachusetts blood the first for Freedom shed.

To war — and with our brethren, then — if only this can be!
Life hangs as nothing in the scale against dear Liberty!
Though hearts be torn asunder, for Freedom we will fight:
Our blood may seal the victory, but God will shield the Right!

LUCY LARCOM

THE secessionists of Maryland were wild with rage, and for a time it seemed that the state might join the Confederacy, but a Federal force under General Butler soon restored order. The incident inspired one of the most impassioned war lyrics written on the Southern side, "My Maryland," by James Ryder Randall.

MY MARYLAND

    THE despot's heel is on thy shore,
        Maryland!
    His torch is at thy temple door,
        Maryland!
    Avenge the patriotic gore
    That flecked the streets of Baltimore,

And be the battle-queen of yore,
     Maryland, my Maryland!

Hark to an exiled son's appeal,
     Maryland!
My Mother State, to thee I kneel,
     Maryland!
For life and death, for woe and weal,
Thy peerless chivalry reveal,
And gird thy beauteous limbs with steel,
     Maryland, my Maryland!...

Dear Mother, burst the tyrant's chain,
     Maryland!
Virginia should not call in vain,
     Maryland!
She meets her sisters on the plain —
"*Sic semper!*" 'tis the proud refrain
That baffles minions back amain,
     Maryland!
Arise in majesty again,
     Maryland, my Maryland!

Come! for thy shield is bright and strong,
     Maryland!
Come! for thy dalliance does thee wrong,
     Maryland!
Come to thine own heroic throng
Stalking with Liberty along,
And chant thy dauntless slogan-song,
     Maryland, my Maryland!

I see the blush upon thy cheek,
     Maryland!
For thou wast ever bravely meek,
     Maryland!
But lo! there surges forth a shriek,
From hill to hill, from creek to creek,

Potomac calls to Chesapeake,
    Maryland, my Maryland!

Thou wilt not yield the Vandal toll,
    Maryland!
Thou wilt not crook to his control,
    Maryland!
Better the fire upon thee roll,
Better the shot, the blade, the bowl,
Than crucifixion of the soul,
    Maryland, my Maryland!

I hear the distant thunder hum,
    Maryland!
The Old Line's bugle, fife, and drum,
    Maryland!
She is not dead, nor deaf, nor dumb;
Huzza! she spurns the Northern scum!
She breathes! She burns! She'll come! She'll come!
    Maryland, my Maryland!

                    JAMES RYDER RANDALL

FEDERAL troops poured into Washington, until a force of fifty thousand was collected there, while the Confederates assembled an army of nearly equal strength at Manassas Junction, thirty miles to the south. On July 15, 1861, the Union army moved forward and on the morning of the 21st, attacked the Confederates, who had intrenched themselves along a little stream called Bull Run. The Southerners stood firm, checked the attack, and finally drove the Union forces from the field in a retreat which soon turned to a rout.

MANASSAS

[July 21, 1861]

THEY have met at last — as storm-clouds
    Meet in heaven,
And the Northmen back and bleeding
    Have been driven;

And their thunders have been stilled,
And their leaders crushed or killed,
And their ranks with terror thrilled,
Rent and riven!

Like the leaves of Vallombrosa
They are lying;
In the moonlight, in the midnight,
Dead and dying;
Like those leaves before the gale,
Swept their legions, wild and pale;
While the host that made them quail
Stood, defying.

When aloft in morning sunlight
Flags were flaunted,
And "swift vengeance on the rebel"
Proudly vaunted:
Little did they think that night
Should close upon their shameful flight,
And rebels, victors in the fight,
Stand undaunted.

But peace to those who perished
In our passes!
Light be the earth above them;
Green the grasses!
Long shall Northmen rue the day
When they met our stern array,
And shrunk from battle's wild affray
At Manassas.
CATHERINE ANN WARFIELD

THE North suddenly realized that the struggle was to be a hard one.
Five hundred thousand volunteers were called for, and General
George B. McClellan was appointed to command the Army of the
Potomac, which was expected to capture Richmond, the capital of

the Confederacy. But month after month passed, McClelian made no move against the enemy, and the public ear was daily irritated by the report, "All quiet along the Potomac."

THE PICKET–GUARD

[November, 1861]

"ALL quiet along the Potomac," they say,
    "Except now and then a stray picket
Is shot, as he walks on his beat to and fro,
    By a rifleman hid in the thicket.
'Tis nothing: a private or two, now and then,
    Will not count in the news of the battle;
Not an officer lost — only one of the men,
    Moaning out, all alone, the death rattle."

All quiet along the Potomac tonight,
    Where the soldiers lie peacefully dreaming;
Their tents in the rays of the clear autumn moon,
    Or the light of the watch-fire, are gleaming.
A tremulous sigh of the gentle night wind
    Through the forest leaves softly is creeping,
While the stars up above, with their glittering eyes,
    Keep guard, for the army is sleeping.

There's only the sound of the lone sentry's tread
    As he tramps from the rock to the fountain,
And thinks of the two in the low trundle-bed
    Far away in the cot on the mountain.
His musket falls slack; his face, dark and grim,
    Grows gentle with memories tender,
As he mutters a prayer for the children asleep —
    For their mother — may Heaven defend her!

The moon seems to shine just as brightly as then,
    That night, when the love yet unspoken
Leaped up to his lips — when low-murmured vows
    Were pledged to be ever unbroken.

Then drawing his sleeve roughly over his eyes,
  He dashes off tears that are welling,
And gathers his gun closer up to its place
  As if to keep down the heart-swelling.

He passes the fountain, the blasted pine-tree;
  The footstep is lagging and weary;
Yet onward he goes, through the broad belt of light,
  Towards the shade of the forest so dreary.
Hark! was it the night wind that rustled the leaves?
  Was it moonlight so wondrously flashing?
It looked like a rifle ... "Ha! Mary, goodbye!"
  The red life-blood is ebbing and plashing.

All quiet along the Potomac tonight —
  No sound save the rush of the river,
While soft falls the dew on the face of the dead —
  The picket's off duty forever!

                              ETHEL LYNN BEERS

But the spring of 1862 was marked by a remarkable combat on the water. At the outbreak of the war, the Federals had destroyed the navy yard at Norfolk, but the Confederates succeeded in raising one vessel, the Merrimac. This they rebuilt, covered with heavy steel rails, armed with ten rifled guns, and named the Virginia. On March 8, 1862, she attacked the Union fleet lying at Newport News and plunged her ram into the side of the Cumberland. Lieutenant Morris, in command of the Cumberland, fought his ship until she sank under him, but the cannon balls glanced harmlessly off the Merrimac's armored sides.

THE CUMBERLAND

[March 8, 1862]

At anchor in Hampton Roads we lay,
  On board of the Cumberland, sloop-of-war;

And at times from the fortress across the bay
  The alarum of drums swept past,
    Or a bugle blast
From the camp on the shore.

Then far away to the south uprose
  A little feather of snow-white smoke,
And we knew that the iron ship of our foes
  Was steadily steering its course
    To try the force
Of our ribs of oak.

Down upon us heavily runs,
  Silent and sullen, the floating fort;
Then comes a puff of smoke from her guns,
  And leaps the terrible death,
    With fiery breath,
From each open port.

We are not idle, but send her straight
  Defiance back in a full broadside!
As hail rebounds from a roof of slate,
  Rebounds our heavier hail
    From each iron scale
Of the monster's hide.

"Strike your flag!" the rebel cries
  In his arrogant old plantation strain.
"Never!" our gallant Morris replies:
    "It is better to sink than to yield!"
  And the whole air pealed
With the cheers of our men.

Then, like a kraken huge and black,
  She crushed our ribs in her iron grasp!
Down went the Cumberland all a wrack,
  With a sudden shudder of death,
    And the cannon's breath
For her dying gasp.

Next morn, as the sun rose over the bay,
  Still floated our flag at the mainmast head.
Lord, how beautiful was Thy day!
    Every waft of the air
    Was a whisper of prayer,
  Or a dirge for the dead.

Ho! brave hearts that went down in the seas!
  Ye are at peace in the troubled stream;
Ho! brave land! with hearts like these,
    Thy flag, that is rent in twain,
    Shall be one again,
  And without a seam!
                    HENRY WADSWORTH LONGFELLOW

THE Merrimac turned her guns upon the other ships of the fleet, and, after heavily damaging all of them, withdrew, intending to return and complete their destruction the next morning.

HOW THE CUMBERLAND WENT DOWN

[March 8, 1862]

GRAY swept the angry waves
  O'er the gallant and the true,
Rolled high in mounded graves
  O'er the stately frigate's crew —
Over cannon, over deck,
Over all that ghastly wreck —
    When the Cumberland went down.

Such a roar the waters rent
  As though a giant died,
When the wailing billows went
  Above those heroes tried;
And the sheeted foam leaped high,
Like white ghosts against the sky —
    As the Cumberland went down.

O shrieking waves that gushed
  Above that loyal band,
Your cold, cold burial rushed
  O'er many a heart on land!
And from all the startled North
A cry of pain broke forth —
    When the Cumberland went down.

And forests old, that gave
  A thousand years of power
To her lordship of the wave
  And her beauty's regal dower,
Bent, as though before a blast,
When plunged her pennoned mast,
    And the Cumberland went down.

And grimy mines that sent
  To her their virgin strength,
And iron vigor lent
  To knit her lordly length,
Wildly stirred with throbs of life,
Echoes of that fatal strife,
    As the Cumberland went down.

Beneath the ocean vast,
  Full many a captain bold,
By many a rotting mast,
  And admiral of old,
Rolled restless in his grave
As he felt the sobbing wave,
    When the Cumberland went down.

And stern Vikings that lay
  A thousand years at rest,
In many a deep blue bay
  Beneath the Baltic's breast,
Leaped on the silver sands,
And shook their rusty brands,
    As the Cumberland went down.
                  S. WEIR MITCHELL

BUT when, on the morning of March 9, 1862, the Merrimac steamed out again into Hampton Roads, a new antagonist confronted her — the Monitor, the eccentric boat designed by James Ericsson, consisting of a revolving ironclad turret mounted on a very low hull — "a cheese-box on a raft." It had arrived from New York the night before. The battle which followed was the first duel of ironclads the world had ever seen, and it ended by the Merrimac retreating to Norfolk, badly damaged.

THE CRUISE OF THE MONITOR

[March 9, 1862]

OUT of a Northern city's bay,
'Neath lowering clouds, one bleak March day,
Glided a craft — the like, I ween,
On ocean's crest was never seen
Since Noah's float, that ancient boat,
Could o'er a conquered deluge gloat.

No raking masts, with clouds of sail,
Bent to the breeze, or braved the gale;
No towering chimney's wreaths of smoke
Betrayed the mighty engine's stroke;
But low and dark, like the crafty shark,
Moved in the waters this novel bark.

The fishers stared as the flitting sprite
Passed their huts in the misty light,
Bearing a turret huge and black,
And said, "The old sea-serpent's back,
Carting away by light of day,
Uncle Sam's fort from New York Bay."

Forth from a Southern city's dock,
Our frigates' strong blockade to mock,
Crept a monster of rugged build,
The work of crafty hands, well skilled —
Old Merrimac, with an iron back
Wooden ships would find hard to crack.

Straight to where the Cumberland lay,
The mail-clad monster made its way;
Its deadly prow struck deep and sure,
And the hero's fighting days were o'er.
Ah! many the braves who found their graves,
With that good ship, beneath the waves!

But with their fate is glory wrought,
Those hearts of oak like heroes fought
With desperate hope to win the day,
And crush the foe that 'fore them lay.
Our flag up run, the last-fired gun,
Tokens how bravely duty was done.

Flushed with success, the victor flew,
Furious, the startled squadron through:
Sinking, burning, driving ashore,
Until that Sabbath day was o'er,
Resting at night to renew the fight
With vengeful ire by morning's light.

Out of its den it burst anew,
When the gray mist the sun broke through,
Steaming to where, in clinging sands,
The frigate Minnesota stands,
A sturdy foe to overthrow,
But in woful plight to receive a blow.

But see! Beneath her bow appears
A champion no danger fears;
A pigmy craft, that seems to be
To this new lord who rules the sea,
Like David of old to Goliath bold —
Youth and giant, by Scripture told.

Round the roaring despot playing,
With willing spirit, helm obeying,

Spurning the iron against it hurled,
While belching turret rapid whirled,
And swift shot's seethe, with smoky wreath,
Told that the shark was showing his teeth —

The Monitor fought.   In grim amaze
The Merrimacs upon it gaze,
Cowering 'neath the iron hail,
Crashing into their coat of mail;
They swore "this craft, the devil's shaft,
Looked like a cheese-box on a raft."

Hurrah! little giant of '62!
Bold Worden with his gallant crew
Forces the fight; the day is won;
Back to his den the monster's gone
With crippled claws and broken jaws,
Defeated in a reckless cause.

Hurrah for the master mind that wrought,
With iron hand, this iron thought!
Strength and safety with speed combined,
Ericsson's gift to all mankind;
To curb abuse, and chains to loose
Hurrah for the Monitor's famous cruise!

                    GEORGE HENRY BOKER

THE reign of terror created by the Merrimac was at an end, and the
ship herself did not last long.   On May 10, 1862, the Confederates
were forced to abandon Norfolk, and the Merrimac was blown up.
The Monitor, which was utterly unseaworthy, foundered in a gale
off Cape Hatteras on December 30.

THE SINKING OF THE MERRIMAC

[May 10, 1862]

GONE down in the flood, and gone out in the flame!
What else could she do, with her fair Northern name?

Her font was a river whose last drop is free:
That river ran boiling with wrath to the sea,
To hear of her baptismal blessing profaned:
A name that was Freedom's, by treachery stained.

'Twas the voice of our free Northern mountains that broke
In the sound of her guns, from her stout ribs of oak:
'Twas the might of the free Northern hand you could feel
In her sweep and her molding, from topmast to keel:
When they made her speak treason (does Hell know of worse?),
How her strong timbers shook with the shame of her curse!

Let her go! Should a deck so polluted again
Ever ring to the tread of our true Northern men?
Let the suicide-ship thunder forth, to the air
And the sea she has blotted, her groan of despair!
Let her last heat of anguish throb out into flame!
Then sink them together — the ship and the name!

LUCY LARCOM

PERHAPS it was this fight in Hampton Roads which drew McClellan's attention in that direction; at any rate, after eight months of hesitation, he decided that the best way to capture Richmond was to remove his army to Fortress Monroe and advance up the peninsula. This he did, with infinite labor and precaution, and finally, on May 31, 1862, got in touch with the Confederates at Fair Oaks. The latter would have won a decisive victory but for the timely arrival of dashing "Phil" Kearny, who rallied the Union forces, led them forward, and swept the Confederates from the field.

KEARNY AT SEVEN PINES

[May 31, 1862]

So THAT soldierly legend is still on its journey —
    That story of Kearny who knew not to yield!
'Twas the day when with Jameson, fierce Berry, and Birney,
    Against twenty thousand he rallied the field.

Where the red volleys poured, where the clamor rose highest,
   Where the dead lay in clumps through the dwarf oak and
      pine,
Where the aim from the thicket was surest and nighest —
   No charge like Phil Kearny's along the whole line.

When the battle went ill, and the bravest were solemn,
   Near the dark Seven Pines, where we still held our ground,
He rode down the length of the withering column,
   And his heart at our war-cry leapt up with a bound;
He snuffed, like his charger, the wind of the powder —
   His sword waved us on and we answered the sign;
Loud our cheer as we rushed, but his laugh rang the louder.
   "There's the devil's own fun, boys, along the whole line!"

How he strode his brown steed! How we saw his blade
      brighten
   In the one hand still left — and the reins in his teeth!
He laughed like a boy when the holidays heighten,
   But a soldier's glance shot from his visor beneath.
Up came the reserves to the mellay infernal,
   Asking where to go in — through the clearing or pine?
"Oh, anywhere! Forward! 'Tis all the same, Colonel:
   You'll find lovely fighting along the whole line!"

Oh, evil the black shroud of night at Chantilly,
   That hid him from sight of his brave men and tried!
Foul, foul sped the bullet that clipped the white lily,
   The flower of our knighthood, the whole army's pride!
Yet we dream that he still — in that shadowy region
   Where the dead arm their ranks at the wan drummer's
      sign —
Rides on, as of old, down the length of his legion,
   And the word still is "Forward!" along the whole line.
                              EDMUND CLARENCE STEDMAN

THE Confederates had found a great leader in the person of General Robert E. Lee, and he soon took the offensive. McClellan promptly began to retreat, and though the Confederates were repulsed after a severe engagement at Malvern Hill, he continued to retire and the attempt against Richmond came to an ignominious close.

MALVERN HILL

[July 1, 1862]

Ye elms that wave on Malvern Hill
   In prime of morn and May,
Recall ye how McClellan's men
   Here stood at bay?
While deep within yon forest dim
   Our rigid comrades lay —
Some with the cartridge in their mouth,
Others with fixed arms lifted South —
   Invoking so
The cypress glades?   Ah, wilds of woe!

The spires of Richmond, late beheld
   Through rifts in musket-haze,
Were closed from view in clouds of dust
   On leaf-walled ways,
Where streamed our wagons in caravans;
   And the Seven Nights and Days
Of march and fast, retreat and fight,
Pinched our grimed faces to ghastly plight —
   Does the elm wood
Recall the haggard beards of blood?

The battle-smoked flag, with stars eclipsed,
   We followed (it never fell!) —
In silence husbanded our strength —
   Received their yell;
Till on this slope we patient turned
   With cannon ordered well;

Reverse we proved was not defeat;
But ah, the sod where thousands meet! —
    Does Malvern Wood
Bethink itself, and muse and brood?

> *We elms of Malvern Hill*
>   *Remember everything;*
> *But sap the twig will fill;*
> *Wag the world how it will,*
>   *Leaves must be green in spring.*
>   HERMAN MELVILLE

MEANWHILE, the Army of Virginia had been formed for the defense of Washington, and placed under the command of General Pope. He endeavored to secure the valley of the Shenandoah, and on August 9, 1862, fought an indecisive battle at Cedar Mountain with the dashing Confederate cavalry leader, "Stonewall" Jackson.

CEDAR MOUNTAIN

[August 9, 1862]

RING the bells, nor ring them slowly;
Toll them not — the day is holy!
Golden-flooded noon is poured
In grand libation to the Lord.

No mourning mothers come today
Whose hopeless eyes forget to pray:
They each hold high the o'erflowing urn,
And bravely to the altar turn.

Ye limners of the ancient saint!
Today another virgin paint;
Where with the lily once she stood
Show now the new beatitude.

Today a mother crowned with pain,
Of silver beauty beyond stain,
Clasping a flower for our land
A-sheathèd in her hand.

Each pointed leaf with sword-like strength,
Guarding the flower throughout its length;
Each sword has won a sweet release
To the flower of beauty and of peace.

Ring the bells, nor ring them slowly,
To the Lord the day is holy;
To the young dead we consecrate
These lives that now we dedicate.

ANNIE FIELDS

LEE's army, released from the defense of Richmond by McClellan's retreat, hastened to face Pope, while Jackson got in Pope's rear, captured Manassas Junction, cut Pope's communications, and on August 30, 1862, defeated the Union forces at the second battle of Bull Run.

"OUR LEFT"

[August 30, 1862]

FROM dawn to dark they stood
That long midsummer day,
While fierce and fast
The battle blast
Swept rank on rank away.

From dawn to dark they fought,
With legions torn and cleft;
And still the wide
Black battle tide
Poured deadlier on "Our Left."

They closed each ghastly gap;
They dressed each shattered rank;
They knew — how well —
That freedom fell
With that exhausted flank.

"Oh, for a thousand men
  Like these that melt away!"
    And down they came,
    With steel and flame,
  Four thousand to the fray!

Right through the blackest cloud
  Their lightning path they cleft;
    And triumph came
    With deathless fame
  To our unconquered "Left."

Ye of your sons secure,
  Ye of your dead bereft —
    Honor the brave
    Who died to save
  Your all upon "Our Left."
                   FRANCIS ORRERY TICKNOR

ON THE following day, Jackson again attacked at Chantilly, an inde
cisive action, lasting all day. During the battle, General "Phil'
Kearny pushed forward to reconnoiter and came upon a Confederate
outpost, which summoned him to surrender. Instead, he clapped
spurs to his horse and endeavored to escape, but was shot and killed.

DIRGE FOR A SOLDIER

[September 1, 1862]

CLOSE his eyes; his work is done!
  What to him is friend or foeman,
Rise of moon, or set of sun,
  Hand of man, or kiss of woman?
    Lay him low, lay him low,
    In the clover or the snow!
    What cares he? he cannot know:
    Lay him low!

As man may, he fought his fight,
　Proved his truth by his endeavor;
Let him sleep in solemn night,
　Sleep forever and forever.
　　Lay him low, lay him low,
　　In the clover or the snow!
　　What cares he? he cannot know:
　　Lay him low!

Fold him in his country's stars,
　Roll the drum and fire the volley!
What to him are all our wars,
　What but death-bemocking folly?
　　Lay him low, lay him low,
　　In the clover or the snow!
　　What cares he? he cannot know:
　　Lay him low!

Leave him to God's watching eye;
　Trust him to the hand that made him.
Mortal love weeps idly by:
　God alone has power to aid him.
　　Lay him low, lay him low,
　　In the clover or the snow!
　　What cares he? he cannot know:
　　Lay him low!

GEORGE HENRY BOKER

POPE's shattered army was drawn back within the defenses of Washington, where McClellan's forces soon joined it. Thousands of recruits were hurried forward to fill the broken ranks.

THE REVEILLE

HARK! I hear the tramp of thousands,
　And of armèd men the hum;

Lo! a nation's hosts have gathered
  Round the quick-alarming drum —
      Saying: "Come,
      Freemen, come!
Ere your heritage be wasted," said the quick-alarming drum.

"Let me of my heart take counsel:
  War is not of life the sum;
Who shall stay and reap the harvest
  When the autumn days shall come?"
      But the drum
      Echoed: "Come!
Death shall reap the braver harvest," said the solemn-
    sounding drum.

"But when won the coming battle,
  What of profit springs therefrom?
What if conquest, subjugation,
  Even greater ills become?"
      But the drum
      Answered: "Come!
You must do the sum to prove it," said the Yankee-answering
    drum.

"What if, 'mid the cannons' thunder,
  Whistling shot and bursting bomb,
When my brothers fall around me,
  Should my heart grow cold and numb?"
      But the drum
      Answered: "Come!
Better there in death united, than in life a recreant.   Come!"

Thus they answered — hoping, fearing,
  Some in faith, and doubting some,
Till a trumpet-voice proclaiming,
  Said: "My chosen people, come!"
      Then the drum,
      Lo! was dumb;
For the great heart of the nation, throbbing, answered:
    "Lord, we come!"

                     BRET HARTE

NEVER was the Union in greater danger. A month before, Lee had been desperately defending Richmond against two armies; now he had defeated them both and was ready to invade the North. It was a masterly campaign, worthy to rank with Washington's at Trenton. He pushed forward with decision, and threw his whole army across the Potomac into Maryland. On September 13, the Confederates passed through Frederick, Maryland, and it was then that the incident recorded in "Barbara Frietchie" is said to have occurred.

BARBARA FRIETCHIE

[September 13, 1862]

Up FROM the meadows rich with corn,
Clear in the cool September morn,

The clustered spires of Frederick stand
Green-walled by the hills of Maryland.

Round about them orchards sweep,
Apple and peach tree fruited deep,

Fair as the garden of the Lord
To the eyes of the famished rebel horde,

On that pleasant morn of the early fall
When Lee marched over the mountain-wall;

Over the mountains winding down,
Horse and foot, into Frederick town.

Forty flags with their silver stars,
Forty flags with their crimson bars,

Flapped in the morning wind: the sun
Of noon looked down, and saw not one.

Up rose old Barbara Frietchie then,
Bowed with her fourscore years and ten;

Bravest of all in Frederick town,
She took up the flag the men hauled down;

In her attic window the staff she set,
To show that one heart was loyal yet.

Up the street came the rebel tread,
Stonewall Jackson riding ahead.

Under his slouched hat left and right
He glanced; the old flag met his sight.

"Halt!" — the dust-brown ranks stood fast.
"Fire!" — out blazed the rifle-blast.

It shivered the window, pane and sash;
It rent the banner with seam and gash.

Quick, as it fell, from the broken staff
Dame Barbara snatched the silken scarf.

She leaned far out on the window-sill,
And shook it forth with a royal will.

"Shoot, if you must, this old gray head,
But spare your country's flag," she said.

A shade of sadness, a blush of shame,
Over the face of the leader came;

The nobler nature within him stirred
To life at that woman's deed and word;

"Who touches a hair of yon gray head
Dies like a dog!   March on!" he said.

All day long through Frederick street
Sounded the tread of marching feet:

All day long that free flag tost
Over the heads of the rebel host.

Ever its torn folds rose and fell
On the loyal winds that loved it well;

And through the hill-gaps sunset light
Shone over it with a warm good-night.

Barbara Frietchie's work is o'er,
And the Rebel rides on his raids no more.

Honor to her! and let a tear
Fall, for her sake, on Stonewall's bier.

Over Barbara Frietchie's grave,
Flag of Freedom and Union, wave!

Peace and order and beauty draw
Round thy symbol of light and law;

And ever the stars above look down
On thy stars below in Frederick town!
                    JOHN GREENLEAF WHITTIER

McCLELLAN, meanwhile, had set his army in motion to head the
Confederates off, and on September 17, the two armies met at An-
tietam in one of the hardest battles of the war, which left Lee badly
shattered.   It was McClellan's first victory, and a notable one.

THE VICTOR OF ANTIETAM

[September 17, 1862]

WHEN tempest winnowed grain from bran,
And men were looking for a man,
Authority called you to the van,
                    McClellan!
Along the line the plaudits ran,
As later when Antietam's cheers began....

Authority called you; then, in mist
And loom of jeopardy — dismissed.
But staring peril soon appalled;
You, the Discarded, she recalled —
Recalled you, nor endured delay;
And forth you rode upon a blasted way,
Arrayed Pope's rout, and routed Lee's array,
   McClellan!
Your tent was choked with captured flags that day,
   McClellan!
Antietam was a telling fray.

Recalled you; and she heard your drum
Advancing through the ghastly gloom.
You manned the walls, you propped the Dome,
You stormed the powerful stormer home,
   McClellan!
Antietam's cannon long shall boom....

Your medaled soldiers love you well,
   McClellan!
Name your name, their true hearts swell;
With you they shook dread Stonewall's spell,
With you they braved the blended yell
Of rebel and maligner fell;
With you in fame or shame they dwell,
   McClellan!
Antietam-braves a brave can tell.

And when your comrades (now so few,
   McClellan —
Such ravage in deep files they rue)
Meet round the board, and sadly view
The empty places; tribute due
They render to the dead — and you!
Absent and silent o'er the blue;
The one-armed lift the wine to *you*
   McClellan,
And great Antietam's cheers renew.
     HERMAN MELVILLE

But with characteristic indecision, McClellan failed to follow up his victory, and Lee made good his retreat across the Potomac. President Lincoln's patience was exhausted; he removed McClellan from command and appointed General Burnside to succeed him.

MARTHY VIRGINIA'S HAND

[September 17, 1862]

"There, on the left!" said the colonel; the battle had shuddered and faded away,
Wraith of a fiery enchantment that left only ashes and blood-sprinkled clay —
"Ride to the left and examine that ridge, where the enemy's sharpshooters stood.
Lord, how they picked off our men, from the treacherous vantage-ground of the wood!
But for their bullets, I'll bet, my batteries sent them something as good.
Go and explore, and report to me then, and tell me how many we killed.
Never a wink shall I sleep till I know our vengeance was duly fulfilled."

Fiercely the orderly rode down the slope of the cornfield — scarred and forlorn,
Rutted by violent wheels, and scathed by the shot that had plowed it in scorn;
Fiercely, and burning with wrath for the sight of his comrades crushed at a blow,
Flung in broken shapes on the ground like ruined memorials of woe;
These were the men whom at daybreak he knew, but never again could know.
Thence to the ridge, where roots out-thrust, and twisted branches of trees
Clutched the hill like clawing lions, firm their prey to seize.

"What's your report?" and the grim colonel smiled when the orderly came back at last.
Strangely the soldier paused: "Well, they were punished."
And strangely his face looked, aghast.

"Yes, our fire told on them; knocked over fifty — laid out in
    line of parade.
Brave fellows, Colonel, to stay as they did! But one I 'most
    wished hadn't stayed.
Mortally wounded, he'd torn off his knapsack; and then, at
    the end, he prayed —
Easy to see, by his hands that were clasped; and the dull,
    dead fingers yet held
This little letter — his wife's — from the knapsack. A pity
    those woods were shelled!"

Silent the orderly, watching with tears in his eyes as his
    officer scanned
Four short pages of writing. "What's this, about 'Marthy
    Virginia's hand'?"
Swift from his honeymoon he, the dead soldier, had gone
    from his bride to the strife;
Never they met again, but she had written him, telling of that
    new life,
Born in the daughter, that bound her still closer and closer
    to him as his wife.
Laying her baby's hand down on the letter, around it she
    traced a rude line:
"If you would kiss the baby," she wrote, "you must kiss this
    outline of mine."

There was the shape of the hand on the page, with the small,
    chubby fingers outspread.
"Marthy Virginia's hand, for her pa" — so the words on the
    little palm said.
Never a wink slept the colonel that night, for the vengeance
    so blindly fulfilled.
Never again woke the old battle-glow when the bullets their
    death-note shrilled.
Long ago ended the struggle, in union of brotherhood happily
    stilled;

Yet from that field of Antietam, in warning and token of
　　love's command,
See! there is lifted the hand of a baby — Marthy Virginia's
　　hand!

GEORGE PARSONS LATHROP

BURNSIDE was entirely incompetent for so large a task, and was
defeated with terrible loss when he hurled his army in an insane at-
tack against the Confederates intrenched on the heights behind
Fredericksburg.　He was at once replaced by Major-General
"Fighting Joe" Hooker, and the Army of the Potomac, of which so
much had been expected, went into winter quarters to reorganize.

AT FREDERICKSBURG

[December 13, 1862]

THE smooth hill is bare, and the cannons are planted,
　　Like Gorgon fates shading its terrible brow;
The word has been passed that the stormers are wanted,
　　And Burnside's battalions are mustering now.
The armies stand by to behold the dread meeting;
　　The work must be done by a desperate few;
The black-mouthèd guns on the height give them greeting —
　　From gun-mouth to plain every grass blade in view.
Strong earthworks are there, and the rifles behind them
　　Are Georgia militia — an Irish brigade —
Their caps have green badges, as if to remind them
　　Of all the brave record their country has made.

The stormers go forward — the Federals cheer them;
　　They breast the smooth hillside — the black mouths are
　　　　dumb;
The riflemen lie in the works till they near them,
　　And cover the stormers as upward they come.
Was ever a death-march so grand and so solemn?
　　At last, the dark summit with flame is enlined;
The great guns belch doom on the sacrificed column,

That reels from the height, leaving hundreds behind.
The armies are hushed — there is no cause for cheering:
    The fall of brave men to brave men is a pain.
Again come the stormers! and as they are nearing
    The flame-sheeted rifle-lines, reel back again.
And so till full noon come the Federal masses —
    Flung back from the height, as the cliff flings a wave;
Brigade on brigade to the death-struggle passes,
    No wavering rank till it steps on the grave.

Then comes a brief lull, and the smoke-pall is lifted,
    The green of the hillside no longer is seen;
The dead soldiers lie as the sea-weed is drifted,
    The earthworks still held by the badges of green.
Have they quailed? is the word.   No: again they are form-
        ing —
    Again comes a column to death and defeat!
What is it in these who shall now do the storming
    That makes every Georgian spring to his feet?

'O God! what a pity!" they cry in their cover,
    As rifles are readied and bayonets made tight;
"'Tis Meagher and his fellows! their caps have green clover;
    'Tis Greek to Greek now for the rest of the fight!"
Twelve hundred the column, their rent flag before them,
    With Meagher at their head, they have dashed at the hill!
Their foemen are proud of the country that bore them;
    But, Irish in love, they are enemies still.
Out rings the fierce word, "Let them have it!" the rifles
    Are emptied point-blank in the hearts of the foe:
It is green against green, but a principle stifles
    The Irishman's love in the Georgian's blow.
The column has reeled, but it is not defeated;
    In front of the guns they re-form and attack;
Six times they have done it, and six times retreated;
    Twelve hundred they came, and two hundred go back.
Two hundred go back with the chivalrous story;
    The wild day is closed in the night's solemn shroud;

A thousand lie dead, but their death was a glory
    That calls not for tears — the Green Badges are proud!

Bright honor be theirs who for honor were fearless,
    Who charged for their flag to the grim cannon's mouth;
And honor to them who were true, though not tearless, —
    Who bravely that day kept the cause of the South.
The quarrel is done — God avert such another;
    The lesson it brought we should evermore heed:
Who loveth the Flag is a man and a brother,
    No matter what birth, or what race, or what creed.
                                JOHN BOYLE O'REILLY

IN THE West the North had made a better showing, largely because a real leader had been discovered in the person of General Ulysses S. Grant.   Grant's greatness consisted not so much in brilliant generalship, as in bull-dog tenacity which never acknowledged defeat, and in a preference for direct attack, as opposed to complicated maneuvers.

CAN'T

How history repeats itself,
    You'll say when you remember Grant,
Who, in his boyhood days, once sought
    Throughout the lexicon for "can't."

He could not find the word that day,
    The earnest boy whose name was Grant;
He never found it through long years,
    With all their power to disenchant.

No hostile host could give him pause;
    Rivers and mountains could not daunt;
He never found that hindering word —
    The steadfast man whose name was Grant.
                            HARRIET PRESCOTT SPOFFORD

NEAR the southern line of Kentucky, the Confederates held two strong forts, Henry and Donelson, and on February 2, 1862, a Union force under General Grant moved forward to attack them. The army was supported by a fleet of gunboats, led by the Essex, which suffered severely, among her dead being Lieutenant S. B. Brittan, Jr., a lad of not quite seventeen.

BOY BRITTAN

[February 6, 1862]

BOY BRITTAN — only a lad — a fair-haired boy — sixteen,
    In his uniform,
Into the storm — into the roaring jaws of grim Fort Henry —
Boldly bears the Federal flotilla —
    Into the battle storm!

Boy Brittan is master's mate aboard of the Essex —
There he stands, buoyant and eager-eyed,
    By the brave captain's side;
Ready to do and dare. *Aye, aye, sir!* always ready —
    In his country's uniform.
Boom! Boom! and now the flag-boat sweeps, and now the Essex,
    Into the battle storm!

Boom! Boom! till river and fort and field are overclouded
By battle's breath; then from the fort a gleam
And a crashing gun, and the Essex is wrapt and shrouded
    In a scalding cloud of steam!

    But victory! victory!
Unto God all praise be ever rendered,
Unto God all praise and glory be!
See, Boy Brittan! see, boy, see!
They strike! Hurrah! the fort has just surrendered!
Shout! Shout! my boy, my warrior boy!
And wave your cap and clap your hands for joy!
Cheer answer cheer and bear the cheer about —

Hurrah! Hurrah! for the fiery fort is ours;
And "Victory!" "Victory!" "Victory!"
     Is the shout.
Shout — for the fiery fort, and the field, and the day are
    ours —
The day is ours — thanks to the brave endeavor of heroes,
    boy, like thee...

     Victory! Victory! ...
But suddenly wrecked and wrapt in seething steam, the Essex
Slowly drifted out of the battle's storm;
Slowly, slowly down — laden with the dead and the dying;
And there, at the captain's feet, among the dead and the
    dying,
The shot-marred form of a beautiful boy is lying —
    There in his uniform!

Laurels and tears for thee, boy,
Laurels and tears for thee!
Laurels of light, moist with the precious dew
Of the inmost heart of the nation's loving heart,
And blest by the balmy breath of the beautiful and the true;
Moist — moist with the luminous breath of the singing
    spheres
     And the nation's starry tears!
And tremble-touched by the pulse-like gush and start
Of the universal music of the heart,
     And all deep sympathy.
Laurels and tears for thee, boy.
    Laurels and tears for thee —
Laurels of light and tears of love forevermore —
    For thee!
              FORCEYTHE WILLSON

A FEW days later, Grant captured Fort Donelson and its entire garrison, and then advanced against Corinth, Mississippi, with Pittsburg Landing as the base of operations. On the morning of April 6, the

Union army was surprised and driven back to the river by a strong
Confederate force under Albert Sidney Johnston, who was killed
during the battle.

ALBERT SIDNEY JOHNSTON

[April 6, 1862]

I HEAR again the tread of war go thundering through the land,
And Puritan and Cavalier are clinching neck and hand,
Round Shiloh church the furious foes have met to thrust and
    slay,
Where erst the peaceful sons of Christ were wont to kneel
    and pray.

The wrestling of the ages shakes the hills of Tennessee,
With all their echoing mounts a-throb with war's wild
    minstrelsy;
A galaxy of stars new-born around the shield of Mars,
And set against the Stars and Stripes the flashing Stars and
    Bars.

'Twas Albert Sidney Johnston led the columns of the Gray,
Like Hector on the plains of Troy, his presence fired the fray;
And dashing horse and gleaming sword spake out his royal
    will
As on the slopes of Shiloh field the blasts of war blew shrill.

"Down with the base invaders!" the Gray shout forth the cry,
"Death to presumptuous rebels!" the Blue ring out reply;
All day the conflict rages and yet again all day,
Though Grant is on the Union side, he cannot stem nor stay.

They are a royal race of men, these brothers face to face,
Their fury speaking through their guns, their frenzy in their
    pace;
The sweeping onset of the Gray bears down the sturdy Blue,
Though Sherman and his legions are heroes through and
    through....

As when the Trojan hero came from that fair city's gates,
With tossing main and flaming crest to scorn the scowling
    fates,
His legions gather round him and madly charge and cheer,
And fill the besieging armies with wild disheveled fear;

Then bares his breast unto the dart the daring spearsman
    sends,
And dying hears his cheering foes, the wailing of his friends,
So Albert Sidney Johnston, the chief of belt and scar,
Lay down to die at Shiloh and turned the scales of war.

Now five and twenty years are gone, and lo, today they
    come
The Blue and Gray in proud array with throbbing fife and
    drum;
But not as rivals, not as foes, as brothers reconciled,
To twine love's fragrant roses where the thorns of hate grew
    wild....

Oh, veterans of the Blue and Gray, who fought on Shiloh field,
The purposes of God are true, His judgment stands revealed;
The pangs of war have rent the veil, and lo, His high decree:
One heart, one hope, one destiny, one flag from sea to sea.

KATE BROWNLEE SHERWOOD

BUELL'S army came up during the night, and Grant was able to assume the offensive next day and drive the enemy, disheartened by the loss of their leader, from the field. Johnston's death left General Beauregard in command.

BEAUREGARD

OUR trust is now in thee,
    Beauregard!
In thy hand the God of Hosts
    Hath placed the sword;

And the glory of thy fame
Has set the world aflame —
Hearts kindle at thy name,
    Beauregard!

The way that lies before
    Is cold and hard;
We are led across the desert
    By the Lord!
But the cloud that shines by night
To guide our steps aright,
Is the pillar of thy might,
    Beauregard!

Thou hast watched the southern heavens
    Evening starred,
And chosen thence thine emblems,
    Beauregard;
And upon thy banner's fold
Is that starry cross enrolled,
Which no Northman shall behold
    Shamed or scarred.

By the blood that crieth loudly
    From the sward,
We have sworn to keep around it
    Watch and ward,
And the standard of thine hand
Yet shall shine above a land,
Like its leader, free and grand,
    Beauregard!

                    CATHERINE ANN WARFIELD

ONE more struggle closed the campaign. On December 29, 1862, the armies of Bragg and Rosecrans met at Murfreesboro, Tennessee, and for four days a desperate battle raged, which ended in the defeat of the Confederates. Among the wounded on the Confederate side, was Isaac Giffen, who was taken by Dr. Francis O. Ticknor into his own home and nursed back to life. He fell two years later in one of the battles before Atlanta.

LITTLE GIFFEN

OUT of the focal and foremost fire,
Out of the hospital walls as dire,
Smitten of grapeshot and gangrene
(Eighteenth battle and *he* sixteen) —
Specter such as you seldom see,
Little Giffen of Tennessee.

"Take him — and welcome!" the surgeons said,
"Little the doctor can help the dead!"
So we took him and brought him where
The balm was sweet on the summer air;
And we laid him down on a wholesome bed —
Utter Lazarus, heel to head!

And we watched the war with bated breath —
Skeleton Boy against skeleton Death.
Months of torture, how many such!
Weary weeks of the stick and crutch;
And still a glint in the steel-blue eye
Told of a spirit that wouldn't die.

And didn't. Nay, more! in death's despite
The crippled skeleton learned to write.
"Dear Mother," at first of course; and then
"Dear Captain," inquiring about "the men."
Captain's answer: "Of eighty and five,
Giffen and I are left alive."

Word of gloom from the war one day:
"Johnston's pressed at the front, they say!"
Little Giffen was up and away;

A tear — his first — as he bade good-bye,
Dimmed the glint of his steel-blue eye.
"I'll write, if spared!"   There was news of the fight;
But none of Giffen — he did not write.

I sometimes fancy that, were I king
Of the princely knights of the Golden Ring,
With the song of the minstrel in mine ear,
And the tender legend that trembles here,
I'd give the best, on his bended knee,
The whitest soul of my chivalry,
For Little Giffen of Tennessee.

FRANCIS ORRERY TICKNOR

THIS ended the campaign.   Both the Union and Confederate armies
were in desperate need of rest and reorganization.   The South, on
the whole, had had the better of the first year's fighting.

THE BATTLE AUTUMN OF 1862

THE flags of war like storm-birds fly,
   The charging trumpets blow;
Yet rolls no thunder in the sky,
   No earthquake strives below.

And, calm and patient, Nature keeps
   Her ancient promise well,
Though o'er her bloom and greenness sweeps
   The battle's breath of hell.

And still she walks in golden hours
   Through harvest-happy farms,
And still she wears her fruits and flowers
   Like jewels on her arms.

What mean the gladness of the plain,
   This joy of eve and morn,
The mirth that shakes the beard of grain
   And yellow locks of corn?

Ah! eyes may well be full of tears,
    And hearts with hate are hot;
But even-paced come round the years,
    And Nature changes not.

She meets with smiles our bitter grief,
    With songs our groans of pain;
She mocks with tint of flower and leaf
    The war-field's crimson stain.

Still, in the cannon's pause, we hear
    Her sweet thanksgiving-psalm;
Too near to God for doubt or fear,
    She shares the eternal calm.

She knows the seed lies safe below
    The fires that blast and burn;
For all the tears of blood we sow
    She waits the rich return.

She sees with clearer eye than ours
    The good of suffering born —
The hearts that blossom like her flowers,
    And ripen like her corn.

Oh, give to us, in times like these,
    The vision of her eyes;
And make her fields and fruited trees
    Our golden prophecies!

Oh, give to us her finer ear!
    Above this stormy din,
We too would hear the bells of cheer
    Ring peace and freedom in.
                JOHN GREENLEAF WHITTIER

CHAPTER III

The Second Year

Though slavery had caused the war, President Lincoln announced, at his inauguration, that he had no intention of interfering with it. But General John C. Frémont, commanding the Western Department, was a famous abolitionist, and on August 31, 1861, he issued a proclamation freeing the slaves of secessionists in Missouri. The President promptly countermanded it and relieved Frémont of his command.

TO JOHN C. FREMONT

[August 31, 1861]

Thy error, Frémont, simply was to act
A brave man's part, without the statesman's tact,
And, taking counsel but of common sense,
To strike at cause as well as consequence.
Oh, never yet since Roland wound his horn
At Roncesvalles, has a blast been blown
Far-heard, wide-echoed, startling as thine own,
Heard from the van of Freedom's hope forlorn
It had been safer, doubtless, for the time
To flatter treason, and avoid offense
To that Dark Power whose underlying crime
Heaves upward its perpetual turbulence.
But if thine be the fate of all who break
The ground for truth's seed, or forerun their years
Till lost in distance, or with stout hearts make
A lane for freedom through the level spears,
Still take thou courage! God has spoken through thee,
Irrevocable, the mighty words, Be free!
The land shakes with them, and the slave's dull ear
Turns from the rice-swamp stealthily to hear.
Who would recall them now must first arrest
The winds that blow down from the free Northwest,

Ruffling the Gulf; or like a scroll roll back
The Mississippi to its upper springs.
Such words fulfil their prophecy, and lack
But the full time to harden into things.
                              JOHN GREENLEAF WHITTIER

BUT after the war had been in progress a year, the President resolved
to throw down the gauntlet to the slave states.   On September 22,
1862, he proclaimed that all slaves would be freed in such states as
were in rebellion against the United States on January 1, 1863.   It
was a war measure pure and simple, and when the South continued
in rebellion, the proclamation went into effect on the first day of the
New Year.

BOSTON HYMN

[Read in Music Hall, Boston, January 1, 1863]

THE word of the Lord by night
    To the watching Pilgrims came,
As they sat by the seaside,
    And filled their hearts with flame.

God said, I am tired of kings,
    I suffer them no more;
Up to my ear the morning brings
    The outrage of the poor.

Think ye I made this ball
    A field of havoc and war,
Where tyrants great and tyrants small
    Might harry the weak and poor?

My angel — his name is Freedom —
    Choose him to be your king;
He shall cut pathways east and west,
    And fend you with his wing.

Lo! I uncover the land,
  Which I had of old time in the West,
As the sculptor uncovers the statue
  When he has wrought his best;

I show Columbia, of the rocks
  Which dip their foot in the seas,
And soar to the air-borne flocks
  Of clouds and the boreal fleece.

I will divide my goods:
  Call in the wretch and slave;
None shall rule but the humble,
  And none but Toil shall have.

I will have never a noble,
  No lineage counted great;
Fishers and choppers and plowmen
  Shall constitute a state.

Go, cut down trees in the forest
  And trim the straightest boughs;
Cut down trees in the forest
  And build me a wooden house.

Call the people together,
  The young men and the sires,
The digger in the harvest field,
  Hireling and him that hires;

And here in a pine state-house
  They shall choose men to rule
In every needful faculty,
  In church and state and school....

I break your bonds and masterships,
  And I unchain the slave:
Free be his heart and hand henceforth
  As wind and wandering wave.

I cause from every creature
   His proper good to flow:
As much as he is and doeth,
   So much he shall bestow.

But, laying hands on another,
   To coin his labor and sweat,
He goes in pawn to his victim
   For eternal years in debt.

Today unbind the captive,
   So only are ye unbound;
Lift up a people from the dust,
   Trump of their rescue, sound!

Pay ransom to the owner
   And fill the bag to the brim.
Who is the owner?   The slave is owner,
   And ever was.   Pay him.

O North! give him beauty for rags,
   And honor, O South! for his shame;
Nevada! coin thy golden crags
   With Freedom's image and name.

Up! and the dusky race
   That sat in darkness long, —
Be swift their feet as antelopes,
   And as behemoth strong.

Come, East and West and North,
   By races, as snowflakes,
And carry my purpose forth,
   Which neither halts nor shakes.

My will fulfilled shall be,
   For, in daylight or in dark,
My thunderbolt has eyes to see
   His way home to the mark.
              RALPH WALDO EMERSON

FINALLY on January 31, 1865, in order definitely to settle the question, Congress adopted an amendment to the Constitution forever abolishing slavery in the United States.   On December 18, 1865, it was announced that the amendment had been ratified by the requisite number of states, and was thenceforward the law of the land.

LAUS DEO!

IT IS done!
Clang of bell and roar of gun
Send the tidings up and down.
How the belfries rock and reel!
How the great guns, peal on peal,
Fling the joy from town to town!

Ring, O bells!
Every stroke exulting tells
Of the burial hour of crime.
Loud and long, that all may hear,
Ring for every listening ear
Of Eternity and Time!

Let us kneel;
God's own voice is in that peal,
And this spot is holy ground.
Lord, forgive us!   What are we,
That our eyes this glory see,
That our ears have heard the sound!...

How they pale,
Ancient myth and song and tale,
In this wonder of our days,
When the cruel rod of war
Blossoms white with righteous law
And the wrath of man is praise!

Blotted out!
All within and all about

Shall a fresher life begin;
    Freer breathe the universe
    As it rolls its heavy curse
On the dead and buried sin!

    It is done!
    In the circuit of the sun
Shall the sound thereof go forth.
    It shall bid the sad rejoice,
    It shall give the dumb a voice,
It shall belt with joy the earth!

    Ring and swing,
    Bells of joy! On morning's wing
Send the song of praise abroad!
    With a sound of broken chains
    Tell the nations that He reigns,
Who alone is Lord and God!
            JOHN GREENLEAF WHITTIER

As THE spring of 1863 opened, the Army of the Potomac gathered itself for another effort, crossed the Rappahannock to attack Lee, and on April 30, 1863, went into camp at Chancellorsville. Lee at once prepared to fight, and a little past midnight of May 1, he dispatched Stonewall Jackson's column to meet the enemy. Jackson had proved himself one of the South's ablest leaders, and every one of his thirty thousand men idolized him.

STONEWALL JACKSON'S WAY

COME, stack arms, men! Pile on the rails,
    Stir up the camp-fire bright;
No growling if the canteen fails,
    We'll make a roaring night.
Here Shenandoah brawls along,
There burly Blue Ridge echoes strong,
To swell the Brigade's rousing song
    Of "Stonewall Jackson's way."

We see him now — the queer slouched hat
    Cocked o'er his eye askew;
The shrewd, dry smile; the speech so pat,
    So calm, so blunt, so true.
The "Blue-Light Elder" knows 'em well;
Says he, "That's Banks — he's fond of shell;
Lord save his soul! we'll give him —" well!
    That's "Stonewall Jackson's way."

Silence! ground arms! kneel all! caps off!
    Old Massa's goin' to pray.
Strangle the fool that dares to scoff!
    Attention! it's his way.
Appealing from his native sod,
In forma pauperis to God:
"Lay bare Thine arm; stretch forth Thy rod!
    Amen!"   That's "Stonewall's way."

He's in the saddle now. Fall in!
    Steady! the whole brigade!
Hill's at the ford, cut off; we'll win
    His way out, ball and blade!
What matter if our shoes are worn?
What matter if our feet are torn?
"Quick step! we're with him before morn!"
    That's "Stonewall Jackson's way."

The sun's bright lances rout the mists
    Of morning, and, by George!
Here's Longstreet, struggling in the lists,
    Hemmed in an ugly gorge.
Pope and his Dutchmen, whipped before;
'Bay'nets and grape!" hear Stonewall roar;
"Charge, Stuart! Pay off Ashby's score!"
    In "Stonewall Jackson's way."

Ah! Maiden, wait and watch and yearn
    For news of Stonewall's band!

Ah! Widow, read, with eyes that burn,
    That ring upon thy hand.
Ah! Wife, sew on, pray on, hope on;
    Thy life shall not be all forlorn;
The foe had better ne'er been born
    That gets in "Stonewall's way."
                JOHN WILLIAMSON PALMER

THE battle began at dawn and lasted all day, without decisive result.
Next day, Jackson made a long flanking movement, and just as twi-
light fell, burst from the woods in overwhelming force and routed the
Federal right wing. For a moment it seemed that all was lost, then
the Eighth Pennsylvania Cavalry got into touch with the Confeder-
ate flank and charged. The regiment was hurled back, terribly
shattered, Major Peter Keenan being among the killed, but the Con-
federate advance had been checked long enough for Pleasanton to
get his artillery into position.

KEENAN'S CHARGE

[May 2, 1863]

THE sun had set:
The leaves with dew were wet —
Down fell a bloody dusk
On the woods, that second of May,
Where "Stonewall's" corps, like a beast of prey,
Tore through with angry tusk.

"They've trapped us, boys!"
Rose from our flank a voice.
With rush of steel and smoke
On came the rebels straight,
Eager as love and wild as hate;
And our line reeled and broke;

Broke and fled.
Not one stayed, — but the dead!

With curses, shrieks, and cries,
Horses and wagons and men
Tumbled back through the shuddering glen,
And above us the fading skies.

There's one hope, still, —
Those batteries parked on the hill!
"Battery, wheel!" ('mid the roar),
"Pass pieces; fix prolonge to fire
Retiring. Trot!"   In the panic dire
A bugle rings "Trot!" — and no more

The horses plunged,
The cannon lurched and lunged,
To join the hopeless rout.
But suddenly rose a form
Calmly in front of the human storm,
With a stern commanding shout:

"Align those guns!"
(We knew it was Pleasanton's.)
The cannoneers bent to obey,
And worked with a will at his word,
And the black guns moved as if *they* had heard.
But, ah, the dread delay!

"To wait is crime;
O God, for ten minutes' time!"
The general looked around.
There Keenan sat, like a stone,
With his three hundred horse alone,
Less shaken than the ground.

"Major, your men?"
"Are soldiers, general." "Then,
Charge, major! Do your best;
Hold the enemy back at all cost,
Till my guns are placed; — else the army is lost.
You die to save the rest!"

By the shrouded gleam of the western skies,
Brave Keenan looked into Pleasanton's eyes
For an instant — clear, and cool, and still;
Then, with a smile, he said: "I will."

"Cavalry, charge!" Not a man of them shrank.
Their sharp, full cheer, from rank on rank,
Rose joyously, with a willing breath, —
Rose like a greeting hail to death.

Then forward they sprang, and spurred, and clashed;
Shouted the officers, crimson-sashed;
Rode well the men, each brave as his fellow,
In their faded coats of the blue and yellow;
And above in the air, with an instinct true,
Like a bird of war their pennon flew.

With clank of scabbards and thunder of steeds,
And blades that shine like sunlit reeds,
And strong brown faces bravely pale,
For fear their proud attempt shall fail,
Three hundred Pennsylvanians close
On twice ten thousand gallant foes.

Line after line the troopers came
To the edge of the wood that was ringed with flame;
Rode in, and saberd, and shot, — and fell:
Nor came one back his wounds to tell.
And full in the midst rose Keenan, tall
In the gloom, like a martyr awaiting his fall,
While the circle-stroke of his saber, swung
'Round his head, like a halo there, luminous hung.

Line after line, aye, whole platoons,
Struck dead in their saddles, of brave dragoons,
By the maddened horses were onward borne
And into the vortex flung, trampled and torn;
As Keenan fought with his men, side by side.
So they rode, till there were no more to ride.

But over them, lying there shattered and mute,
What deep echo rolls? 'Tis a death-salute
From the cannon in place; for, heroes, you braved
Your fate not in vain; the army was saved!

Over them now, — year following year, —
Over their graves the pine-cones fall,
And the whippoorwill chants his specter-call;
But they stir not again; they raise no cheer:
They have ceased.   But their glory shall never cease,
Nor their light be quenched in the light of peace.
The rush of their charge is resounding still,
That saved the army at Chancellorsville.
                    GEORGE PARSONS LATHROP

THE Confederates paused in face of the terrible fire, and Jackson and
his staff pushed forward to reconnoiter the position.   As he was re-
turning to his lines in the dusk of evening, he and his companions
were mistaken for Union troops by his own men, and fired upon.
Jackson fell, pierced by three bullets.

"THE BRIGADE MUST NOT KNOW, SIR!'

[May 2, 1863]

"WHO'VE ye got there?" — "Only a dying brother,
    Hurt in the front just now."
"Good boy! he'll do.   Somebody tell his mother
    Where he was killed, and how."

"Whom have you there?" — "A crippled courier, Major,
    Shot by mistake, we hear.
He was with Stonewall."   "Cruel work they've made here;
    Quick with him to the rear!"

"Well, who comes next?" — "Doctor, speak low, speak low,
    sir;
    Don't let the men find out!

It's Stonewall!" — "God!" — "The brigade must not know,
    sir,
  While there's a foe about!"

Whom have we here — shrouded in martial manner,
    Crowned with a martyr's charm?
A grand dead hero, in a living banner,
    Born of his heart and arm:

The heart whereon his cause hung — see how clingeth
    That banner to his bier!
The arm wherewith his cause struck — hark! how ringeth
    His trumpet in their rear!

What have we left?   His glorious inspiration,
    His prayers in council met.
Living, he laid the first stones of a nation;
    And dead, he builds it yet.

UNKNOWN

EARLY on the morning of Sunday, May 3, the Confederates again attacked and drove the Union army back across the river, with a loss of seventeen thousand men.   But the victory was outweighed by the loss of Stonewall Jackson, who died May 10.   It was perhaps the supreme irony of the war that the best-loved leader on the Southern side should have been killed by his own men.   His last words were, "Let us cross the river and rest in the shade."

UNDER THE SHADE OF THE TREES

[May 10, 1863]

WHAT are the thoughts that are stirring his breast?
    What is the mystical vision he sees?
— "Let us pass over the river and rest
    Under the shade of the trees."

Has he grown sick of his toils and his tasks?
  Sighs the worn spirit for respite or ease?
Is it a moment's cool halt that he asks,
  Under the shade of the trees?

Is it the gurgle of waters whose flow
  Ofttime has come to him, borne on the breeze,
Memory listens to, lapsing so low,
  Under the shade of the trees?

Nay — though the rasp of the flesh was so sore,
  Faith, that had yearnings far keener than these,
Saw the soft sheen of the Thitherward Shore
  Under the shade of the trees; —

Caught the high psalms of ecstatic delight —
  Heard the harps harping like soundings of seas —
Watched earth's assoilèd ones walking in white
  Under the shade of the trees.

Oh, was it strange he should pine for release,
  Touched to the soul with such transports as these —
He who so needed the balsam of peace,
  Under the shade of the trees?

Yea, it was noblest for him — it was best
  (Questioning naught of our Father's decrees),
There to pass over the river and rest
  Under the shade of the trees!

                              MARGARET JUNKIN PRESTON

LEE paused only to rest his forces and then, for the second time, invaded Maryland, swept down the Shenandoah Valley, and finally concentrated his army at Gettysburg. There the Union army waited to receive him, and a terrific battle followed, lasting three days, and culminating in a great Confederate charge, led by General

George Pickett and his Virginians. It was repulsed with terrible slaughter, the Confederates withdrew in good order and recrossed the Potomac into Virginia.

THE HIGH TIDE AT GETTYSBURG

[July 3, 1863]

A CLOUD possessed the hollow field,
The gathering battle's smoky shield:
    Athwart the gloom the lightning flashed,
    And through the cloud some horsemen dashed,
And from the heights the thunder pealed.

Then, at the brief command of Lee,
Moved out that matchless infantry,
    With Pickett leading grandly down,
    To rush against the roaring crown
Of those dread heights of destiny.

Far heard above the angry guns,
A cry across the tumult runs:
    The voice that rang through Shiloh's woods,
    And Chickamauga's solitudes:
The fierce South cheering on her sons!

Ah, how the withering tempest blew
Against the front of Pettigrew!
    A Khamsin wind that scorched and singed
    Like that infernal flame that fringed
The British squares at Waterloo!

A thousand fell where Kemper led;
A thousand died where Garnett bled;
    In blinding flame and strangling smoke,
    The remnant through the batteries broke,
And crossed the works with Armistead.

"Once more in Glory's van with me!"
    Virginia cried to Tennessee:

"We two together, come what may,
Shall stand upon those works today!"
The reddest day in history.

Brave Tennessee! In reckless way
Virginia heard her comrade say:
  "Close round this rent and riddled rag!"
  What time she set her battle flag
Amid the guns of Doubleday.

But who shall break the guards that wait
Before the awful face of Fate?
  The tattered standards of the South
  Were shriveled at the cannon's mouth,
And all her hopes were desolate.

In vain the Tennesseean set
His breast against the bayonet;
  In vain Virginia charged and raged,
  A tigress in her wrath uncaged,
Till all the hill was red and wet!

Above the bayonets, mixed and crossed,
Men saw a gray, gigantic ghost
  Receding through the battle-cloud,
  And heard across the tempest loud
The death-cry of a nation lost!

The brave went down! Without disgrace
They leaped to Ruin's red embrace:
  They only heard Fame's thunders wake,
  And saw the dazzling sunburst break
In smiles on Glory's bloody face!

They fell, who lifted up a hand
And bade the sun in heaven to stand;
  They smote and fell, who set the bars
  Against the progress of the stars,
And stayed the march of Motherland!

They stood, who saw the future come
On through the fight's delirium;
   They smote and stood, who held the hope
   Of nations on that slippery slope,
Amid the cheers of Christendom!

God lives!   He forged the iron will,
That clutched and held that trembling hill!
   God lives and reigns! He built and lent
   The heights for Freedom's battlement,
Where floats her flag in triumph still!

Fold up the banners!   Smelt the guns!
Love rules.   Her gentler purpose runs.
   A mighty mother turns in tears,
   The pages of her battle years,
Lamenting all her fallen sons!
               WILL HENRY THOMPSON

LEE had left twenty-five thousand of his best soldiers dead or
wounded on the field of battle — veteran fighters whom he was
never able to replace.   There was never again any chance of Con-
federate success, and for this reason Gettysburg may fairly be said
to have been the decisive battle of the Civil War.

GETTYSBURG

[July 1, 2, 3, 1863]

THERE was no union in the land,
   Though wise men labored long
With links of clay and ropes of sand
   To bind the right and wrong.

There was no temper in the blade
   That once could cleave a chain;
Its edge was dull with touch of trade
   And clogged with rust of gain.

The sand and clay must shrink away
    Before the lava tide:
By blows and blood and fire assay
    The metal must be tried.

Here sledge and anvil met, and when
    The furnace fiercest roared,
God's undiscerning workingmen
    Reforged His people's sword.

Enough for them to ask and know
    The moment's duty clear —
The bayonets flashed it here below,
    The guns proclaimed it here:

To do and dare, and die at need,
    But while life lasts, to fight —
For right or wrong a simple creed,
    But simplest for the right.

They faltered not who stood that day
    And held this post of dread;
Nor cowards they who wore the gray
    Until the gray was red.

For every wreath the victor wears
    The vanquished half may claim;
And every monument declares
    A common pride and fame.

We raise no altar stones to Hate,
    Who never bowed to Fear:
No province crouches at our gate,
    To shame our triumph here.

Here standing by a dead wrong's grave
    The blindest now may see,
The blow that liberates the slave
    But sets the master free!

When ills beset the nation's life
　　Too dangerous to bear,
The sword must be the surgeon's knife,
　　Too merciful to spare.

O Soldier of our common land,
　　'Tis thine to bear that blade
Loose in the sheath, or firm in hand,
　　But ever unafraid.

When foreign foes assail our right,
　　One nation trusts to thee —
To wield it well in worthy fight —
　　The sword of Meade and Lee!

JAMES JEFFREY ROCHE

AMONG the thousands who took part in that terrible three days' struggle none was more remarkable than old John Burns, a veteran of the War of 1812 and of the Mexican War, who, rejected at the outbreak of the Civil War on account of his age, nevertheless took down his rifle and helped repel the invaders when they approached his home at Gettysburg.

JOHN BURNS OF GETTYSBURG

HAVE you heard the story that gossips tell
Of Burns of Gettysburg? No? Ah, well:
Brief is the glory that hero earns,
Briefer the story of poor John Burns:
He was the fellow who won renown —
The only man who didn't back down
When the rebels rode through his native town;
But held his own in the fight next day,
When all his townsfolk ran away.
That was in July, sixty-three —
The very day that General Lee,
Flower of Southern chivalry,

Baffled and beaten, backward reeled
From a stubborn Meade and a barren field.

I might tell how, but the day before,
John Burns stood at his cottage door,
Looking down the village street,
Where, in the shade of his peaceful vine,
He heard the low of his gathered kine,
And felt their breath with incense sweet;
Or I might say, when the sunset burned
The old farm gable, he thought it turned
The milk that fell like a babbling flood
Into the milk-pail, red as blood!
Or how he fancied the hum of bees
Were bullets buzzing among the trees.
But all such fanciful thoughts as these
Were strange to a practical man like Burns,
Who minded only his own concerns,
Troubled no more by fancies fine
Than one of his calm-eyed, long-tailed kine —
Quite old-fashioned and matter-of-fact,
Slow to argue, but quick to act.
That was the reason, as some folks say,
He fought so well on that terrible day.

And it was terrible.   On the right
Raged for hours the heady fight,
Thundered the battery's double bass —
Difficult music for men to face;
While on the left — where now the graves
Undulate like the living waves
That all that day unceasing swept
Up to the pits the rebels kept —
Round-shot plowed the upland glades,
Sown with bullets, reaped with blades;
Shattered fences here and there
Tossed their splinters in the air;
The very trees were stripped and bare;

The barns that once held yellow grain
Were heaped with harvests of the slain;
The cattle bellowed on the plain,
The turkeys screamed with might and main,
The brooding barn-fowl left their rest
With strange shells bursting in each nest.

Just where the tide of battle turns,
Erect and lonely, stood old John Burns.
How do you think the man was dressed?
He wore an ancient, long buff vest,
Yellow as saffron — but his best;
And, buttoned over his manly breast,
Was a bright blue coat with a rolling collar,
And large gilt buttons — size of a dollar —
With tails that the country-folk called "swaller."
He wore a broad-brimmed, bell-crowned hat,
White as the locks on which it sat.
Never had such a sight been seen
For forty years on the village green,
Since old John Burns was a country beau,
And went to the "quiltings" long ago.

Close at his elbows all that day,
Veterans of the Peninsula,
Sunburnt and bearded, charged away;
And striplings, downy of lip and chin —
Clerks that the Home-Guard mustered in —
Glanced, as they passed, at the hat he wore,
Then at the rifle his right hand bore;
And hailed him, from out their youthful lore,
With scraps of a slangy repertoire:
"How are you, White Hat?" "Put her through!"
"Your head's level!" and "Bully for you!"
Called him "Daddy," — begged he'd disclose
The name of the tailor who made his clothes,
And what was the value he set on those:

While Burns, unmindful of jeer or scoff,
Stood there picking the rebels off —
With his long brown rifle, and bell-crown hat,
And the swallow-tails they were laughing at.

'Twas but a moment, for that respect
Which clothes all courage their voices checked;
And something the wildest could understand
Spake in the old man's strong right hand,
And his corded throat, and the lurking frown
Of his eyebrows under his old bell-crown;
Until, as they gazed, there crept an awe
Through the ranks in whispers, and some men saw,
In the antique vestments and long white hair,
The Past of the Nation in battle there;
And some of the soldiers since declare
That the gleam of his old white hat afar,
Like the crested plume of the brave Navarre,
That day was their oriflamme of war.

So raged the battle.   You know the rest:
How the rebels, beaten and backward pressed,
Broke at the final charge and ran.
At which John Burns — a practical man —
Shouldered his rifle, unbent his brows,
And then went back to his bees and cows.

That is the story of old John Burns;
This is the moral the reader learns:
In fighting the battle, the question's whether
You'll show a hat that's white, or a feather.

BRET HARTE

On November 19, 1863, a portion of the battle-field of Gettysburg
was consecrated as a national military cemetery with impressive
ceremonies. A long and eloquent address was delivered by Edward
Everett, and then President Lincoln arose and spoke simply and
briefly, almost extemporaneously, but so fittingly and with such

consummate patriotism, that his words have been emblazoned in American history beside the great utterances of Washington and Jefferson and Patrick Henry.

THE GETTYSBURG ADDRESS

FOURSCORE and seven years ago our fathers brought forth on this continent a new nation, conceived in liberty, and dedicated to the proposition that all men are created equal. Now we are engaged in a great civil war, testing whether that nation, or any nation so conceived and so dedicated, can long endure.

We are met on a great battle-field of that war. We have come to dedicate a portion of that field as a final resting-place for those who here gave their lives that that nation might live.

It is altogether fitting and proper that we should do this. But in a larger sense, we cannot dedicate, we cannot consecrate, we cannot hallow this ground. The brave men, living and dead, who struggled here, have consecrated it far above our poor power to add or detract. The world will little note, nor long remember, what we say here, but it can never forget what they did here. It is for us, the living, rather, to be dedicated here to the unfinished work which they who fought here have thus far so nobly advanced.

It is rather for us to be here dedicated to the great task remaining before us; — that from these honored dead, we take increased devotion to that cause for which they gave the last full measure of devotion; — that we here highly resolve that these dead shall not have died in vain, that this nation, under God, shall have a new birth of freedom, and that government of the people, by the people, for the people, shall not perish from the earth.

ABRAHAM LINCOLN

By a strange coincidence, on the very day of the victory at Gettys-
burg, July 3, 1863, the great Confederate stronghold of Vicksburg,
on the Mississippi, surrendered to General Grant, who had been be-
sieging it since the middle of May.   The entire Confederate garrison,
twenty-seven thousand strong, was taken prisoner.

VICKSBURG

For sixty days and upwards,
   A storm of shell and shot
Rained round us in a flaming shower,
   But still we faltered not.
"If the noble city perish,"
   Our grand young leader said,
"Let the only walls the foe shall scale
   Be ramparts of the dead!"

For sixty days and upwards,
   The eye of heaven waxed dim;
And e'en throughout God's holy morn,
   O'er Christian prayer and hymn,
Arose a hissing tumult,
   As if the fiends in air
Strove to engulf the voice of faith
   In the shrieks of their despair.

There was wailing in the houses,
   There was trembling on the marts,
While the tempest raged and thundered,
   'Mid the silent thrill of hearts;
But the Lord, our shield, was with us,
   And ere a month had sped,
Our very women walked the streets
   With scarce one throb of dread.

And the little children gamboled,
   Their faces purely raised,
Just for a wondering moment,
   As the huge bombs whirled and blazed;

Then turned with silvery laughter
  To the sports which children love,
Thrice-mailed in the sweet, instinctive thought
  That the good God watched above.

Yet the hailing bolts fell faster,
  From scores of flame-clad ships,
And about us, denser, darker,
  Grew the conflict's wild eclipse,
Till a solid cloud closed o'er us,
  Like a type of doom and ire,
Whence shot a thousand quivering tongues
  Of forked and vengeful fire.

But the unseen hands of angels
  Those death-shafts turned aside,
And the dove of heavenly mercy
  Ruled o'er the battle tide:
In the houses ceased the wailing,
  And through the war-scarred marts
The people strode, with step of hope,
  To the music in their hearts.

PAUL HAMILTON HAYNE

Two months later, Chattanooga was occupied by the Army of the Cumberland, under General Rosecrans, who pushed forward to the Chickamauga Valley.   There, on September 18, he was attacked by a strong Confederate army, and, after two days' fighting, compelled to retreat.   General Thomas, in command of the left wing, saved the army from serious disaster by standing firm and repelling assault after assault, winning the title of "The Rock of Chickamauga."

THE BALLAD OF CHICKAMAUGA

[September 19, 20, 1863]

BY CHICKAMAUGA's crooked stream the martial trumpets
    blew;
The North and South stood face to face, with War's dread
    work to do.

O lion-strong, unselfish, brave, twin athletes battle-wise,
Brothers yet enemies, the fire of conflict in their eyes,
All banner-led and bugle-stirred, they set them to the fight,
Hearing the god of slaughter laugh from mountain height to
    height.

The ruddy, fair-haired, giant North breathed loud and strove
    amain;
The swarthy shoulders of the South did heave them to the
    strain;
An earthquake shuddered underfoot, a cloud rolled overhead:
And serpent-tongues of flame cut through and lapped and
    twinkled red,
Where back and forth a bullet-stream went singing like
    a breeze,
What time the snarling cannon-balls to splinters tore the trees.

"Make way, make way!" a voice boomed out, "I'm marching
    to the sea!"
The answer was a rebel yell and Bragg's artillery.
Where Negley struck, the cohorts gray like storm-tossed
    clouds were rent;
Where Buckner charged, a cyclone fell, the blue to tatters
    went;
The noble Brannan cheered his men, Pat Cleburne answered
    back,
And Lytle stormed, and life was naught in Walthall's bloody
    track.

Old Taylor's Ridge rocked to its base, and Pigeon Mountain
    shook;
And Helm went down, and Lytle died, and broken was Mc-
    Cook.
Van Cleve moved like a hurricane, a tempest blew with
    Hood,
Awful the sweep of Breckenridge across the flaming wood.
Never before did battle-roar such chords of thunder make,
Never again shall tides of men over such barriers break.

Stand fast, stand fast!" cried Rosecrans; and Thomas said,
    "I will!"
And, crash on crash, his batteries dash their broadsides down
    the hill.
Brave Longstreet's splendid rush tore through whatever
    barred its track,
Till the Rock of Chickamauga hurled the roaring columns back,
And gave the tide of victory a red tinge of defeat,
Adding a noble dignity to that hard word, retreat.

Two days they fought, and evermore those days shall stand
    apart,
Keynotes of epic chivalry within the nation's heart.
Come, come, and set the carven rocks to mark this glorious
    spot:
Here let the deeds of heroes live, their hatreds be forgot.
Build, build, but never monument of stone shall last as long
As one old soldier's ballad borne on breath of battle-song.

                                MAURICE THOMPSON

GRANT had been severely injured by a fall from a horse, but this de-
feat brought him into the field again, though he was still on crutches.
The Confederates had taken a strong position on Lookout Mountain,
overlooking Chattanooga, and on November 24, Grant attacked,
sending Hooker's brigade up the side of the mountain, which it cap-
tured at dawn the following day.   It was the last battle of the cam-
paign.

THE BATTLE OF LOOKOUT MOUNTAIN

[November 24, 1863]

"GIVE me but two brigades," said Hooker, frowning at forti-
    fied Lookout;
"And I'll engage to sweep that mountain clear of that mock-
    ing rebel rout."
At early morning came an order that set the General's face
    aglow:
"Now," said he to his staff, "draw out my soldiers. Grant
    says that I may go."

Hither and thither dashed each eager Colonel, to join his
    regiment,
While a low rumor of the daring purpose ran on from tent to
    tent.
For the long roll was sounding through the valley, and the
    keen trumpet's bray,
And the wild laughter of the swarthy veterans, who cried,
    "We fight today!"

The solid tramp of infantry, the rumble of the great jolting gun,
The sharp, clear order, and the fierce steeds neighing, "Why's
    not the fight begun?"
All these plain harbingers of sudden conflict broke on the
    startled ear;
And last arose a sound that made your blood leap, the ringing
    battle-cheer.

The lower works were carried at one onset; like a vast roaring
    sea
Of steel and fire, our soldiers from the trenches swept out
    the enemy;
And we could see the gray-coats swarming up from the moun-
    tain's leafy base,
To join their comrades in the higher fastness — for life or
    death the race!

Then our long line went winding up the mountain, in a huge
    serpent track,
And the slant sun upon it flashed and glimmered as on a
    dragon's back.
Higher and higher the column's head pushed onward, ere the
    rear moved a man;
And soon the skirmish lines their straggling volleys and
    single shots began.

Then the bald head of Lookout flamed and bellowed, and all
    its batteries woke,
And down the mountain poured the bomb-shells, puffing
    into our eyes their smoke;

And balls and grape-shot rained upon our column, that bore
    the angry shower
As if it were no more than that soft dropping which scarcely
    stirs the flower....

We saw our troops had gained a foothold almost beneath the
    topmost ledge,
And back and forth the rival lines went surging upon the
    dizzy edge.
We saw, sometimes, our men fall backwards slowly, and
    groaned in our despair;
Or cheered when now and then a stricken rebel plunged out
    in open air,
Down, down, a thousand empty fathoms dropping — his
    God alone knows where!

At eve thick haze upon the mountain gathered, with rising
    smoke stained black,
And not a glimpse of the contending armies shone through
    the swirling rack.
Night fell o'er all; but still they flashed their lightnings and
    rolled their thunders loud,
Though no man knew upon which side was going that battle
    in the cloud.

Night — what a night! — of anxious thought and wonder
    but still no tidings came
From the bare summit of the trembling mountain, still
    wrapped in mist and flame.
But towards the sleepless dawn, stillness, more dreadful than
    the fierce sound of war,
Settled o'er Nature, as if she stood breathless before the
    morning star.

As the sun rose, dense clouds of smoky vapor boiled from the
    valley's deeps,
Dragging their torn and ragged edges slowly up through the
    tree-clad steeps;

And rose and rose, till Lookout, like a vision, above us grandly
    stood,
And over his bleak crags and storm-blanched headlands
    burst the warm golden flood.

Thousands of eyes were fixed upon the mountain, and thou-
    sands held their breath,
And the vast army, in the valley watching, seemed touched
    with sudden death.
High o'er us soared great Lookout, robed in purple, a glory on
    his face,
A human meaning in his hard, calm features, beneath that
    heavenly grace.

Out on a crag walked something — what? an eagle, that
    treads yon giddy height?
Surely no man! but still he clambered forward into the full,
    rich light.
Then up he started with a sudden motion, and from the
    blazing crag
Flung to the morning breeze and sunny radiance the dear old
    starry flag!

Ah! then what followed?   Scarred and war-worn soldiers, like
    girls, flushed through their tan,
And down the thousand wrinkles of the battles a thousand
    tear-drops ran.
Men seized each other in returned embraces, and sobbed for
    very love;
A spirit, which made all that moment brothers, seemed
    falling from above.

And as we gazed, around the mountain's summit our glitter-
    ing files appeared,
Into the rebel works we saw them moving; and we — we
    cheered, we cheered!
And they above waved all their flags before us, and joined
    our frantic shout,
Standing, like demigods, in light and triumph upon their own
    Lookout!

GEORGE HENRY BOKER

CHAPTER IV

The Final Struggle

The fourth year of the war found the North in position to push the struggle to a conclusion. There were eight hundred thousand Union soldiers in the field, well trained and well equipped, while the Confederate forces had been reduced to scarcely half as many.

PUT IT THROUGH

[1864]

Come, Freemen of the land,
Come, meet the last demand —
Here's a piece of work in hand;
    Put it through!
Here's a log across the way,
We have stumbled on all day;
Here's a plowshare in the clay —
    Put it through!

Here's a country that's half free,
And it waits for you and me
To say what its fate shall be;
    Put it through!
While one traitor thought remains,
While one spot its banner stains,
One link of all its chains —
    Put it through!

Hear our brothers in the field,
Steel your swords as theirs are steeled,
Learn to wield the arms they wield —
    Put it through!
Lock the shop and lock the store,
And chalk this upon the door —
"We've enlisted for the war!"
    Put it through!

For the birthrights yet unsold,
For the history yet untold,
For the future yet unrolled,
    Put it through!
Lest our children point with shame
On the fathers' dastard fame,
Who gave up a nation's name,
    Put it through!

                    EDWARD EVERETT HALE

THE North planned a double attack.   Grant was made Lieutenant-General and prepared to advance on Richmond, while to General Sherman was assigned the task of capturing Atlanta, Georgia, and invading the heart of the Confederacy.   Sherman was before Atlanta by the middle of July, 1864, and on the 20th, repulsed a desperate sally made by the Confederates.

LOGAN AT PEACH TREE CREEK

A VETERAN'S STORY

[July 20, 1864]

You know that day at Peach Tree Creek,
When the Rebs with their circling, scorching wall
Of smoke-hid cannon and sweep of flame
Drove in our flanks, back! back! and all
Our toil seemed lost in the storm of shell —
That desperate day McPherson fell!

Our regiment stood in a little glade
Set round with half-grown red oak trees —
An awful place to stand, in full fair sight,
While the minie bullets hummed like bees,
And comrades dropped on either side —
That fearful day McPherson died!

The roar of the battle, steady, stern,
Rung in our ears.   Upon our eyes

The belching cannon smoke, the half-hid swing
Of deploying troops, the groans, the cries,
The hoarse commands, the sickening smell —
That blood-red day McPherson fell!

But we stood there! — when out from the trees,
Out of the smoke and dismay to the right
Burst a rider — His head was bare, his eye
Had a blaze like a lion fain for fight;
His long hair, black as the deepest night,
Streamed out on the wind.   And the might
Of his plunging horse was a tale to tell,
And his voice rang high like a bugle's swell;
"Men, the enemy hem us on every side;
We'll whip 'em yet!   Close up that breach —
Remember your flag — don't give an inch!
The right flank's gaining and soon will reach —
Forward boys, and give 'em hell!" —
Said Logan after McPherson fell.

We laughed and cheered and the red ground shook
As the general plunged along the line
Through the deadliest rain of screaming shells;
For the sound of his voice refreshed us all,
And we filled the gap like a roaring tide,
And saved the day McPherson died!

But that was twenty years ago,
And part of a horrible dream now past.
For Logan, the lion, the drums throb low
And the flag swings low on the mast;
He has followed his mighty chieftain through
The mist-hung stream, where gray and blue
One color stand,
And North to South extends the hand.
It's right that deeds of war and blood
Should be forgot, but, spite of all,
I think of Logan, now, as he rode

That day across the field; I hear the call
Of his trumpet voice — see the battle shine
In his stern, black eyes, and down the line
Of cheering men I see him ride,
As on the day McPherson died.

HAMLIN GARLAND

SHERMAN'S pressure upon Atlanta grew more and more merciless,
and finally, on September 2, 1864, the Confederates evacuated the
city.   Sherman immediately occupied it, and prepared for a ma-
neuver which was destined to be the most famous of the war.   He
determined to destroy Atlanta, and, marching across Georgia, to
capture one or more of the important seaport towns.   His first objec-
tive was Savannah, two hundred and fifty miles away, and on No-
vember 16, 1864, the "march to the sea" began.

SHERMAN'S MARCH TO THE SEA

[November 16–December 22, 1864]

OUR camp-fires shone bright on the mountain
    That frowned on the river below,
As we stood by our guns in the morning,
    And eagerly watched for the foe;
When a rider came out of the darkness
    That hung over mountain and tree,
And shouted: "Boys, up and be ready!
    For Sherman will march to the sea."

Then cheer upon cheer for bold Sherman
    Went up from each valley and glen,
And the bugles reëchoed the music
    That came from the lips of the men;
For we knew that the stars in our banner
    More bright in their splendor would be,
And that blessings from Northland would greet us
    When Sherman marched down to the sea.

Then forward, boys! forward to battle!
  We marched on our wearisome way,
We stormed the wild hills of Resaca,
  God bless those who fell on that day!
Then Kenesaw, dark in its glory,
  Frowned down on the flag of the free,
And the East and the West bore our standard
  And Sherman marched on to the sea.

Still onward we pressed till our banners
  Swept out from Atlanta's grim walls,
And the blood of the patriot dampened
  The soil where the traitor flag falls.
We paused not to weep for the fallen,
  Who slept by each river and tree,
Yet we twined them a wreath of the laurel
  As Sherman marched down to the sea.

Oh, proud was our army that morning,
  That stood where the pine darkly towers,
When Sherman said: "Boys, you are weary
  But today fair Savannah is ours!"
Then sang we the song of our chieftain,
  That echoed o'er river and lea,
And the stars in our banner shone brighter
  When Sherman marched down to the sea.
                                SAMUEL H. M. BYERS

THROUGH the heart of Georgia the army moved, leaving behind it a path of ruin forty miles in width. It was warfare of the most ruthless and destructive kind, and brought panic to the South.

THE SONG OF SHERMAN'S ARMY

A PILLAR of fire by night,
  A pillar of smoke by day,
Some hours of march — then a halt to fight,
  And so we hold our way;

Some hours of march — then a halt to fight,
  As on we hold our way.

Over mountain and plain and stream,
  To some bright Atlantic bay,
With our arms aflash in the morning beam,
  We hold our festal way;
With our arms aflash in the morning beam,
  We hold our checkless way!

There is terror wherever we come,
  There is terror and wild dismay
When they see the Old Flag and hear the drum
  Announce us on our way;
When they see the Old Flag and hear the drum
  Beating time to our onward way.

Never unlimber a gun
  For those villainous lines in gray;
Draw sabers! and at 'em upon the run!
  'Tis thus we clear our way;
Draw sabers, and soon you will see them run,
  As we hold our conquering way.

The loyal, who long have been dumb,
  Are loud in their cheers today;
And the old men out on their crutches come,
  To see us hold our way;
And the old men out on their crutches come,
  To bless us on our way.

Around us in rear and flanks,
  Their futile squadrons play,
With a sixty-mile front of steady ranks,
  We hold our checkless way;
With a sixty-mile front of serried ranks,
  Our banner clears the way.

Hear the spattering fire that starts
  From the woods and the copses gray,

There is just enough fighting to quicken our hearts,
  As we frolic along the way!
There is just enough fighting to warm our hearts,
  As we rattle along the way.

  Upon different roads, abreast,
    The heads of our columns gay,
  With fluttering flags, all forward pressed,
    Hold on their conquering way;
  With fluttering flags to victory pressed,
    We hold our glorious way.

  Ah, traitors! who bragged so bold
    In the sad war's early day,
  Did nothing predict you should ever behold
    The Old Flag come this way?
  Did nothing predict you should yet behold
    Our banner come back this way?

  By heaven! 'tis a gala march,
    'Tis a picnic or a play;
  Of all our long war 'tis the crowning arch,
    Hip, hip! for Sherman's way!
  Of all our long war this crowns the arch —
    For Sherman and Grant, hurrah!
                CHARLES GRAHAM HALPINE

GENERAL BEAUREGARD, gathering what forces he could, endeavored
to halt the invasion, but Sherman pressed on irresistibly. On De-
cember 22, 1864, he marched into Savannah, which the Confederates
had hastily abandoned, and on Christmas Day telegraphed Presi-
dent Lincoln, "I beg to present to you, as a Christmas gift, the city
of Savannah."

SHERMAN'S IN SAVANNAH

[December 22, 1864]

LIKE the tribes of Israel,
  Fed on quails and manna,

Sherman and his glorious band
Journeyed through the rebel land,
Fed from Heaven's all-bounteous hand,
   Marching on Savannah!

As the moving pillar shone,
Streamed the starry banner
All day long in rosy light,
Flaming splendor all the night,
Till it swooped in eagle flight
   Down on doomed Savannah!

Glory be to God on high!
Shout the loud Hosanna!
Treason's wilderness is past,
Canaan's shore is won at last,
Peal a nation's trumpet-blast —
   Sherman's in Savannah!

Soon shall Richmond's tough old hide
Find a tough old tanner!
Soon from every rebel wall
Shall the rag of treason fall,
Till our banner flaps o'er all
   As it crowns Savannah!

           OLIVER WENDELL HOLMES

SHERMAN paused at Savannah to fortify the place and reorganize his army; then, on January 15, 1865, he started northward into South Carolina. A month later, Columbia was occupied and then Sherman moved forward on Charleston, which the Confederate troops were compelled to abandon.

CAROLINA

[January, 1865]

THE despot treads thy sacred sands,
Thy pines give shelter to his bands,
Thy sons stand by with idle hands,
   Carolina!

He breathes at ease thy airs of balm,
He scorns the lances of thy palm;
Oh! who shall break thy craven calm,
  Carolina!
Thy ancient fame is growing dim,
A spot is on thy garment's rim;
Give to the winds thy battle-hymn,
  Carolina!

Call on thy children of the hill,
Wake swamp and river, coast and rill,
Rouse all thy strength and all thy skill,
  Carolina!
Cite wealth and science, trade and art,
Touch with thy fire the cautious mart,
And pour thee through the people's heart,
  Carolina!
Till even the coward spurns his fears,
And all thy fields, and fens, and meres
Shall bristle like thy palm with spears,
  Carolina!

I hear a murmur as of waves
That grope their way through sunless caves,
Like bodies struggling in their graves,
  Carolina!
And now it deepens; slow and grand
It swells, as, rolling to the land,
An ocean broke upon thy strand,
  Carolina!
Shout! Let it reach the startled Huns!
And roar with all thy festal guns!
It is the answer of thy sons,
  Carolina!

      HENRY TIMROD

THE cotton in the town was burned, many houses caught fire, and a magazine exploded, killing two hundred people. The city was virtually a ruin when the last of the Confederate troops — "poor old Dixie's bottom dollar" — withdrew. Sherman marched in and occupied it on February 18, 1865.

ROMANCE

[February 18, 1865]

"TALK of pluck!" pursued the Sailor,
    Set at euchre on his elbow,
    "I was on the wharf at Charleston,
    Just ashore from off the runner.

"It was gray and dirty weather,
    And I heard a drum go rolling,
    Rub-a-dubbing in the distance,
    Awful dour-like and defiant.

"In and out among the cotton,
    Mud, and chains, and stores, and anchors,
    Tramped a squad of battered scarecrows —
    Poor old Dixie's bottom dollar!

"Some had shoes, but all had rifles,
    Them that wasn't bald was beardless,
    And the drum was rolling 'Dixie,'
    And they stepped to it like men, sir!

"Rags and tatters, belts and bayonets,
    On they swung, the drum a-rolling,
    Mum and sour. It looked like fighting,
    And they meant it too, by thunder!"

WILLIAM ERNEST HENLEY

GRANT, meanwhile, had begun his advance before Richmond. On May 1, 1864, the Army of the Potomac, one hundred and thirty thousand strong, advanced into the Wilderness, south of the Rapidan, and there, on May 5, Lee hurled his forces upon them. A few days later, at Spottsylvania, Lee seized the colors of a Texas regiment and started to lead an assault in person. The men protested and promised to carry the position if Lee would retire. They advanced shouting, "Lee to the rear!" and kept their word.

LEE TO THE REAR

[Spottsylvania, May 12, 1864]

Dawn of a pleasant morning in May
Broke through the Wilderness cool and gray;
While perched in the tallest tree-tops, the birds
Were caroling Mendelssohn's "Songs without Words."

Far from the haunts of men remote,
The brook brawled on with a liquid note;
And Nature, all tranquil and lovely, wore
The smile of the spring, as in Eden of yore.

Little by little, as daylight increased,
And deepened the roseate flush in the East —
Little by little did morning reveal
Two long glittering lines of steel;

Where two hundred thousand bayonets gleam,
Tipped with the light of the earliest beam,
And the faces are sullen and grim to see
In the hostile armies of Grant and Lee.

All of a sudden, ere rose the sun,
Pealed on the silence the opening gun —
A little white puff of smoke there came,
And anon the valley was wreathed in flame.

Down on the left of the Rebel lines,
Where a breastwork stands in a copse of pines,
Before the Rebels their ranks can form,
The Yankees have carried the place by storm.

Stars and Stripes on the salient wave,
Where many a hero has found a grave,
And the gallant Confederates strive in vain
The ground they have drenched with their blood, to regain.

Yet louder the thunder of battle roared —
Yet a deadlier fire on the columns poured;
Slaughter infernal rode with Despair,
Furies twain, through the murky air.

Not far off, in the saddle there sat
A gray-bearded man in a black slouched hat;
Not much moved by the fire was he,
Calm and resolute Robert Lee.

Quick and watchful he kept his eye
On the bold Rebel brigades close by, —
Reserves that were standing (and dying) at ease,
While the tempest of wrath toppled over the trees.

For still with their loud, deep, bull-dog bay,
The Yankee batteries blazed away,
And with every murderous second that sped
A dozen brave fellows, alas! fell dead.

The grand old graybeard rode to the space
Where Death and his victims stood face to face,
And silently waved his old slouched hat —
A world of meaning there was in that!

"Fellow me! Steady!   We'll save the day!"
This was what he seemed to say;
And to the light of his glorious eye
The bold brigades thus made reply:

"We'll go forward, but you must go back" —
And they moved not an inch in the perilous track;
"Go to the rear, and we'll send them to hell!"
And the sound of the battle was lost in their yell.

Turning his bridle, Robert Lee
Rode to the rear.   Like waves of the sea,
Bursting the dikes in their overflow,
Madly his veterans dashed on the foe.

And backward in terror that foe was driven,
Their banners rent and their columns riven,
Wherever the tide of battle rolled
Over the Wilderness, wood and wold.

Sunset out of a crimson sky
Streamed o'er a field of ruddier dye,
And the brook ran on with a purple stain,
From the blood of ten thousand foemen slain.

Seasons have passed since that day and year —
Again o'er its pebbles the brook runs clear,
And the field in a richer green is drest
Where the dead of a terrible conflict rest.

Hushed is the roll of the Rebel drum,
The sabers are sheathed, and the cannon are dumb;
And Fate, with his pitiless hand, has furled
The flag that once challenged the gaze of the world;

But the fame of the Wilderness fight abides;
And down into history grandly rides,
Calm and unmoved as in battle he sat,
The gray-bearded man in the black slouched hat.

JOHN REUBEN THOMPSON

FOR two weeks a fearful struggle raged.   The Union losses were very heavy, but on May 11, Grant wired to the Secretary of War, "I propose to fight it out on this line, if it takes all summer."   Lee, to create a diversion, threw a large body of cavalry into the Shenandoah Valley, and Grant dispatched Sheridan to head them off.   On October 19, the Confederates attacked unexpectedly at Cedar Creek, while Sheridan himself was at Winchester, but he managed to arrive in time to rally his troops and save the day. The invaders retreated to Virginia.

SHERIDAN'S RIDE

[October 19, 1864]

UP FROM the South, at break of day,
Bringing to Winchester fresh dismay,
The affrighted air with a shudder bore,
Like a herald in haste to the chieftain's door,
The terrible grumble, and rumble, and roar,
Telling the battle was on once more,
    And Sheridan twenty miles away.

And wider still those billows of war
Thundered along the horizon's bar;
And louder yet into Winchester rolled
The roar of that red sea uncontrolled,
Making the blood of the listener cold,
As he thought of the stake in that fiery fray,
    With Sheridan twenty miles away.

But there is a road from Winchester town,
A good, broad highway leading down:
And there, through the flush of the morning light,
A steed as black as the steeds of night
Was seen to pass, as with eagle flight;
As if he knew the terrible need,
He stretched away with his utmost speed.
Hills rose and fell, but his heart was gay,
    With Sheridan fifteen miles away.

Still sprang from those swift hoofs, thundering south,
The dust like smoke from the cannon's mouth,
Or the trail of a comet, sweeping faster and faster,
Foreboding to traitors the doom of disaster.
The heart of the steed and the heart of the master

Were beating like prisoners assaulting their walls,
Impatient to be where the battle-field calls;
Every nerve of the charger was strained to full play,
    With Sheridan only ten miles away.

Under his spurning feet, the road
Like an arrowy Alpine river flowed,
And the landscape sped away behind
Like an ocean flying before the wind;
And the steed, like a bark fed with furnace ire,
Swept on, with his wild eye full of fire;
But, lo! he is nearing his heart's desire;
He is snuffing the smoke of the roaring fray,
    With Sheridan only five miles away.

The first that the general saw were the groups
Of stragglers, and then the retreating troops;
What was done? what to do? a glance told him both.
Then striking his spurs with a terrible oath,
He dashed down the line, 'mid a storm of huzzas,
And the wave of retreat checked its course there, becaus.
The sight of the master compelled it to pause.
With foam and with dust the black charger was gray;
By the flash of his eye, and the red nostril's play,
He seemed to the whole great army to say:
"I have brought you Sheridan all the way
    From Winchester down to save the day."

Hurrah! hurrah for Sheridan!
Hurrah! hurrah for horse and man!
And when their statues are placed on high
Under the dome of the Union sky,
The American soldier's Temple of Fame,
There, with the glorious general's name,
Be it said, in letters both bold and bright:
"Here is the steed that saved the day
    By carrying Sheridan into the fight,
      From Winchester — twenty miles away!"
           THOMAS BUCHANAN READ

GRANT steadily tightened his grip on Richmond, and Lee at last perceived that to hold the capital longer would be to sacrifice his army. He withdrew during the night of April 2, 1865, and the Union troops entered the city unopposed next day.

THE FALL OF RICHMOND

THE TIDINGS RECEIVED IN THE NORTHERN METROPOLIS
(APRIL, 1865)

WHAT mean these peals from every tower,
   And crowds like seas that sway?
The cannon reply; they speak the heart
   Of the People impassioned, and say —
A city in flags for a city in flames,
   Richmond goes Babylon's way —
     Sing and pray.

O weary years and woeful wars,
   And armies in the grave;
But hearts unquelled at last deter
The helmed dilated Lucifer —
   Honor to Grant the brave,
Whose three stars now like Orion's rise
   When wreck is on the wave —
     Bless his glaive.

Well that the faith we firmly kept,
   And never our aim forswore
For the Terrors that trooped from each recess
When fainting we fought in the Wilderness,
   And Hell made loud hurrah;
But God is in Heaven, and Grant in the Town,
   And Right through Might is Law —
     God's way adore.

HERMAN MELVILLE

Lee tried desperately to escape the force which Grant at once sent in pursuit, but soon found himself surrounded. To fight would have been folly. Instead he asked for a parley, and surrendered to Grant at two o'clock on the afternoon of Palm Sunday, April 9, 1865.

THE SURRENDER AT APPOMATTOX

[April 9, 1865]

As BILLOWS upon billows roll,
  On Victory victory breaks;
Ere yet seven days from Richmond's fall
  And crowning triumph wakes
The loud joy-gun, whose thunders run
  By sea-shore, streams, and lakes.
    The hope and great event agree
    In the sword that Grant received from Lee.

The warring eagles fold the wing,
  But not in Cæsar's sway;
Not Rome o'ercome by Roman arms we sing,
  As on Pharsalia's day,
But Treason thrown, though a giant grown,
  And Freedom's larger play.
    All human tribes glad token see
    In the close of the wars of Grant and Lee.
                              HERMAN MELVILLE

In DISBANDING his army, Lee issued a farewell address, copies of which are still treasured in many a Southern home. Even in the North, he was recognized as a great general and true gentleman. After the war, he became president of a college at Lexington, Virginia, and died there in 1870.

ROBERT E. LEE

A GALLANT foeman in the fight,
  A brother when the fight was o'er,
The hand that led the host with might
  The blessed torch of learning bore.

No shriek of shells nor roll of drums,
  No challenge fierce, resounding far,
When reconciling Wisdom comes
  To heal the cruel wounds of war.

Thought may the minds of men divide,
  Love makes the heart of nations one,
And so, thy soldier grave beside,
  We honor thee, Virginia's son.
                    JULIA WARD HOWE

THE South had believed to the very last that it would win the war,
but Lee's surrender abruptly ended all such dreams.   Nevertheless
peace was welcome, even though it brought ruin in its train.   At
least there would be no more bloodshed.

ACCEPTATION

WE DO accept thee, heavenly Peace!
  Albeit thou comest in a guise
  Unlooked for — undesired, our eyes
Welcome through tears the sweet release
From war, and woe, and want — surcease,
For which we bless thee, blessèd Peace!

We lift our foreheads from the dust;
  And as we meet thy brow's clear calm,
  There falls a freshening sense of balm
Upon our spirits.   Fear — distrust —
The hopeless present on us thrust —
We'll meet them as we can, and *must*.

War has not wholly wrecked us: still
  Strong hands, brave hearts, high souls are ours —
  Proud consciousness of quenchless powers —
A Past whose memory makes us thrill —
Futures uncharacterfrom, to fill
With heroisms — if we will.

Then courage, brothers! — Though each breast
  Feel oft the rankling thorn, despair,
  That failure plants so sharply there —
No pain, no pang shall be confest:
We'll work and watch the brightening west,
And leave to God and Heaven the rest.

            MARGARET JUNKIN PRESTON

THE war was won, but the joy of the North was soon dimmed by a great tragedy. On the evening of April 14, 1865, less than a week after Lee's surrender, President Lincoln attended a performance of a comedy called "Our American Cousin," at Ford's Theater at Washington. As the play was drawing to a close, the audience was startled by a pistol shot, and an instant later saw a man leap from the President's box to the stage. The man was an actor named John Wilkes Booth. He had shot the President through the head, and the latter died next day without regaining consciousness.

O CAPTAIN! MY CAPTAIN!

[April 14, 1865]

O CAPTAIN! my Captain! our fearful trip is done,
The ship has weathered every rack, the prize we sought is won,
The port is near, the bells I hear, the people all exulting,
While follow eyes the steady keel, the vessel grim and daring;
    But O heart! heart! heart!
      O the bleeding drops of red,
    Where on the deck my Captain lies,
      Fallen cold and dead.

O Captain! my Captain! rise up and hear the bells;
Rise up — for you the flag is flung — for you the bugle trills,
For you bouquets and ribboned wreaths — for you the shores
    a-crowding,
For you they call, the swaying mass, their eager faces turning;
    Here Captain! dear father!
      This arm beneath your head!
    It is some dream that on the deck
      You've fallen cold and dead.

My Captain does not answer, his lips are pale and still,
My father does not feel my arm, he has no pulse nor will,
The ship is anchored safe and sound, its voyage closed and
    done,
From fearful trip the victor ship comes in with object won;
    Exult O shores, and ring O bells!
    But I with mournful tread,
Walk the deck my Captain lies,
    Fallen cold and dead.

WALT WHITMAN

ON WEDNESDAY, April 19, a simple funeral service was held at the
White House, and for two days thereafter the body of the murdered
President lay in state in the rotunda of the Capitol.

THE DEAR PRESIDENT

ABRAHAM LINCOLN, the Dear President,
Lay in the Round Hall at the Capitol,
And there the people came to look their last....

Through the dark April day, a ceaseless throng,
They passed the coffin, saw the sleeping face,
And, blessing it, in silence moved away.

And one, a poet, spoke within his heart:
"It harmed him not to praise him when alive,
And me it cannot harm to praise him dead.

"Too oft the muse has blushed to speak of men —
No muse shall blush to speak her best of him,
And still to speak her best of him is dumb.

"O lofty wisdom's low simplicity!
O awful tenderness of noted power! —
No man e'er held so much of power so meek.

"He was the husband of the husbandless,
He was the father of the fatherless:
Within his heart he weighed the common woe.

"His call was like a father's to his sons!
As to a father's voice, they, hearing, came —
Eager to offer, strive, and bear, and die.

"The mild bond-breaker, servant of his Lord,
He took the sword, but in the name of Peace,
And touched the fetter, and the bound was free.

"Oh, place him not among the historic kings,
Strong, barbarous chiefs and bloody conquerors,
But with the Great and pure Republicans:

"Those who have been unselfish, wise, and good.
Bringers of Light and Pilots in the dark,
Bearers of Crosses, Servants of the World.

"And always, in his Land of birth and death,
Be his fond name — warmed in the people's hearts —
Abraham Lincoln, the Dear President."

JOHN JAMES PIATT

THEN the funeral train started for Lincoln's home at Springfield,
Illinois, stopping at Philadelphia, New York, and other towns along
the route, great crowds everywhere gathering to honor the dead
President.

ABRAHAM LINCOLN

OH, SLOW to smite and swift to spare,
Gentle and merciful and just!
Who, in the fear of God, didst bear
The sword of power, a nation's trust!

In sorrow by thy bier we stand,
    Amid the awe that hushes all,
And speak the anguish of a land
    That shook with horror at thy fall.

Thy task is done; the bond are free:
    We bear thee to an honored grave,
Whose proudest monument shall be
    The broken fetters of the slave.

Pure was thy life; its bloody close
    Hath placed thee with the sons of light,
Among the noble host of those
    Who perished in the cause of Right.

                    WILLIAM CULLEN BRYANT

THE burial took place at Springfield on May 4, and his body still rests there, his tomb sharing with that of George Washington at Mount Vernon the veneration of the American people.

HUSH'D BE THE CAMPS TODAY

[May 4, 1865]

HUSH'D be the camps today,
And soldiers, let us drape our war-worn weapons,
And each with musing soul retire to celebrate
Our dear commander's death.

No more for him life's stormy conflicts,
Nor victory, nor defeat — no more time's dark events,
Charging like ceaseless clouds across the sky.

But sing, poet, in our name,
Sing of the love we bore him — because you, dweller in
        camps, know it truly.

As they invault the coffin there,
Sing — as they close the doors of earth upon him — one verse,
For the heavy hearts of soldiers.

                    WALT WHITMAN

THE true quality of Lincoln's greatness has been more and more appreciated with the passing years. The captains, "with their guns and drums" have passed, but he grows greater and greater.

LINCOLN

[From the "Commemoration Ode"]

NATURE, they say, doth dote,
And cannot make a man
Save on some worn-out plan,
Repeating us by rote:
For him her Old-World molds aside she threw,
And, choosing sweet clay from the breast
Of the unexhausted West,
With stuff untainted shaped a hero new,
Wise, steadfast in the strength of God, and true....

His was no lonely mountain-peak of mind,
Thrusting to thin air o'er our cloudy bars,
A sea-mark now, now lost in vapors blind;
Broad prairie rather, genial, level-lined,
Fruitful and friendly for all human kind,
Yet also nigh to heaven and loved of loftiest stars....

Great captains, with their guns and drums,
Disturb our judgment for the hour,
But at last silence comes;
These are all gone, and, standing like a tower,
Our children shall behold his fame,
The kindly-earnest, brave, foreseeing man,
Sagacious, patient, dreading praise, not blame,
New birth of our new soil, the first American.

JAMES RUSSELL LOWELL

LINCOLN

I KNEW the man. I see him as he stands
With gifts of mercy in his outstretched hands;

A kindly light within his gentle eyes,
Sad as the toil in which his heart grew wise;
His lips half-parted with the constant smile
That kindled truth, but foiled the deepest guile;
His head bent forward, and his willing ear
Divinely patient right and wrong to hear:
Great in his goodness, humble in his state,
Firm in his purpose, yet not passionate,
He led his people with a tender hand,
And won by love a sway beyond command;
Summoned by lot to mitigate a time
Frenzied by rage, unscrupulous with crime,
He bore his mission with so meek a heart
That Heaven itself took up his people's part,
And when he faltered, helped him ere he fell,
Eking his efforts out by miracle.
No king this man, by grace of God's intent;
No, something better, freeman — President!
A nature, modeled on a higher plan,
Lord of himself, an inborn gentleman!

GEORGE HENRY BOKER

ON MAY 24, the united armies of Grant and Sherman, two hundred
thousand strong, were reviewed at Washington by President John-
son and his cabinet.

A SECOND REVIEW OF THE GRAND ARMY

[May 24, 1865]

I READ last night of the Grand Review
In Washington's chiefest avenue —
Two hundred thousand men in blue,
    I think they said was the number —
Till I seemed to hear their trampling feet,
The bugle blast and the drum's quick beat,
The clatter of hoofs in the stony street,
The cheers of people who came to greet,

And the thousand details that to repeat
   Would only my verse encumber —
Till I fell in a revery, sad and sweet,
   And then to a fitful slumber.

When, lo! in a vision I seemed to stand
In the lonely Capitol. On each hand
Far stretched the portico, dim and grand
Its columns ranged like a martial band
Of sheeted specters, whom some command
   Had called to a last reviewing.
And the streets of the city were white and bare;
No footfall echoed across the square;
But out of the misty midnight air
I heard in the distance a trumpet blare,
And the wandering night-winds seemed to bear
   The sound of a far tattooing.

Then I held my breath with fear and dread;
For into the square, with a brazen tread,
There rode a figure whose stately head
   O'erlooked the review that morning,
That never bowed from its firm-set seat
When the living column passed its feet,
Yet now rode steadily up the street
   To the phantom bugle's warning:

Till it reached the Capitol square, and wheeled,
And there in the moonlight stood revealed
A well-known form that in State and field
   Had led our patriot sires:
Whose face was turned to the sleeping camp,
Afar through the river's fog and damp,
That showed no flicker, nor waning lamp,
   Nor wasted bivouac fires.

And I saw a phantom army come,
With never a sound of fife or drum,

But keeping time to a throbbing hum
  Of wailing and lamentation:
The martyred heroes of Malvern Hill,
Of Gettysburg and Chancellorsville,
The men whose wasted figures fill
  The patriot graves of the nation.

And there came the nameless dead — the men
Who perished in fever-swamp and fen,
The slowly-starved of the prison-pen;
  And, marching beside the others,
Came the dusky martyrs of Pillow's fight,
With limbs enfranchised and bearing bright:
I thought — perhaps 'twas the pale moonlight —
  They looked as white as their brothers!

And so all night marched the Nation's dead,
With never a banner above them spread,
Nor a badge, nor a motto brandishèd;
No mark — save the bare uncovered head
  Of the silent bronze Reviewer;
With never an arch save the vaulted sky;
With never a flower save those that lie
On the distant graves — for love could buy
  No gift that was purer or truer.

So all night long swept the strange array;
So all night long, till the morning gray,
I watch'd for one who had passed away,
  With a reverent awe and wonder, —
Till a blue cap waved in the lengthening line,
And I knew that one who was kin of mine
Had come; and I spake — and lo! that sign
  Awakened me from my slumber.

                                   BRET HARTE

THE war left many wounds, but time is a great healer, and even as early as 1867, the women of Columbus, Mississippi, decorated alike the graves of the Confederate and Union soldiers buried there.

THE BLUE AND THE GRAY

By the flow of the inland river,
  Whence the fleets of iron have fled,
Where the blades of the grave-grass quiver,
  Asleep are the ranks of the dead.
    Under the sod and the dew,
      Waiting the Judgment Day:
    Under the one, the Blue;
      Under the other, the Gray.

These in the robings of glory,
  Those in the gloom of defeat,
All with the battle-blood gory,
  In the dusk of eternity meet:
    Under the sod and the dew,
      Waiting the Judgment Day:
    Under the laurel, the Blue;
      Under the willow, the Gray.

From the silence of sorrowful hours
  The desolate mourners go,
Lovingly laden with flowers,
  Alike for the friend and the foe:
    Under the sod and the dew,
      Waiting the Judgment Day:
    Under the roses, the Blue;
      Under the lilies, the Gray.

So, with an equal splendor,
  The morning sun-rays fall,
With a touch impartially tender,
  On the blossoms blooming for all:

Under the sod and the dew,
  Waiting the Judgment Day:
Broidered with gold, the Blue;
  Mellowed with gold, the Gray....

No more shall the war-cry sever,
  Or the winding rivers be red;
They banish our anger forever
  When they laurel the graves of our dead!
Under the sod and the dew,
  Waiting the Judgment Day:
Love and tears for the Blue;
  Tears and love for the Gray.

FRANCIS MILES FINCH

ON MAY 5, 1868, General John A. Logan, Commander-in-Chief of
the Grand Army of the Republic, issued an order appointing May 30
for services throughout the North in decorating the graves of the
fallen soldiers, and that date has been observed annually ever since.
In the Southern States, Memorial Day is observed at different times,
but in all the states, North and South, one day is set apart every year
as a day of remembrance.

ODE

[Sung on the occasion of decorating the graves of the Confederate dead,
at Magnolia Cemetery, Charleston, South Carolina, 1867]

SLEEP sweetly in your humble graves,
  Sleep, martyrs of a fallen cause;
Though yet no marble column craves
  The pilgrim here to pause.

In seeds of laurel in the earth
  The blossom of your fame is blown,
And somewhere, waiting for its birth,
  The shaft is in the stone!

Meanwhile, behalf the tardy years
  Which keep in trust your storied tombs,
Behold! your sisters bring their tears,
  And these memorial blooms.

Small tributes! but your shades will smile
  More proudly on these wreaths today,
Than when some cannon-molded pile
  Shall overlook this bay.

Stoop, angels, hither from the skies!
  There is no holier spot of ground
Than where defeated valor lies,
  By mourning beauty crowned!
                HENRY TIMROD

DECORATION DAY

SLEEP, comrades, sleep and rest
  On this Field of the Grounded Arms,
Where foes no more molest,
  Nor sentry's shot alarms!

Ye have slept on the ground before,
  And started to your feet
At the cannon's sudden roar,
  Or the drum's redoubling beat.

But in this camp of Death
  No sound your slumber breaks;
Here is no fevered breath,
  No wound that bleeds and aches.

All is repose and peace;
  Untrampled lies the sod;
The shouts of battle cease,
  It is the truce of God!

Rest, comrades, rest and sleep!
　　The thoughts of men shall be
As sentinels to keep
　　Your rest from danger free.

Your silent tents of green
　　We deck with fragrant flowers;
Yours has the suffering been,
　　The memory shall be ours.
　　　　　HENRY WADSWORTH LONGFELLOW

PART V
AMERICA GOES CRUSADING

THE EAGLE'S SONG

THE lioness whelped, and the sturdy cub
Was seized by an eagle and carried up,
And homed for a while in an eagle's nest,
And slept for a while on an eagle's breast;
And the eagle taught it the eagle's song:
"To be stanch, and valiant, and free, and strong!"

The lion whelp sprang from the eyrie nest,
From the lofty crag where the queen birds rest;
He fought the King on the spreading plain,
And drove him back o'er the foaming main.
He held the land as a thrifty chief,
And reared his cattle, and reaped his sheaf,
Nor sought the help of a foreign hand,
Yet welcomed all to his own free land!

Two were the sons that the country bore
To the Northern lakes and the Southern shore;
And Chivalry dwelt with the Southern son,
And Industry lived with the Northern one.
Tears for the time when they broke and fought!
Tears was the price of the union wrought!
And the land was red in a sea of blood,
Where brother for brother had swelled the flood!

And now that the two are one again,
Behold on their shield the word "Refrain!"
And the lion cubs twain sing the eagle's song:
"To be stanch, and valiant, and free, and strong!"
For the eagle's beak, and the lion's paw,
And the lion's fangs, and the eagle's claw,
And the eagle's swoop, and the lion's might,
And the lion's leap, and the eagle's sight,
Shall guard the flag with the word "Refrain!"
Now that the two are one again!

RICHARD MANSFIELD

CHAPTER I

The Making of a Giant

NEVER before in history has a nation grown so rapidly as did the United States in the years following the Civil War. The adventurous and ambitious of the whole world sought her shores, eager for the liberty, the security, the opportunity which she offered to all alike. Other nations began to look askance at this young giant and to wonder how such strength would be employed.

O MOTHER OF A MIGHTY RACE

O MOTHER of a mighty race,
Yet lovely in thy youthful grace!
The elder dames, thy haughty peers,
Admire and hate thy blooming years.
    With words of shame
And taunts of scorn they join thy name.

For on thy cheeks the glow is spread
That tints thy morning hills with red;
Thy step — the wild deer's rustling feet,
Within thy woods, are not more fleet;
    Thy hopeful eye
Is bright as thine own sunny sky.

Ay, let them rail — those haughty ones,
While safe thou dwellest with thy sons.
They do not know how loved thou art,
How many a fond and fearless heart
    Would rise to throw
Its life between thee and the foe.

They know not, in their hate and pride,
What virtues with thy children bide;
How true, how good, thy graceful maids

Make bright, like flowers, the valley-shades;
    What generous men
Spring, like thine oaks, by hill and glen; —

What cordial welcomes greet the guest
By thy lone rivers of the West;
How faith is kept, and truth revered,
And man is loved, and God is feared,
    In woodland homes,
And where the ocean border foams.

There's freedom at thy gates, and rest
For Earth's downtrodden and opprest,
A shelter for the hunted head,
For the starved laborer toil and bread.
    Power, at thy bounds,
Stops and calls back his baffled hounds.

O fair young mother! on thy brow
Shall sit a nobler grace than now.
Deep in the brightness of thy skies
The thronging years in glory rise,
    And, as they fleet,
Drop strength and riches at thy feet.
WILLIAM CULLEN BRYANT

WASHINGTON and Jefferson had warned their countrymen against alliances with other nations; President Monroe had warned the governments of Europe to attempt no conquests in the western hemisphere. But growing commerce and improved communications were bringing the nations closer together. A great step forward was the completion of the first Atlantic cable, from Ireland to Newfoundland, an enterprise undertaken and carried through by Cyrus West Field.

HOW CYRUS LAID THE CABLE

[July 29, 1866]

COME, listen all unto my song;
    It is no silly fable;

'Tis all about the mighty cord
 They call the Atlantic Cable.

Bold Cyrus Field he said, says he,
 "I have a pretty notion
That I can run a telegraph
 Across the Atlantic Ocean."

Then all the people laughed, and said
 They'd like to see him do it;
He might get half-seas over, but
 He never could go through it.

To carry out his foolish plan
 He never would be able;
He might as well go hang himself
 With his Atlantic Cable.

But Cyrus was a valiant man,
 A fellow of decision;
And heeded not their mocking words,
 Their laughter and derision.

Twice did his bravest efforts fail,
 And yet his mind was stable;
He wa'n't the man to break his heart
 Because he broke his cable.

"Once more, my gallant boys!" he cried;
 "*Three times* — you know the fable
(I'll make it *thirty*," muttered he,
 "But I will lay the cable!").

Once more they tried, — hurrah! hurrah!
 What means this great commotion?
The Lord be praised! the cable's laid
 Across the Atlantic Ocean!

Loud ring the bells, — for, flashing through
    Six hundred leagues of water,
Old Mother England's benison
    Salutes her eldest daughter!

O'er all the land the tidings speed,
    And soon, in every nation,
They'll hear about the cable with
    Profoundest admiration!

Now, long live President and Queen;
    And long live gallant Cyrus;
And may his courage, faith, and zeal
    With emulation fire us;

And may we honor evermore
    The manly, bold, and stable;
And tell our sons, to make them brave,
    How Cyrus laid the cable!

                JOHN GODFREY SAXE

In 1867 a vast new territory was added to the Union when Alaska was purchased from Russia for the sum of $7,200,000. It was regarded as a land of snow and ice, and many doubted whether it would ever be of any value to the United States, but thirty years later gold was discovered there, and the rush to the Klondike duplicated that to California in '49.

AN ARCTIC VISION

[June 20, 1867]

WHERE the short-legged Esquimaux
Waddle in the ice and snow,
And the playful Polar bear
Nips the hunter unaware;...
Polar dock, where Nature slips
From the ways her icy ships;
Land of fox and deer and sable,

Shore end of our western cable —
Let the news that flying goes
Thrill through all your Arctic floes,
And reverberate the boast
From the cliffs off Beechy's coast,
Till the tidings, circling round
Every bay of Norton Sound,
Throw the vocal tide-wave back
To the isles of Kodiac.
Let the stately Polar bears
Waltz around the pole in pairs,
And the walrus, in his glee,
Bare his tusk of ivory;
While the bold sea-unicorn
Calmly takes an extra horn;...
Slide, ye solemn glaciers, slide,
One inch farther to the tide...
All ye icebergs, make salaam —
You belong to Uncle Sam!

On the spot where Eugene Sue
Led his wretched Wandering Jew,
Stands a form whose features strike
Russ and Esquimaux alike,
He it is whom Skalds of old
In their Runic rhymes foretold;
Lean of flank and lank of jaw,
See the real Northern Thor!...
Leaning on his icy hammer
Stands the hero of this drama,
And above the wild duck's clamor,
In his own peculiar grammar,
With its linguistic disguises,
Lo, the Arctic prologue rises:

"Wal, I reckon 'taint so bad,
Seein' ez 'twas all they had;
True, the Springs are rather late,

And early Falls predominate;
But the ice crop's pretty sure,
And the air is kind o' pure;
'Tain't so very mean a trade,
When the land is all surveyed.
There's a right smart chance for fur-chase
All along this recent purchase,
And, unless the stories fail,
Every fish from cod to whale;
Rocks, too; mebbe quartz; let's see —
'Twould be strange if there should be —
Seems I've heerd such stories told;
Eh! — why, bless us — yes, it's gold!"

While the blows are falling thick
From his California pick,
You may recognize the Thor
Of the vision that I saw —
Freed from legendary glamour,
See the real magician's hammer.

                              BRET HARTE

ON OCTOBER 8 and 9, 1871, a terrible disaster overtook Chicago,
which had grown to be the greatest city in the West, when a fire
broke out which spread beyond control and almost entirely destroyed
it.   Two hundred people were killed and a hundred thousand ren-
dered homeless.   But the whole country rallied to her aid, and the
city quickly rose from the ashes, greater than ever.

CHICAGO

[October 8-10, 1871]

MEN said at vespers: "All is well!"
In one wild night the city fell;
Fell shrines of prayer and marts of gain
Before the fiery hurricane.

On threescore spires had sunset shone,
Where ghastly sunrise looked on none.

Men clasped each other's hands, and said:
"The City of the West is dead!"

Brave hearts who fought, in slow retreat,
The fiends of fire from street to street,
Turned, powerless, to the blinding glare,
The dumb defiance of despair.

A sudden impulse thrilled each wire
That signaled round that sea of fire;
Swift words of cheer, warm heart-throbs came;
In tears of pity died the flame!

From East, from West, from South and North,
The messages of hope shot forth,
And, underneath the severing wave,
The world, full-handed, reached to save.

Fair seemed the old; but fairer still
The new, the dreary void shall fill
With dearer homes than those o'erthrown,
For love shall lay each corner-stone.

Rise, stricken city! from thee throw
The ashen sackcloth of thy woe;
And build, as to Amphion's strain,
To songs of cheer thy walls again!

How shriveled in thy hot distress
The primal sin of selfishness!
How instant rose, to take thy part,
The angel in the human heart!

Ah! not in vain the flames that tossed
Above thy dreadful holocaust;
The Christ again has preached through thee
The Gospel of Humanity!

Then lift once more thy towers on high,
And fret with spires the western sky,
To tell that God is yet with us,
And love is still miraculous!

JOHN GREENLEAF WHITTIER

A YEAR later, on November 9, 1872, Boston suffered a similar dis-
aster, when sixty-five acres in the very heart of the city were laid
waste, with a loss of $80,000,000. But the nation rushed to Boston's
aid, just as it had to Chicago's, and the city was quickly rebuilt.

AFTER THE FIRE

[November 9, 1872]

WHILE far along the eastern sky
I saw the flags of Havoc fly,
As if his forces would assault
The sovereign of the starry vault
And hurl Him back the burning rain
That seared the cities of the plain,
I read as on a crimson page
The words of Israel's scepterd sage: —

For riches make them wings, and they
Do as an eagle fly away.

O vision of that sleepless night,
What hue shall paint the mocking light
That burned and stained the orient skies
Where peaceful morning loves to rise,
As if the sun had lost his way
And dawned to make a second day —
Above how red with fiery glow,
How dark to those it woke below!

On roof and wall, on dome and spire,
Flashed the false jewels of the fire;
Girt with her belt of glittering panes,
And crowned with starry-gleaming vanes,

Our northern queen in glory shone
With new-born splendors not her own,
And stood, transfigured in our eyes,
A victim decked for sacrifice!...

Again I read the words that came
Writ in the rubric of the flame:
Howe'er we trust to mortal things,
Each hath its pair of folded wings;
Though long their terrors rest unspread
Their fatal plumes are never shed;
At last, at last, they stretch in flight,
And blot the day and blast the night!

Hope, only Hope, of all that clings
Around us, never spreads her wings;
Love, though he break his earthly chain,
Still whispers he will come again;
But Faith that soars to seek the sky
Shall teach our half-fledged souls to fly,
And find, beyond the smoke and flame,
The cloudless azure whence they came!

OLIVER WENDELL HOLMES

THE Indians had been concentrated on reservations in the West, but in the autumn of 1874, gold was discovered on the Sioux reservation in the Black Hills, and the Government decided to transfer the Sioux to another reservation. Under the advice of their chief, Sitting Bull, they refused to stir. A detachment of the Seventh Cavalry, under Lieutenant-Colonel George A. Custer, was sent against them, and came suddenly upon their encampment on June 25, 1876. A terrific fight followed, in which Custer and all his men were slain.

CUSTER'S LAST CHARGE

[June 25, 1876]

DEAD! Is it possible? He, the bold rider,
Custer, our hero, the first in the fight,

Charming the bullets of yore to fly wider,
　　Far from our battle-king's ringlets of light!
Dead, our young chieftain, and dead, all forsaken!
　　No one to tell us the way of his fall!
Slain in the desert, and never to waken,
　　Never, not even to victory's call!

Proud for his fame that last day that he met them!
　　All the night long he had been on their track,
Scorning their traps and the men that had set them,
　　Wild for a charge that should never give back.
There on the hilltop he halted and saw them —
　　Lodges all loosened and ready to fly:
Hurrying scouts with the tidings to awe them,
　　Told of his coming before he was nigh.

All the wide valley was full of their forces,
　　Gathered to cover the lodges' retreat! —
Warriors running in haste to their horses,
　　Thousands of enemies close to his feet!
Down in the valleys the ages had hollowed,
　　There lay the Sitting Bull's camp for a prey!
Numbers!　What recked he?　What recked those who fol-
　　lowed —
　　Men who had fought ten to one ere that day?

Out swept the squadrons, the fated three hundred,
　　Into the battle-line steady and full;
Then down the hillside exultingly thundered,
　　Into the hordes of the old Sitting Bull!
Wild Ogalallah, Arapahoe, Cheyenne,
　　Wild Horse's braves, and the rest of their crew,
Shrank from that charge like a herd from a lion —
　　Then closed around, the grim horde of wild Sioux!

Right to their center he charged, and then facing —
　　Hark to those yells! and around them, O see!
Over the hilltops the Indians come racing.

Coming as fast as the waves of the sea!
Red was the circle of fire around them;
  No hope of victory, no ray of light,
Shot through that terrible black cloud without them,
  Brooding in death over Custer's last fight.

Then did he blench?   Did he die like a craven,
  Begging those torturing fiends for his life?
Was there a soldier who carried the Seven
  Flinched like a coward or fled from the strife?
No, by the blood of our Custer, no quailing!
  There in the midst of the Indians they close,
Hemmed in by thousands, but ever assailing,
  Fighting like tigers, all 'bayed amid foes!

Thicker and thicker the bullets came singing;
  Down go the horses and riders and all;
Swiftly the warriors around them were ringing,
  Circling like buzzards awaiting their fall.
See the wild steeds of the mountain and prairie,
  Savage eyes gleaming from forests of mane;
Quivering lances with pennons so airy,
  War-painted warriors charging amain.

Backward, again and again, they were driven,
  Shrinking to close with the lost little band;
Never a cap that had worn the bright Seven
  Bowed till its wearer was dead on the strand.
Closer and closer the death circle growing,
  Ever the leader's voice, clarion clear,
Rang out his words of encouragement glowing,
  "We can but die once, boys — we'll sell our lives dear!"

Dearly they sold them like Berserkers raging,
  Facing the death that encircled them round;
Death's bitter pangs by their vengeance assuaging,
  Marking their tracks by their dead on the ground.
Comrades, our children shall yet tell their story,—

Custer's last charge on the old Sitting Bull;
And ages shall swear that the cup of his glory
Needed but that death to render it full.

FREDERICK WHITTAKER

THE Indians, of course, were forced to yield eventually to the superior power of the American Government. There was another outbreak a few years later, and that was the last. The few survivors turned to peaceful occupations, or were content to live in idleness upon the Government's bounty.

INDIAN NAMES

YE SAY they all have passed away,
    That noble race and brave,
That their light canoes have vanished
    From off the crested wave;
That, 'mid the forests where they roamed,
    There rings no hunter's shout;
But their name is on your waters,
    Ye may not wash it out.

'Tis where Ontario's billow
    Like ocean's surge is curled;
Where strong Niagara's thunders wake
    The echo of the world;
Where red Missouri bringeth
    Rich tribute from the West,
And Rappahannock sweetly sleeps
    On green Virginia's breast.

Ye say their conelike cabins,
    That clustered o'er the vale,
Have fled away like withered leaves
    Before the autumn's gale:
But their memory liveth on your hills,
    Their baptism on your shore;
Your everlasting rivers speak
    Their dialect of yore.

Old Massachusetts wears it
  Within her lordly crown,
And broad Ohio bears it
  'Mid all her young renown;
Connecticut hath wreathed it
  Where her quiet foliage waves,
And bold Kentucky breathes it hoarse,
  Through all her ancient caves.

Wachusett hides its lingering voice
  Within his rocky heart,
And Alleghany graves its tone
  Throughout his lofty chart;
Monadnock on his forehead hoar
  Doth seal the sacred trust:
Your mountains build their monument,
  Though ye destroy their dust.

LYDIA HUNTLEY SIGOURNEY

IN 1876, a great industrial exposition was held at Philadelphia to mark the hundredth anniversary of the signing of the Declaration of Independence.   Richard Wagner composed a march for the opening exercises on May 10, and Whittier's "Centennial Hymn" was sung by a chorus of a thousand voices.

CENTENNIAL HYMN

OUR fathers' God! from out whose hand
The centuries fall like grains of sand,
We meet today, united, free,
And loyal to our land and Thee,
To thank Thee for the era done,
And trust Thee for the opening one.

Here, where of old, by Thy design,
The fathers spake that word of Thine
Whose echo is the glad refrain
Of rended bolt and falling chain,

To grace our festal time, from all
The zones of earth our guests we call.

Be with us while the New World greets
The Old World thronging all its streets,
Unveiling all the triumphs won
By art or toil beneath the sun;
And unto common good ordain
This rivalship of hand and brain.

Thou, who hast here in concord furled
The war flags of a gathered world,
Beneath our Western skies fulfill
The Orient's mission of good-will,
And, freighted with love's Golden Fleece,
Send back its Argonauts of peace.

For art and labor met in truce,
For beauty made the bride of use,
We thank Thee; but, withal, we crave
The austere virtues strong to save,
The honor proof to place or gold,
The manhood never bought nor sold!

Oh make Thou us, through centuries long,
In peace secure, in justice strong;
Around our gift of freedom draw
The safeguards of Thy righteous law:
And, cast in some diviner mold,
Let the new cycle shame the old!

JOHN GREENLEAF WHITTIER

On May 24, 1883, the great suspension bridge spanning the East River and connecting Brooklyn with New York City was opened to the public. It had been thirteen years in construction, and remains to this day a masterpiece of strength and beauty.

THE BROOKLYN BRIDGE

[May 24, 1883]

A GRANITE cliff on either shore:
    A highway poised in air;
Above, the wheels of traffic roar;
    Below, the fleets sail fair; —
And in and out, forevermore,
The surging tides of ocean pour,
And past the towers the white gulls soar,
    And winds the sea-clouds bear.

O peerless this majestic street,
    This road that leaps the brine!
Upon its heights twin cities meet,
    And throng its grand incline —
To east, to west, with swiftest feet,
Though ice may crash and billows beat,
Though blinding fogs the wave may greet
    Or golden summer shine.

Sail up the Bay with morning's beam,
    Or rocky Hellgate by —
Its columns rise, its cables gleam,
    Great tents athwart the sky!
And lone it looms, august, supreme,
When, with the splendor of a dream,
Its blazing cressets gild the stream
    Till evening shadows fly.

By Nile stand proud the pyramids,
    But they were for the dead;
The awful gloom that joy forbids,
    The mourners' silent tread,

The crypt, the coffin's stony lids —
Sad as a soul the maze that thrids
Of dark Amenti, ere it rids
    Its way of judgment dread.

This glorious arch, these climbing towers
    Are all for life and cheer!
Part of the New World's nobler dowers;
    Hint of millennial year
That comes apace, though evil lowers —
When loftier aims and larger powers
Will mold and deck this earth of ours,
    And heaven at length bring near!

Unmoved its cliffs shall crown the shore;
    Its arch the chasm dare;
Its network hang the blue before,
    As gossamer in air;
While in and out, forevermore,
The surging tides of ocean pour,
And past its towers the white gulls soar
    And winds the sea-clouds bear!
                    EDNA DEAN PROCTOR

DURING all these years, America had been evolving ideals of liberty
and philanthropy. She had welcomed to her shores the oppressed of
other nations. She had won freedom within her own boundaries at
terrible cost. She began to feel — what no nation had ever felt before
— a responsibility for freedom everywhere. And so the time came
when she was to embark upon her first crusade.

STANZAS ON FREEDOM

MEN! whose boast it is that ye
Come of fathers brave and free,
If there breathe on earth a slave,
Are ye truly free and brave?

If ye do not feel the chain
When it works a brother's pain,
Are ye not base slaves indeed,
Slaves unworthy to be freed?

Women! who shall one day bear
Sons to breathe New England air,
If ye hear, without a blush,
Deeds to make the roused blood rush
Like red lava through your veins,
For your sisters now in chains —
Answer! are ye fit to be
Mothers of the brave and free?

Is true Freedom but to break
Fetters for our own dear sake,
And, with leathern hearts, forget
That we owe mankind a debt?
No! true freedom is to share
All the chains our brothers wear,
And, with heart and hand, to be
Earnest to make others free!

They are slaves who fear to speak
For the fallen and the weak;
They are slaves who will not choose
Hatred, scoffing and abuse,
Rather than in silence shrink
From the truth they needs must think;
They are slaves who dare not be
In the right with two or three.

JAMES RUSSELL LOWELL

CHAPTER II

THE CRUSADE AGAINST SPAIN

FOR three centuries and a half Spain had held possession of the island of Cuba, and the people of the United States had watched with sympathy the struggles of the Cubans to throw off the Spanish yoke. In 1895, revolution on the island flared out more fiercely than ever before, and under such leaders as Gomez, Maceo, and Garcia, the Cubans gained control of many of the provinces.

CUBA TO COLUMBIA

[April, 1896]

A VOICE went over the waters —
    A stormy edge of the sea —
Fairest of Freedom's daughters,
    Have you no help for me?
Do you not hear the rusty chain
    Clanking about my feet?
Have you not seen my children slain,
    Whether in cell or street?
Oh, if you were sad as I,
    And I as you were strong,
You would not have to call or cry —
    You would not suffer long!

"Patience?" — have I not learned it,
    Under the crushing years?
Freedom — have I not earned it,
    Toiling with blood and tears?
"Not of you?" — my banners wave
    Not on Egyptian shore,
Or by Armenia's mammoth grave —
    But at your very door!
Oh, if you were needy as I,
    And I as you were strong,

You should not suffer, bleed, and die,
   Under the hoofs of wrong!

Is it that you have never
   Felt the oppressor's hand,
Fighting, with fond endeavor,
   To cling to your own sweet land?
Were you not half dismayed,
   There in the century's night,
Till to your view a sister's aid
   Came, like a flash of light?
Oh, what gift could ever be grand
   Enough to pay the debt,
If out of the starry Western land,
   Should come my Lafayette!

                WILL CARLETON

SPAIN made the mistake of placing General Valeriano Weyler in command in Cuba, with orders to put down the rebellion at any cost. Weyler had an evil reputation for cruelty, and he proceeded to make it more evil by various measures whose brutality was exploited by a Cuban propaganda service, assisted by various newspapers, until American indignation was at white heat.

CUBA LIBRE

COMES a cry from Cuban water —
   From the warm, dusk Antilles —
From the lost Atlanta's daughter,
   Drowned in blood as drowned in seas;
Comes a cry of purpled anguish —
   See her struggles, hear her cries!
Shall she live, or shall she languish?
   Shall she sink, or shall she rise?

She shall rise, by all that's holy!
   She shall live and she shall last;
Rise as we, when crushed and lowly,
   From the blackness of the past.

Bid her strike!   Lo, it is written
  Blood for blood and life for life.
Bid her smite, as she is smitten;
  Behold, our stars were born of strife!

Once we flashed her lights of freedom,
  Lights that dazzled her dark eyes
Till she could but yearning heed them,
  Reach her hands and try to rise.
Then they stabbed her, choked her, drowned her
  Till we scarce could hear a note.
Ah! these rusting chains that bound her!
  Oh! these robbers at her throat!

And the kind who forged these fetters?
  Ask five hundred years for news.
Stake and thumbscrew for their betters!
  Inquisitions!   Banished Jews!
Chains and slavery!   What reminder
  Of one red man in that land?
Why, these very chains that bind her
  Bound Columbus, foot and hand!

Shall she rise as rose Columbus,
  From his chains, from shame and wrong —
Rise as Morning, matchless, wondrous —
  Rise as some rich morning song —
Rise a ringing song and story,
  Valor, Love personified?
Stars and stripes, espouse her glory,
  Love and Liberty allied.

Joaquin Miller

The situation of Americans in Havana began to cause uneasiness, and the battleship Maine was sent to give them any protection which might be necessary.   The Maine reached Havana on the morning of January 24, 1898, entered the harbor and anchored at a spot designated by the Spanish authorities.   On the morning of February 16, the news flashed over the country that she had been blown up at her anchorage, and that 266 of her men had been killed.

THE MEN OF THE MAINE

[February 15, 1898]

Not in the dire, ensanguined front of war,
Conquered or conqueror,
'Mid the dread battle-peal, did they go down
To the still under-seas, with fair Renown
To weave for them the hero-martyr's crown.
They struck no blow
'Gainst an embattled foe;
With valiant-hearted Saxon hardihood
They stood not as the Essex sailors stood,
So sore bestead in that far Chilian bay;
Yet no less faithful they,
These men who, in a passing of the breath,
Were hurtled upon death.

No warning the salt-scented sea-wind bore,
No presage whispered from the Cuban shore
Of the appalling fate
That in the tropic night-time lay in wait
To bear them whence they shall return no more.
Some lapsed from dreams of home and love's clear star
Into a realm where dreams eternal are;
And some into a world of wave and flame
Wherethrough they came
To living agony that no words can name.
Tears for them all,
And the low-tunèd dirge funereal!

Their place is now
With those who wear, green-set about the brow,
The deathless immortelles, —
The heroes torn and scarred

Whose blood made red the barren ocean dells,
Fighting with him the gallant Ranger bore,
Daring to do what none had dared before,
To wave the New World banner, freedom-starred,
At England's very door!
Yea, with such noble ones their names shall stand
As those who heard the dying Lawrence speak
His burning words upon the Chesapeake,
And grappled in the hopeless hand-to-hand;
With those who fell on Erie and Champlain
Beneath the pouring, pitiless battle-rain:
With such as these, our lost men of the Maine!

What though they faced no storm of iron hail
That freedom and the right might still prevail?
The path of duty it was theirs to tread
To death's dark vale through ways of travail led,
And they are ours — our dead!
If it be true that each loss holds a gain,
It must be ours through saddened eyes to see
From out this tragic holocaust of pain
The whole land bound in closer amity!

CLINTON SCOLLARD

A WAVE of wrath swept over the American people, but Captain Sigsbee, of the destroyed ship, asked that judgment be suspended until the cause of the disaster had been investigated.　On the list of the dead were many names of Irish origin, such as Kelly, and Burke, and Shea.

THE FIGHTING RACE

[February 16, 1898]

"READ out the names!" and Burke sat back,
　　And Kelly drooped his head,
While Shea — they call him Scholar Jack —
　　Went down the list of the dead.

Officers, seamen, gunners, marines,
    The crews of the gig and yawl,
The bearded man and the lad in his teens,
    Carpenters, coal passers — all.
Then, knocking the ashes from out his pipe,
    Said Burke in an offhand way:
"We're all in that dead man's list by Cripe!
    Kelly and Burke and Shea."
"Well, here's to the Maine, and I'm sorry for Spain,"
    Said Kelly and Burke and Shea.

"Wherever there's Kellys there's trouble," said Burke.
    "Wherever fighting's the game,
Or a spice of danger in grown man's work,"
    Said Kelly, "you'll find my name."
"And do we fall short," said Burke, getting mad,
    "When it's touch and go for life?"
Said Shea, "It's thirty-odd years, bedad,
    Since I charged to drum and fife
Up Marye's Heights, and my old canteen
    Stopped a rebel ball on its way;
There were blossoms of blood on our sprigs of green —
    Kelly and Burke and Shea —
And the dead didn't brag." "Well, here's to the flag!"
    Said Kelly and Burke and Shea.

"I wish 'twas in Ireland, for there's the place,"
    Said Burke, "that we'd die by right,
In the cradle of our soldier race,
    After one good stand-up fight.
My grandfather fell on Vinegar Hill,
    And fighting was not his trade;
But his rusty pike's in the cabin still,
    With Hessian blood on the blade."
"Aye, aye," said Kelly, "the pikes were great
    When the word was 'clear the way!'
We were thick on the roll in ninety-eight —
    Kelly and Burke and Shea."

"Well, here's to the pike and the sword and the like!"
   Said Kelly and Burke and Shea.

And Shea, the scholar, with rising joy,
   Said, "We were at Ramillies;
We left our bones at Fontenoy
   And up in the Pyrenees;
Before Dunkirk, on Landen's plain,
   Cremona, Lille, and Ghent;
We're all over Austria, France, and Spain,
   Wherever they pitched a tent.
We've died for England from Waterloo
   To Egypt and Dargai;
And still there's enough for a corps or crew,
   Kelly and Burke and Shea."
"Well, here's to good honest fighting blood!"
   Said Kelly and Burke and Shea.

"Oh, the fighting races don't die out,
   If they seldom die in bed,
For love is first in their hearts, no doubt,"
   Said Burke; then Kelly said:
"When Michael, the Irish Archangel, stands,
   The angel with the sword,
And the battle-dead from a hundred lands
   Are ranged in one big horde,
Our line, that for Gabriel's trumpet waits,
   Will stretch three deep that day,
From Jehoshaphat to the Golden Gates —
   Kelly and Burke and Shea."
"Well, here's thank God for the race and the sod!"
   Said Kelly and Burke and Shea.

                              JOSEPH I. C. CLARKE

SPAIN announced that the Maine had been blown up by an explosion of her magazines, caused probably by carelessness on the part of her officers, but the American people waited in ominous silence.

TO SPAIN — A LAST WORD

IBERIAN! palter no more!   By thine hands, thine alone, they
    were slain!
Oh, 'twas a deed in the dark —
        Yet mark!
We will show you a way — only one — by which ye may blot
    out the stain!

Build them a monument whom to death-sleep, in their sleep,
    ye betrayed!
Proud and stern let it be —
        Cuba free!
So, only, the stain shall be razed — so, only, the great debt
    be paid!

EDITH M. THOMAS

AT LAST the investigating board announced that "the Maine was destroyed by the explosion of a submarine mine, which caused the partial explosion of two or more of the forward magazines." On April 19, Congress adopted a resolution recognizing the independence of the Cubans, and empowering the President to use the entire land and naval forces of the United States to drive Spain from the island.   War was formally declared a few days later.

BATTLE SONG

WHEN the vengeance wakes, when the battle breaks,
    And the ships sweep out to sea;
When the foe is neared, when the decks are cleared,
    And the colors floating free;
When the squadrons meet, when it's fleet to fleet
    And front to front with Spain,
From ship to ship, from lip to lip,
    Pass on the quick refrain,
"Remember, remember the Maine!"

When the flag shall sign, "Advance in line;
   Train ships on an even keel;"
When the guns shall flash and the shot shall crash
   And bound on the ringing steel;
When the rattling blasts from the armored masts
   Are hurling their deadliest rain,
Let their voices loud, through the blinding cloud,
   Cry ever the fierce refrain,
"Remember, remember the Maine!"

God's sky and sea in that storm shall be
   Fate's chaos of smoke and flame,
But across that hell every shot shall tell,
   Not a gun can miss its aim;
Not a blow shall fail on the crumbling mail,
   And the waves that engulf the slain
Shall sweep the decks of the blackened wrecks,
   With the thundering, dread refrain,
"Remember, remember the Maine!"

                                        ROBERT BURNS WILSON

A SHIVER of alarm ran through the courts of Europe.   There was
something threatening in the spectacle of this young Republic going
to war, without thought of profit or reward, to free another people.
So Europe, especially France and Germany, had backed Spain from
the first; now there was talk of an alliance to assist her.   But before
anything could be accomplished, Spain had gone down to the swift-
est defeat that ever overwhelmed a great nation.

THE FLAG

Up with the banner of the free!
   Its stars and stripes unfurled!
And let the battle beauty blaze
   Above a startled world.
No more around its towering staff
   The folds shall twine again,
Till falls beneath its righteous wrath
   The gonfalon of Spain.

That flag with constellated stars
  Shines ever in the van!
And like the rainbow in the storm,
  Presages peace to man.
For still amid the cannon's roar
  It sanctifies the fight,
And flames along the battle lines,
  The emblem of the Right.

It seeks no conquest, knows no fear;
  Cares not for pomp or state;
As pliant as the atmosphere,
  As resolute as Fate.
Where'er it floats, on land or sea,
  No stain its honor mars,
And Freedom smiles, her fate secure,
  Beneath its steadfast stars.

HARRY LYNDON FLASH

THE first blow was struck with amazing suddenness, in a totally un-
expected quarter.   Thousands of miles away across the Pacific lay
another island dependency of Spain, the Philippines, of which Amer-
icans had not often heard.   On April 26, a cablegram to Commo-
dore George Dewey, in command of the American Asiatic squadron
at Hong Kong, ordered him to proceed to the Philippines and de-
stroy the Spanish fleet there.   The squadron reached Manila on the
night of April 30, steamed straight into the harbor, and at dawn
attacked the Spanish ships, which were sunk one after another.

DEWEY AT MANILA

[May 1, 1898]

I

'TWAS the very verge of May
  When the bold Olympia led
Into Boca Grande gray
  Dewey's squadron, dark and dread, —
Creeping past Corregidor,
Guardian of Manila's shore.

Do they sleep who wait the fray?
   Is the moon so dazzling bright
That our cruisers' battle-gray
   Melts into the misty light?...
Ah! the rockets flash and soar!
Wakes at last Corregidor!

All too late their screaming shell
   Tears the silence with its track;
This is but the *gate* of hell,
   We've no leisure to turn back.
Answer, Boston — then once more
Slumber on, Corregidor!

And as, like a slowing tide,
   Onward still the vessels creep,
Dewey, watching, falcon-eyed,
   Orders — "Let the gunners sleep;
For we meet a foe at four
Fiercer than Corregidor."

Well they slept, for well they knew
   What the morrow taught us all, —
He was wise (as well as true)
   Thus upon the foe to fall.
Long shall Spain the day deplore
Dewey ran Corregidor.

II

May is dancing into light
   As the Spanish Admiral
From a dream of phantom fight
   Wakens at his sentry's call.
Shall he leave Cavité's lee,
Hunt the Yankee fleet at sea?

O Montojo, to thy deck,
   That today shall float its last!

Quick! To quarters! Yonder speck
    Grows a hull of portent vast.
Hither, toward Cavité's lee
Comes the Yankee hunting thee!

Not for fear of hidden mine
    Halts our doughty Commodore.
He, of old heroic line,
    Follows Farragut once more,
Hazards all on victory,
Here within Cavité's lee.

If he loses, all is gone;
    He will win because he must.
And the shafts of yonder dawn
    Are not quicker than his thrust.
Soon, Montojo, he shall be
With thee in Cavité's lee.

Now, Manila, to the fray!
    Show the hated Yankee host
This is not a holiday —
    Spanish blood is more than boast.
Fleet and mine and battery,
Crush him in Cavité's lee!

Lo, hell's geysers at our fore
    Pierce the plotted path — in vain,
Nerving every man the more
    With the memory of the Maine!
Now at last our guns are free
Here within Cavité's lee.

"Gridley," says the Commodore,
    "You may fire when ready."   Then
Long and loud, like lions' roar
    When a rival dares the den,
Breaks the awful cannonry
Full across Cavité's lee.

Who shall tell the daring tale
  Of our Thunderbolt's attack,
Finding, when the chart should fail,
  By the lead his dubious track,
Five ships following faithfully
Five times o'er Cavité's lee;

Of our gunners' deadly aim;
  Of the gallant foe and brave
Who, unconquered, faced with flame,
  Seek the mercy of the wave —
Choosing honor in the sea
Underneath Cavité's lee?

Let the meed the victors gain
  Be the measure of their task.
Less of flinching, stouter strain,
  Fiercer combat — who could ask?
And "surrender" — 'twas a word
That Cavité ne'er had heard.

Noon — the woeful work is done!
  Not a Spanish ship remains;
But, of their eleven, none
  Ever was so truly Spain's!
Which is prouder, they or we,
Thinking of Cavité's lee?

ENVOY

But remember, when we've ceased
  Giving praise and reckoning odds,
Man shares courage with the beast,
  Wisdom cometh from the gods.
Who would win, on land or wave,
Must be wise as well as brave.
                    ROBERT UNDERWOOD JOHNSON

BY NOON the entire Spanish fleet was destroyed, the shore batteries silenced, and a white flag floated over the citadel of Cavité.   Dewey had not lost a man and had won the greatest naval battle in American history.

DEWEY IN MANILA BAY

HE TOOK a thousand islands and he didn't lose a man
    (Raise your heads and cheer him as he goes!) —
He licked the sneaky Spaniard till the fellow cut and ran,
    For fighting's part of what a Yankee knows.

He fought 'em and he licked 'em, without any fuss or flam
    (It was only his profession for to win),
He sank their boats beneath 'em, and he spared 'em as they
        swam,
    And then he sent his ambulances in.

He had no word to cheer him and had no bands to play,
    He had no crowds to make his duty brave;
But he risked the deep torpedoes at the breaking of the day,
    For he knew he had our self-respect to save.

He flew the angry signal crying justice for the Maine,
    He flew it from his flagship as he fought.
He drove the tardy vengeance in the very teeth of Spain,
    And he did it just because he thought he ought.

He busted up their batteries and sank eleven ships
    (He knew what he was doing, every bit);
He set the Maxims going like a hundred cracking whips,
    And every shot that crackled was a hit.

He broke 'em and he drove 'em, and he didn't care at all,
    He only liked to do as he was bid;
He crumpled up their squadron and their batteries and all —
    He knew he had to lick 'em and he did.

And when the thing was finished and they flew the frightened
    flag,
  He slung his guns and sent his foot ashore,
And he gathered in their wounded, and he quite forgot to brag,
  For he thought he did his duty, nothing more.

Oh, he took a thousand islands and he didn't lose a man
  (Raise your heads and cheer him as he goes!) —
He licked the sneaky Spaniard till the fellow cut and ran,
  For fighting's part of what a Yankee knows!
                            R. V. RISLEY

ANOTHER fleet had been collected at Key West, under command of
Admiral Sampson, ready to proceed to Cuba, and on April 21 — the
very day war was declared — orders came for it to sail. It put to sea
next morning, steamed off to Havana, and proceeded to blockade the
Cuban coast.

THE SPIRIT OF THE MAINE

IN BATTLE-LINE of somber gray
  Our ships-of-war advance,
As Red Cross Knights in holy fray
  Charged with avenging lance.
And terrible shall be thy plight,
  O fleet of cruel Spain!
Forever in our van doth fight
  The Spirit of the Maine!

As when beside Regillus Lake
  The Great Twin Brethren came
A righteous fight for Rome to make
  Against the Deed of Shame —
So now a ghostly ship shall doom
  The fleet of treacherous Spain:
Before her guilty soul doth loom
  The Spirit of the Maine!

A wraith arrayed in peaceful white,
    As when asleep she lay
Above the traitorous mine that night
    Within Havana Bay,
She glides before the avenging fleet,
    A sign of woe to Spain,
Brave though her sons, how shall they meet
    The Spirit of the Maine!

                              TUDOR JENKS

A SPANISH fleet had also put to sea, and managed to elude the Ameri-
can squadron and slip into the harbor of Santiago, where it was
promptly blockaded.   Santiago was strongly defended, and an army
under General William Shafter sailed from Tampa, Florida, on June
7, to assist in its capture.

COMRADES

Now from their slumber waking —
    The long sleep men thought death —
The War Gods rise, inhaling deep
    The cannon's fiery breath!
Their mighty arms uplifted,
    Their gleaming eyes aglow
With the steadfast light of battle,
    As it blazed long years ago!

Now from the clouds they summon
    The Captains of the Past,
Still sailing in their astral ships
    The star-lit spaces vast;
And from Valhalla's peaceful plains
    The Great Commanders come,
And marshal again their armies
    To the beat of the muffled drum.

His phantom sails unfurling
    McDonough sweeps amain

Where once his Yankee sailors fought
    The battle of Champlain!
And over Erie's waters,
    Again his flagship sweeps,
While Perry on the quarter-deck
    His endless vigil keeps.

Silent as mists that hover
    When twilight shadows fall,
The ghosts of the royal armies
    Foregather at the call;
And their glorious chiefs are with them,
    From conflicts lost or won,
As they gather round one mighty shade,
    The shade of Washington!...

Side by side with the warships
    That sail for the hostile fleet,
The ships of the Past are sailing
    And the dauntless comrades meet;
And standing shoulder to shoulder,
    The armèd spirits come,
And march with our own battalions
    To the beat of the muffled drum!

                    HENRY R. DORR

THE transports reached Santiago June 20, and the army disem-
barked. One brigade was under command of General Joseph
Wheeler, an old Confederate cavalryman, and one of the squadrons
under him was the famous "Rough Riders," of which Theodore
Roosevelt was lieutenant-colonel. Wheeler's brigade moved for-
ward at once without waiting for orders, but was soon held up by the
Spanish intrenchments.

WHEELER'S BRIGADE AT SANTIAGO

BENEATH the blistering tropical sun
    The column is standing ready,

Awaiting the fateful command of one
　　Whose word will ring out
　　　To an answering shout
　　To prove it alert and steady.
And a stirring chorus all of them sung
　　With singleness of endeavor,
Though some to "The Bonny Blue Flag" had swung
　　And some to "The Union For Ever."

The order came sharp through the desperate air
　　And the long ranks rose to follow,
Till their dancing banners shone more fair
　　　Than the brightest ray
　　　Of the Cuban day
　　On the hill and jungled hollow;
And to "Maryland" some in the days gone by
　　Had fought through the combat's rumble,
And some for "Freedom's Battle-Cry"
　　Had seen the broad earth crumble.

Full many a widow weeps in the night
　　Who had been a man's wife in the morning;
For the banners we loved we bore to the height
　　　Where the enemy stood
　　　As a hero should,
　　His valor his country adorning;
But drops of pride with your tears of grief,
　　Ye American women, mix ye!
For the North and South, with a Southron chief,
　　Kept time to the tune of "Dixie."

WALLACE RICE

AFTER great confusion and several days' delay, the remainder of the army came up, and on the afternoon of June 30, a general advance was ordered. By dawn of July 1, the troops were in position and the attack began.

DEEDS OF VALOR AT SANTIAGO
[July 1, 1898]

WHO cries that the days of daring are those that are faded
    far,
That never a light burns planet-bright to be hailed as the
    hero's star?
Let the deeds of the dead be laureled, the brave of the elder
    years,
But a song, we say, for the men of today, who have proved
    themselves their peers!

High in the vault of the tropic sky is the garish eye of the sun,
And down with its crown of guns afrown looks the hilltop to
    be won;
There is the trench where the Spaniard lurks, his hold and
    his hiding-place,
And he who would cross the space between must meet death
    face to face.

The black mouths belch and thunder, and the shrapnel shrieks
    and flies;
Where are the fain and the fearless, the lads with the dauntless
    eyes?
Will the moment find them wanting! Nay, but with valor
    stirred!
Like the leashed hound on the coursing-ground they wait
    but the warning word.

"Charge!" and the line moves forward, moves with a shout
    and a swing,
While sharper far than the cactus-thorn is the spiteful bullet's
    sting.

Now they are out in the open, and now they are breasting
 the slope,
While into the eyes of death they gaze as into the eyes of
 of hope.

Never they wait nor waver, but on they clamber and on,
With "Up with the flag of the Stripes and Stars, and down
 with the flag of the Don!"
What should they bear through the shot-rent air but rout
 to the ranks of Spain,
For the blood that throbs in their hearts is the blood of the
 boys of Anthony Wayne!

See, they have taken the trenches! Where are the foemen?
 Gone!
And now "Old Glory" waves in the breeze from the heights
 of San Juan!
And so, while the dead are laureled, the brave of the elder
 years,
A song, we say, for the men of today who have proved them-
 selves their peers.

CLINTON SCOLLARD

THE morning was consumed in blundering about under the Spanish fire, in a vain endeavor to carry out the orders of a general lying in a hammock, overcome by the heat, far to the rear. Finally, the subordinate commanders acted for themselves. Lawton, Ludlow, and Chaffee took the fort of El Caney, and the Rough Riders charged the fort on San Juan Hill and captured it.

THE CHARGE AT SANTIAGO

[July 1, 1898]

WITH shot and shell, like a loosened hell,
 Smiting them left and right,
They rise or fall on the sloping wall
 Of beetling bush and height!

They do not shrink at the awful brink
   Of the rifle's hurtling breath,
But onward press, as their ranks grow less,
   To the open arms of death!

Through a storm of lead, o'er maimed and dead,
   Onward and up they go,
Till hand to hand the unflinching band
   Grapple the stubborn foe.
O'er men that reel,' mid glint of steel,
   Bellow or boom of gun,
They leap and shout over each redoubt
   Till the final trench is won!

O charge sublime! Over dust and grime
   Each hero hurls his name
In shot or shell, like a molten hell,
   To the topmost heights of fame!
And prone or stiff, under bush and cliff,
   Wounded or dead men lie,
While the tropic sun on a grand deed done
   Looks with his piercing eye!
               WILLIAM HAMILTON HAYNE

IN SPITE of this success, General Shafter cabled Washington that he
had decided to withdraw. But the dismay which this message
caused was turned to rejoicing by another from Admiral Sampson.
At nine o'clock on the morning of Sunday, July 3, the Spanish fleet
came rushing out of the harbor in a desperate effort to escape. The
Americans closed in, and a battle began which ended in the total
destruction of the Spanish ships.

SANTIAGO

[July 3, 1898]

IN THE *stagnant pride of an outworn race*
   The Spaniard sailed the sea:
Till we haled him up to God's judgment place —
   And smashed him by God's decree!

Out from the harbor, belching smoke,
　　Came dashing seaward the Spanish ships —
And from all our decks a great shout broke,
Then our hearts came up and set us a-choke
　　For joy that we had them at last at grips!

No need for signals to get us away —
　　We were off at score, with our screws a-gleam!
Through the blistering weeks we'd watched the bay
And our captains had need not a word to say —
　　Save to bellow and curse down the pipes for steam!

Leading the pack in its frightened flight
　　The Colon went foaming away to the west —
Her tall iron bulwarks, black as night,
And her great black funnels, sharp in sight
　　'Gainst the green-clad hills in their peace and rest.

Her big Hontaria blazed away
　　At the Indiana, our first in line.
The short-ranged shot drenched our decks with spray —
While our thirteen-inchers, in answering play,
　　Ripped straight through her frame to her very spine!...

Straight to its end went our winning fight
　　With the thunder of guns in a mighty roar.
Our hail of iron, casting withering blight,
Turning the Spanish ships in their flight
　　To a shorter death on the rock-bound shore.

The Colon, making her reckless race
　　With the Brooklyn and Oregon close a-beam,
Went dashing landward — and stopped the chase
By grinding her way to her dying-place
　　In a raging outburst of flame and steam.

So the others, facing their desperate luck,
　　Drove headlong on to their rock-dealt death —

The Vizcaya, yielding before she struck,
The riddled destroyers, a huddled ruck,
    Sinking, and gasping for drowning breath.

So that flying battle surged down the coast,
    With its echoing roar from the Cuban land;
So the dying war-ships gave up the ghost;
So we shattered and mangled the Philistine host —
    So the fight was won that our Sampson planned!
                              THOMAS A. JANVIER

THE American battleships were practically uninjured, and the fleet
had lost only one man — the only mortality on the American side
during the two battles which resulted in the total destruction of the
Spanish navy.   The Spanish loss was 350 killed, 160 wounded, 1774
taken prisoners.

THE FLEET AT SANTIAGO [1]

[July 3, 1898]

THE heart leaps with the pride of their story,
    Predestinate lords of the sea!
They are heirs of the flag and its glory,
    They are sons of the soil it keeps free;
For their deeds the serene exaltation
    Of a cause that was stained with no shame,
For their dead the proud tears of a nation,
    Their fame shall endure with its fame.

The fervor that grim, unrelenting,
    The founders in homespun had fired,
With blood the free compact cementing,
    Was the flame that their souls had inspired.

[1] From *Such Stuff as Dreams*, by Charles E. Russell, copyright 1901 and
1929.   Used by special permission of the publishers, The Bobbs-Merrill
Company.

They were sons of the dark tribulations,
  Of the perilous days of the birth
Of a nation sprung free among nations,
  A new hope to the children of earth!

They were nerved by the old deeds of daring,
  Every tale of Decatur they knew,
Every ship that, the bright banner bearing,
  Shot to keep it afloat in the blue;
They were spurred by the splendor undying
  Of Somers' fierce fling in the bay,
And the Watchword that Lawrence died crying,
  And of Cushing's calm courage were they.

By the echo of guns at whose thunder
  Old monarchies crumbled and fell,
When the warships were shattered asunder
  And their pennants went down in the swell;
By the strength of the race that, unfearing,
  Faces death till the death of the last,
Or has sunk with the fierce Saxon cheering,
  Its colors still nailed to the mast —

So they fought — and the stern race immortal
  Of Cromwell and Hampton and Penn
Has thrown open another closed portal,
  Stricken chains from a new race of men.
So they fought, so they won, so above them
  Blazed the light of a consecrate aim;
Empty words! Who may tell how we love them,
  How we thrill with the joy of their fame!
                    CHARLES E. RUSSELL

THE superior speed of the American ships and the high quality of American marksmanship, as compared to the Spanish, decided the battle. Here, as at Manila, the victory had been won by "the men behind the guns."

THE MEN BEHIND THE GUNS

A CHEER and salute for the Admiral, and here's to the Captain
    bold,
And never forget the Commodore's debt when the deeds of
    might are told!
They stand to the deck through the battle's wreck when the
    great shells roar and screech —
And never they fear when the foe is near to practice what they
    preach:
But off with your hat and three times three for Columbia's
    true-blue sons,
The men below who batter the foe — the men behind the
    guns!

Oh, light and merry of heart are they when they swing into
    port once more,
When, with more than enough of the "green-backed stuff,"
    they start for their leave-o'-shore;
And you'd think, perhaps, that the blue-bloused chaps who
    loll along the street
Are a tender bit, with salt on it, for some fierce "mustache"
    to eat —
Some warrior bold, with straps of gold, who dazzles and fairly
    stuns
The modest worth of the sailor boys — the lads who serve
    the guns.

But say not a word till the shot is heard that tells the fight is
    on,
Till the long, deep roar grows more and more from the ships
    of "Yank" and "Don,"
Till over the deep the tempests sweep of fire and bursting
    shell,

And the very air is a mad Despair in the throes of a living hell;
Then down, deep down, in the mighty ship, unseen by the
    midday suns,
You'll find the chaps who are giving the raps — the men
    behind the guns!

Oh, well they know how the cyclones blow that they loose from
    their cloud of death,
And they know is heard the thunder-word their fierce ten-
    incher saith!
The steel decks rock with the lightning shock, and shake with
    the great recoil,
And the sea grows red with the blood of the dead and reaches
    for his spoil —
But not till the foe has gone below or turns his prow and runs,
Shall the voice of peace bring sweet release to the men behind
    the guns!

JOHN JEROME ROONEY

SPAIN had collapsed like the house of cards that she was, and sued
for peace. On August 12, a protocol was signed and hostilities
ceased. Eight days later, the American squadron steamed into
New York Harbor.

WHEN THE GREAT GRAY SHIPS COME IN

[New York Harbor, August 20, 1898]

To EASTWARD ringing, to westward winging, o'er mapless
    miles of sea,
On winds and tides the gospel rides that the furthermost isles
    are free,
And the furthermost isles make answer, harbor, and height,
    and hill,
Breaker and beach cry each to each, "'Tis the Mother who
    calls! Be still!"
Mother! new-found, beloved, and strong to hold from harm,
Stretching to these across the seas the shield of her sovereign
    arm,

Who summoned the guns of her sailor sons, who bade her
    navies roam,
Who calls again to the leagues of main, and who calls them
    this time Home!

And the great gray ships are silent, and the weary watchers
    rest,
The black cloud dies in the August skies, and deep in the
    golden west
Invisible hands are limning a glory of crimson bars,
And far above is the wonder of a myriad wakened stars!
Peace!   As the tidings silence the strenuous cannonade,
Peace at last! is the bugle blast the length of the long block-
    ade,
And eyes of vigil weary are lit with the glad release,
From ship to ship and from lip to lip it is "Peace! Thank
    God for peace."

Ah, in the sweet hereafter Columbia still shall show
The sons of these who swept the seas how she bade them rise
    and go —
How, when the stirring summons smote on her children's
    ear,
South and North at the call stood forth, and the whole land
    answered, "Here!"
For the soul of the soldier's story and the heart of the sailor's
    song
Are all of those who meet their foes as right should meet with
    wrong,
Who fight their guns till the foeman runs, and then, on the
    decks they trod,
Brave faces raise, and give the praise to the grace of their
    country's God!

Yes, it is good to battle, and good to be strong and free,
To carry the hearts of a people to the uttermost ends of sea.
To see the day steal up the bay where the enemy lies in wait,
To run your ship to the harbor's lip and sink her across the
    strait: —

But better the golden evening when the ships round heads
>   for home,
And the long gray miles slip swiftly past in a swirl of seething
>   foam,
And the people wait at the haven's gate to greet the men who
>   win!
Thank God for peace! Thank God for peace, when the great
>   gray ships come in!

GUY WETMORE CARRYL

A TREATY of peace was signed on December 10, by which Spain, in
spite of European protest, was compelled to relinquish all sovereignty
over Cuba, and to cede Porto Rico, Guam, and the Philippine Islands
to the United States, receiving in payment for the latter the sum of
twenty million dollars. For a time it seemed that America's first
crusade had been a complete triumph, but she soon found herself
involved in a struggle entirely unforeseen and deeply repugnant to
many of her citizens.

LAND OF OUR FATHERS

To DEITIES of gauds and gold,
>   Land of our Fathers, do not bow!
But unto those beloved of old
>   Bend thou the brow!

Austere they were of front and form;
>   Rigid as iron in their aim;
Yet in them pulsed a blood as warm
>   And pure as flame; —

Honor, whose foster-child is Truth;
>   Unselfishness in place and plan;
Justice, with melting heart of ruth;
>   And Faith in man!

Give these thy worship, then no fears
>   Of future foes need fright thy soul!

Triumphant thou shalt mount the years
    Toward thy high goal!

                    CLINTON SCOLLARD

THE people of the Philippines for many years had been fighting
against Spanish oppression, and a band of them, under Emilio
Aguinaldo, had assisted at the capture of Manila, supposing that
Spanish defeat would mean Philippine independence. Instead, they
found that they had merely changed masters, and at once took up
arms against the Americans. To employ the troops of the Republic
against a people fighting for freedom, and to shoot them down as
"rebels," occasioned in the United States a great outburst of indig-
nation.

"REBELS"

SHOOT down the "rebels" — men who dare
    To claim their native land!
Why should the white invader spare
    A dusky heathen band?

You bought them from the Spanish King,
    You bought the men he stole;
You bought perchance a ghastlier thing —
    The Duke of Alva's soul!

"Freedom!" you cry, and train your gun
    On men who would be freed,
And in the name of Washington
    Achieve a Weyler's deed.

Boast of the benefits you spread,
    The faith of Christ you hold;
Then seize the very soil you tread
    And fill your arms with gold.

Go, prostitute your mother-tongue,
    And give the "rebel" name

To those who to their country clung,
   Preferring death to shame.

And call him "loyal," him who brags
   Of countrymen betrayed —
The patriot of the money-bags,
   The loyalist of trade.

Oh, for the good old Roman days
   Of robbers bold and true,
Who scorned to oil with pious phrase
   The deeds they dared to do...

I hate the oppressor's iron rod,
   I hate his murderous ships,
But most of all I hate, O God,
   The lie upon his lips!...

              ERNEST CROSBY

BUT powerful interests desired the Philippines for purposes of trade, and demagogues in and out of Congress shouted that wherever the American flag had been raised it must remain. The administration found it impossible to draw back, and hostilities were vigorously pressed. On February 5, 1899, General Ricarti's division of the Filipino army was encountered near Santa Ana and completely routed. It was here that Lieutenant W. G. Miles performed the exploit described in the following poem.

BALLAD OF LIEUTENANT MILES

[February 5, 1899]

WHEN you speak of dauntless deeds,
   When you tell of stirring scenes,
Tell this story of the isles
Where the endless summer smiles —
Tell of young Lieutenant Miles
   In the far-off Philippines!

'Twas the Santa Ana fight! —
    All along the Tagal line
From the thickets dense and dire
Gushed the fountains of their fire;
You could mark their rifles' ire,
    You could hear their bullets whine.

Little wonder there was pause!
    Some were wounded, some were dead;
"Call Lieutenant Miles!"   He came,
In his eyes a fearless flame.
"Yonder block-house is our aim!"
    The battalion leader said.

"You must take it — how you will;
    You must break this damnèd spell!"
"Volunteers!" cried Miles.   'Twas vain,
For that narrow tropic lane
'Twixt the bamboo and the cane
    Was a very lane of hell.

There were five stood forth at last;
    God above, but they were men!
"Come!" — exultantly he saith! —
Did they falter?   Not a breath!
Down the path of hurtling death
    The Lieutenant led them then.

Two have fallen — now a third!
    Forward dash the other three;
In the onrush of that race
Ne'er a swerve nor stay of pace.
And the Tagals — dare they face
    Such a desperate company?

Panic gripped them by the throat —
    Every Tagal rifleman;
And as though they seemed to see

In those charging foemen three
An avenging destiny,
   Fierce and fast and far they ran.

So a salvo for the six!
   So a round of ringing cheers!
Heroes of the distant isles
Where the endless summer smiles —
Gallant young Lieutenant Miles
And his valiant volunteers!

CLINTON SCOLLARD

FOR three years the war went on, with massacre, ambush, and lonely murder — a sordid and cruel struggle — a sorry ending to a great adventure. But the natives, of course, had no chance of success, and the capture of Aguinaldo March 23, 1901, put an end to organized resistance, though there were sporadic outbreaks for several years longer.

ON A SOLDIER FALLEN IN THE PHILIPPINES

STREETS of the roaring town,
Hush for him, hush, be still!
He comes, who was stricken down
Doing the word of our will.
Hush! Let him have his state.
Give him his soldier's crown,
The grists of trade can wait
Their grinding at the mill,
But he cannot wait for his honor, now the trumpet has been
    blown.
Wreathe pride now for his granite brow, lay love on his breast
    of stone.

Toll! Let the great bells toll
Till the clashing air is dim,
Did we wrong this parted soul?
We will make it up to him.

Toll! Let him never guess
What work we set him to.
Laurel, laurel, yes;
He did what we bade him do.
Praise, and never a whispered hint but the fight he fought
was good;
Never a word that the blood on his sword was his country's
own heart's blood.

A flag for the soldier's bier
Who dies that his land may live;
Oh, banners, banners here,
That he doubt not nor misgive!
That he heed not from the tomb
The evil days draw near
When the nation, robed in gloom,
With its faithless past shall strive.
Let him never dream that his bullet's scream went wide of its
island mark,
Home to the heart of his sinning land where she stumbled
and sinned in the dark.

WILLIAM VAUGHN MOODY

THE country was placed under a civil government and the work of organizing and developing it begun. It has, of course, profited immensely in a material way from the American occupation, but its people have never ceased to demand independence. Some day, no doubt, it will be given them, and the liabilities of America's first crusade will be finally liquidated.

THE ISLANDS OF THE SEA

God is shaping the great future of the Islands of the Sea;
He has sown the blood of martyrs and the fruit is liberty;
In thick clouds and in darkness He has sent abroad His
word;
He has given a haughty nation to the cannon and the sword.

He has seen a people moaning in the thousand deaths they
    die;
He has heard from child and woman a terrible dark cry;
He has given the wasted talent of the steward faithless
    found
To the youngest of the nations with His abundance crowned.

He called her to do justice where none but she had power;
He called her to do mercy to her neighbor at the door;
He called her to do vengeance for her own sons foully dead;
Thrice did He call unto her ere she inclined her head.

She has gathered the vast Midland, she has searched her
    borders round;
There has been a mighty hosting of her children on the ground;
Her search-lights lie along the sea, her guns are loud on land;
To do her will upon the earth her armies round her stand.

The fleet, at her commandment, to either ocean turns;
Belted around the mighty world her line of battle burns;
She has loosed the hot volcanoes of the ships of flaming hell;
With fire and smoke and earthquake shock her heavy venge-
    ance fell.

O joyfullest May morning when before our guns went down
The Inquisition priesthood and the dungeon-making crown,
While through red lights of battle our starry dawn burst out,
Swift as the tropic sunrise that doth with glory shout!

Be jubilant, free Cuba, our feet are on thy soil;
Up mountain road, through jungle growth, our bravest for
    thee toil;
There is no blood so precious as their wounds pour forth for
    thee;
Sweet be thy joys, free Cuba — sorrows have made thee free.

Nor Thou, O noble Nation, who wast so slow to wrath,
With grief too heavy-laden follow in duty's path;

Not for ourselves our lives are; not for Thyself art Thou;
The Star of Christian Ages is shining on Thy brow.

Rejoice, O mighty Mother, that God hath chosen Thee
To be the western warder of the Islands of the Sea;
He lifteth up, He casteth down, He is the King of Kings,
Whose dread commands o'er awe-struck lands are borne on
    eagle's wings.

GEORGE EDWARD WOODBERRY

CHAPTER III

Twenty Years of Peace

No country in the world entered upon the twentieth century with a brighter future than did the United States. Conscious of strength and vigor, busy and prosperous, long years of peace and happiness seemed to stretch ahead.

A TOAST TO OUR NATIVE LAND

Huge and alert, irascible yet strong,
We make our fitful way 'mid right and wrong
One time we pour out millions to be free,
Then rashly sweep an empire from the sea!
One time we strike the shackles from the slaves,
And then, quiescent, we are ruled by knaves.
Often we rudely break restraining bars,
And confidently reach out toward the stars.

Yet under all there flows a hidden stream
Sprung from the Rock of Freedom, the great dream
Of Washington and Franklin, men of old
Who knew that freedom is not bought with gold.
This is the Land we love, our heritage,
Strange mixture of the gross and fine, yet sage
And full of promise — destined to be great.
Drink to Our Native Land! God Bless the State!
        Robert Bridges ("Droch")

More than ever did Americans believe in their own country as the land of freedom, the land of opportunity. More and more were they inclined to keep aloof from the rivalries and jealousies of Europe.

"AMERICA FOR ME"

'Tis fine to see the Old World, and travel up and down
Among the famous palaces and cities of renown,

To admire the crumbly castles and the statues of the kings —
But now I think I've had enough of antiquated things.

So it's home again, and home again, America for me!
My heart is turning home again, and there I long to be,
In the land of youth and freedom beyond the ocean bars,
Where the air is full of sunlight and the flag is full of stars.

Oh, London is a man's town, there's power in the air;
And Paris is a woman's town, with flowers in her hair;
And it's sweet to dream in Venice, and it's great to study
      Rome;
But when it comes to living, there is no place like home.

I like the German fir-woods, in green battalions drilled;
I like the gardens of Versailles, with flashing fountains
      filled;
But oh, to take your hand, my dear, and ramble for a day
In the friendly western woodland where Nature has her
      way!

I know that Europe's wonderful, yet something seems to
      lack:
The Past is too much with her, and the people looking
      back.
But the glory of the Present is to make the Future free —
We love our land for what she is and what she is to be.

Oh, it's home again, and home again, America for me!
I want a ship that's westward bound to plow the rolling sea,
To the blessèd Land of Room Enough beyond the ocean bars,
Where the air is full of sunlight and the flag is full of stars.
                      HENRY VAN DYKE

BUT in the very first year of the new century, a bolt from the blue
fell upon the country when, on September 6, 1901, President William
McKinley was shot down by an anarchist while holding a public
reception at the Buffalo Exposition, and died a week later.

McKINLEY

[September 6, 1901]

'TIS not the President alone
   Who, stricken by that bullet, fell;
The assassin's shot that laid him prone
   Pierced a great nation's heart as well;
And when the baleful tidings sped
   From lip to lip throughout the crowd,
Then, as they deemed their ruler dead,
   'Twas Liberty that cried aloud.

Aye, Liberty! for where the foam
   Of oceans twain marks out the coast
'Tis there, in Freedom's very home,
   That anarchy has maimed its host;
There 'tis that it has turned to bite
   The hand that fed it; there repaid
A country's welcome with black spite;
   There, Judas-like, that land betrayed.

For 'tis no despot that's laid low,
   But a free nation's chosen chief;
A free man, stricken by a blow
   Base, dastardly, past all belief.
And Tyranny exulting hears
   The tidings flashed across the sea;
While stern Repression hugs her fears,
   And mouths them in a harsh decree.

Meanwhile the cloud, though black as death,
   Is lined with hopes, hopes light as life,
And Liberty that, scant of breath,
   Had watched the issue of the strife,

Fills the glad air with grateful cries
To find the sun no more obscured,
And with new yearnings in her eyes
Climbs to her watch-tower — reassured.

UNKNOWN

London *Truth.*

THE assassin was a youth named Leon Czolgosz, a professed anarchist lately come from Poland, and the whole country suddenly awoke to the danger of admitting unquestioned the squalid horde which was swarming across the sea and making America an asylum for the vice and crime of Europe. The restriction of this unwelcome immigration began at once, and has continued ever since with increasing rigor and effectiveness.

UNGUARDED GATES

WIDE open and unguarded stand our gates,
Named of the four winds, North, South, East, and West;
Portals that lead to an enchanted land
Of cities, forests, fields of living gold,
Vast prairies, lordly summits touched with snow,
Majestic rivers sweeping proudly past
The Arab's date-palm and the Norseman's pine —
A realm wherein are fruits of every zone,
Airs of all climes, for lo! throughout the year
The red rose blossoms somewhere — a rich land,
A later Eden planted in the wilds,
With not an inch of earth within its bound
But if a slave's foot press it sets him free.
Here, it is written, Toil shall have its wage,
And Honor honor, and the humblest man
Stand level with the highest in the law.
Of such a land have men in dungeons dreamed,
And with the vision brightening in their eyes
Gone smiling to the fagot and the sword.

Wide open and unguarded stand our gates,
And through them presses a wild motley throng —

Men from the Volga and the Tartar steppes,
Featureless figures of the Hoang-Ho,
Malayan, Scythian, Teuton, Kelt, and Slav,
Flying the Old World's poverty and scorn;
These bringing with them unknown gods and rites,
Those, tiger passions, here to stretch their claws.
In street and alley what strange tongues are loud,
Accents of menace alien to our air,
Voices that once the Tower of Babel knew!

O Liberty, white Goddess! is it well
To leave the gates unguarded? On thy breast
Fold Sorrow's children, soothe the hurts of fate,
Lift the downtrodden, but with hands of steel
Stay those who to thy sacred portals come
To waste the gifts of freedom. Have a care
Lest from thy brow the clustered stars be torn
And trampled in the dust. For so of old
The thronging Goth and Vandal trampled Rome,
And where the temples of the Cæsars stood
The lean wolf unmolested made her lair.

THOMAS BAILEY ALDRICH

THEODORE ROOSEVELT, who had been Vice-President, succeeded to
the Presidency, and a year later sponsored a project of vast impor-
tance to the country — the construction of a ship canal across the
Isthmus of Panama. A French company had secured a concession
from Colombia, which owned the isthmus, in 1879, and began dig-
ging the canal, but its resources had been exhausted, largely through
mismanagement, and work had long since ceased.

PANAMA

HERE the oceans twain have waited
All the ages to be mated —
Waited long and waited vainly,
Though the script was written plainly:

"This, the portal of the sea,
Opes for him who holds the key;
Here the empire of the earth
Waits in patience for its birth."

But the Spanish monarch, dimly
Seeing little, answered grimly:
"North and South the land is Spain's;
As God gave it, it remains.
He who seeks to break the tie,
By mine honor, he shall die!"

So the centuries rollèd on,
And the gift of great Colon,
Like a spendthrift's heritage,
Dwindled slowly, age by age,
Till the flag of red and gold
Fell from hands unnerved and old,
And the granite-pillared gate
Waited still the key of fate.

Who shall hold that magic key
But the child of destiny,
In whose veins has mingled long
All the best blood of the strong?
He who takes his place by grace
Of no singlè tribe or race,
But by many a rich bequest
From the bravest and the best.
Sentinel of duty, here
Must he guard a hemisphere.

Let the old world keep its ways;
Naught to him its blame or praise;
Naught its greed, or hate, or fear;
For all swords be sheathèd here.
Yea, the gateway shall be free
Unto all, from sea to sea;

And no fratricidal slaughter
Shall defile its sacred water;
But — the hand that ope'd the gate
Shall forever hold the key!

JAMES JEFFREY ROCHE

IN 1902, the French company was bought out by the United States
for the exorbitant sum of forty million dollars, and when Colombia
made difficulties about renewing the concession, Roosevelt encour-
aged the revolt of the Isthmus and the organization of the Republic
of Panama, securing control of the canal route for the United States.
In 1914, the canal was completed and opened for traffic. It short-
ened the sea route between the Atlantic and Pacific coasts by ten
thousand miles.

DARIEN

A.D. 1513–A.D. 1901

[The American Senate has ratified the isthmus treaty. — WASHINGTON
TELEGRAM.]

"SILENT upon a peak in Darien,"
    The Spanish steel red in his conquering hand,
    While golden, green and gracious the vast land
Of that new world comes sudden into ken —
Stands Nuñez da Balboa. North and south
    He sees at last the full Pacific roll
    In blue and silver on each shelf and shoal,
And the white bar of the broad river's mouth,
And the long, ranked palm-trees. "Queen of Heaven," he
    cried,
    "Today thou giv'st me this for all my pain,
    And I the glorious guerdon give to Spain,
A new earth and new sea to be her pride,
War ground and treasure-house." And while he spoke
The world's heart knew a mightier dawn was broke.

"Silent, upon a peak in Darien" —
    Four hundred years being fled, a Greater stood
        On that same height; and did behold the flood

Of blue waves leaping; Mother of all men!
Wise Nature!   And she spake, "The gift I gave
  To Nuñez da Balboa could not keep
  Spain from her sins; now must the ages sweep
To larger legend, tho' her own was brave.
Here on this ridge I do foresee fresh birth.
  That which departed shall bring side by side,
  The sea shall sever what hills did divide;
Shall link in love."   And there was joy on earth;
Whilst England and Columbia, quitting fear,
Kissed — and let in the eager waters there.

EDWIN ARNOLD

So THE country entered the second decade of the century, and the time drew near when it was to launch a second crusade, far greater than the first one, which would take it three thousand miles across the Atlantic to face the most warlike nation of modern times.

NATIONAL SONG

AMERICA, my own!
  Thy spacious grandeurs rise
Faming the proudest zone
  Pavilioned by the skies;
Day's flying glory breaks
  Thy vales and mountains o'er,
And gilds thy streams and lakes
  From ocean shore to shore.

Praised be thy wood and wold,
  Thy corn and wine and flocks,
The yellow blood of gold
  Drained from thy cañon rocks;
Thy trains that shake the land,
  Thy ships that plough the main,
Triumphant cities grand
  Roaring with noise of gain.

Earth's races look to Thee:
　　The peoples of the world
Thy risen splendors see
　　And thy wide flag unfurled;
Thy sons, in peace or war,
　　That emblem who behold,
Bless every shining star,
　　Cheer every streaming fold!

Float high, O gallant flag,
　　O'er Carib Isles of palm,
O'er bleak Alaskan crag,
　　O'er far-off lone Guam;
Where Mauna Loa pours
　　Black thunder from the deeps;
O'er Mindanao's shores,
　　O'er Luzon's coral steeps.

Float high, and be the sign
　　Of love and brotherhood —
The pledge, by right divine
　　Of Power, to do good;
For aye and everywhere,
　　On continent and wave,
Armipotent to dare,
　　Imperial to save!

WILLIAM HENRY VENABLE

CHAPTER IV

THE CRUSADE AGAINST GERMANY

IN THE summer of 1914, a great war broke out suddenly in Europe, with Germany and Austria on one side and England, France, Belgium, and Russia on the other. Other nations soon joined the fray, until nearly the whole continent was involved. Millions of men were in the field, and the war was carried on from the very first with a savagery and destructiveness unparalleled in history.

SONNETS WRITTEN IN THE FALL OF 1914

AWAKE, ye nations, slumbering supine,
Who round enring the European fray!
Heard ye the trumpet sound? "The Day! the Day!
The last that shall on England's empire shine!
The Parliament that broke the Right Divine
Shall see her realm of reason swept away,
The lesser nations shall the sword obey —
The sword o'er all carve the great world's design!"
So on the English Channel boasts the foe
On whose imperial brow death's helmet nods.
Look where his hosts o'er bloody Belgium go,
And mix a nation's past with blazing sods!
A kingdom's waste! a people's homeless woe!
Man's broken Word, and violated gods!

Hearken, the feet of the Destroyer tread
The wine-press of the nations; fast the blood
Pours from the side of Europe; in full flood
On the Septentrional watershed
The rivers of fair France are running red!
England, the mother-eyrie of our brood,
That on the summit of dominion stood,
Shakes in the blast: heaven battles overhead!
Lift up thy head, O Rheims, of ages heir

That treasured up in thee their glorious sum;
Upon whose brow, prophetically fair,
Flamed the great morrow of the world to come;
Haunt with thy beauty this volcanic air
Ere yet thou close, O Flower of Christendom!

As when the shadow of the sun's eclipse
Sweeps on the earth, and spreads a spectral air,
As if the universe were dying there,
On continent and isle the darkness dips,
Unwonted gloom, and on the Atlantic slips;
So in the night the Belgian cities flare
Horizon-wide; the wandering people fare
Along the roads, and load the fleeing ships.
And westward borne that planetary sweep,
Darkening o'er England and her times to be,
Already steps upon the ocean-deep!
Watch well, my country, that unearthly sea,
Lest when thou thinkest not, and in thy sleep,
Unapt for war, that gloom enshadow thee!

George Edward Woodberry

For many years the nations of Europe, urged on by age-old hatreds, had been arming against each other, but it was Germany which finally delivered the attack, and to most Americans it seemed clear that the struggle was one of despotism, as typified by Germany and Austria, against democracy, as typified by France and England.

ABRAHAM LINCOLN WALKS AT MIDNIGHT

[In Springfield, Illinois]

It is portentous, and a thing of state
That here at midnight, in our little town,
A mourning figure walks, and will not rest,
Near the old court-house pacing up and down,

Or by his homestead, or in shadowed yards
He lingers where his children used to play;

Or through the market, on the well-worn stones
He stalks until the dawn-stars burn away.

A bronzed, lank man! His suit of ancient black,
A famous high top-hat and plain worn shawl
Make him the quaint great figure that men love.
The prairie-lawyer, master of us all.

He cannot sleep upon his hillside now.
He is among us: — as in times before!
And we who toss and lie awake for long
Breathe deep, and start, to see him pass the door.

His head is bowed. He thinks on men and kings.
Yea, when the sick world cries, how can he sleep?
Too many peasants fight, they know not why,
Too many homesteads in black terror weep.

The sins of all the war-lords burn his heart.
He sees the dreadnaughts scouring every main.
He carries on his shawl-wrapped shoulders now
The bitterness, the folly and the pain.

He cannot rest until a spirit-dawn
Shall come; — the shining hope of Europe free:
The league of sober folk, the Workers' Earth
Bringing long peace to Cornland, Alp, and Sea.

It breaks his heart that kings must murder still,
That all his hours of travail here for men
Seem yet in vain. And who will bring white peace
That he may sleep upon his hill again?

                              VACHEL LINDSAY

AMERICAN opinion was especially aroused by Germany's cynical dis-
regard of her pledge to respect the neutrality of Belgium, and by her
policy of "frightfulness" on land and sea. Of this America herself

was soon to have a taste, for on February 28, 1915, an American ves-
sel, the William P. Frye, carrying a cargo of wheat from Seattle to
Queenstown, was sunk by a German raider in the South Atlantic.

THE WILLIAM P. FRYE

[February 28, 1915]

I SAW her first abreast the Boston Light
At anchor; she had just come in, turned head,
And sent her hawsers creaking, clattering down.
I was so near to where the hawse-pipes fed
The cable out from her careening bow,
I moved up on the swell, shut steam and lay
Hove to in my old launch to look at her.
She'd come in light, a-skimming up the Bay
Like a white ghost with topsails bellying full;
And all her noble lines from bow to stern
Made music in the wind; it seemed she rode
The morning air like those thin clouds that turn
Into tall ships when sunrise lifts the clouds
From calm sea-courses.

There, in smoke-smudged coats,
Lay funneled liners, dirty fishing craft,
Blunt cargo-luggers, tugs, and ferry-boats.
Oh, it was good in that black-scuttled lot
To see the Frye come lording on her way
Like some old queen that we had half forgot
Come to her own.   A little up the Bay
The Fort lay green, for it was springtime then;
The wind was fresh, rich with the spicy bloom
Of the New England coast that tardily
Escapes, late April, from an icy tomb.
The State-House glittered on old Beacon Hill,
Gold in the sun.... 'Twas all so fair awhile;
But she was fairest — this great square-rigged ship
That had blown in from some far happy isle
Or from the shores of the Hesperides.

They caught her in a South Atlantic road
Becalmed, and found her hold brimmed up with wheat;
"Wheat's contraband," they said, and blew her hull
To pieces, murdered one of our stanch fleet,
Fast dwindling, of the big old sailing ships
That carry trade for us on the high sea
And warped out of each harbor in the States.

It wasn't law, so it seems strange to me —
A big mistake.   Her keel's struck bottom now
And her four masts sunk fathoms, fathoms deep
To Davy Jones.   The dank seaweed will root
On her oozed decks, and the cross-surges sweep
Through the set sails; but never, never more
Her crew will stand away to brace and trim,
Nor sea-blown petrels meet her thrashing up
To windward on the Gulf Stream's stormy rim;
Never again she'll head a no'theast gale,
Or like a spirit loom up, sliding dumb,
And ride in safe beyond the Boston Light,
To make the harbor glad because she's come.
                              JEANNE ROBERT FOSTER

OTHER American ships suffered a similar fate, and the crowning out-
rage came on May 7, 1915, when the great Cunard liner Lusitania
was torpedoed without warning off the coast of Ireland, and 1153
men, women and children drowned.   Of these, 114 were Americans.

THE WHITE SHIPS AND THE RED

[May 7, 1915]

WITH drooping sail and pennant
    That never a wind may reach,
They float in sunless waters
    Beside a sunless beach.
Their mighty masts and funnels
    Are white as driven snow,

And with a pallid radiance
  Their ghostly bulwarks glow.

Here is a Spanish galleon
  That once with gold was gay,
Here is a Roman trireme
  Whose hues outshone the day.
But Tyrian dyes have faded,
  And prows that once were bright
With rainbow stains wear only
  Death's livid, dreadful white.

White as the ice that clove her
  That unforgotten day,
Among her pallid sisters
  The grim Titanic lay.
And through the leagues above her
  She looked aghast, and said:
"What is this living ship that comes
  Where every ship is dead?"

The ghostly vessels trembled
  From ruined stern to prow;
What was this thing of terror
  That broke their vigil now?
Down through the startled ocean
  A mighty vessel came,
Not white, as all dead ships must be,
  But red, like living flame!

The pale green waves about her
  Were swiftly, strangely dyed,
By the great scarlet stream that flowed
  From out her wounded side.
And all her decks were scarlet
  And all her shattered crew.
She sank among the white ghost ships
  And stained them through and through.

The grim Titanic greeted her.
"And who art thou?" she said;
"Why dost thou join our ghostly flee
Arrayed in living red?
We are the ships of sorrow
Who spend the weary night,
Until the dawn of Judgment Day,
Obscure and still and white."

"Nay," said the scarlet visitor,
"Though I sink through the sea,
A ruined thing that was a ship,
I sink not as did ye.
For ye met with your destiny
By storm or rock or fight,
So through the lagging centuries
Ye wear your robes of white.

"But never crashing iceberg
Nor honest shot of foe,
Nor hidden reef has sent me
The way that I must go.
My wound that stains the waters,
My blood that is like flame,
Bear witness to a loathly deed,
A deed without a name.

"I went not forth to battle,
I carried friendly men,
The children played about my decks,
The women sang — and then —
And then — the sun blushed scarlet
And Heaven hid its face,
The world that God created
Became a shameful place!

"My wrong cries out for vengeance,
The blow that sent me here

Was aimed in hell. My dying scream
    Has reached Jehovah's ear.
Not all the seven oceans
    Shall wash away that stain;
Upon a brow that wears a crown
    I am the brand of Cain."

When God's great voice assembles
    The fleet on Judgment Day,
The ghosts of ruined ships will rise
    In sea and strait and bay.
Though they have lain for ages
    Beneath the changeless flood,
They shall be white as silver,
    But one — shall be like blood.

JOYCE KILMER

PRESIDENT WOODROW WILSON warned Germany that the United States would not endure further disregard of her rights as a neutral, but on January 31, 1917, Germany announced that unrestricted submarine warfare against all ships encountered on the sea would begin next day. The German Ambassador was at once handed his passports, and on April 5, after three American ships had been sunk without warning, war against Germany was declared. On June 14, the First Division of American regulars started for France.

THE ROAD TO FRANCE

THANK God our liberating lance
Goes flaming on the way to France!
To France — the trail the Gurkhas found!
To France — old England's rallying ground!
To France — the path the Russians strode!
To France — the Anzac's glory road!
To France — where our Lost Legion ran
To fight and die for God and man!
To France — with every race and breed
That hates Oppression's brutal creed!

Ah, France — how could our hearts forget
The path by which came Lafayette?
How could the haze of doubt hang low
Upon the road of Rochambeau?
At last, thank God!   At last we see
There is no tribal Liberty!
No beacon lighting just our shores!
No Freedom guarding but our doors!
The flame she kindled for our sires
Burns now in Europe's battle fires!
The soul that led our fathers west
Turns back to free the world's oppressed!

Allies, you have not called in vain;
We share your conflict and your pain.
"Old Glory," through new stains and rents,
Partakes of Freedom's sacraments.
Into that hell his will creates
We drive the foe — his lusts, his hates.
Last come, we will be last to stay,
Till Right has had her crowning day.
Replenish, comrades, from our veins,
The blood the sword of despot drains,
And make our eager sacrifice
Part of the freely-rendered price
You pay to lift humanity —
You pay to make our brothers free!
See, with what proud hearts we advance
      To France!

DANIEL HENDERSON

It was a war which appealed deeply to the idealism of the American people.   They felt that they were fighting to sustain those principles. of liberty and equality which the Declaration of Independence had proclaimed to be every man's birthright.

AMERICA RESURGENT

She is risen from the dead!
Loose the tongue and lift the head;
     Let the sons of light rejoice.
She has heard the challenge clear;
She has answered, "I am here";
     She has made the stainless choice.

Bound with iron and with gold —
But her limbs they could not hold
     When the word of words was spoken;
Freedom calls —
The prison walls
     Tumble, and the bolts are broken!

Hail her!   She is ours again —
Hope and heart of harassed men
     And the tryants' doom and terror.
Send abroad the old alarms;
Call to arms, to arms, to arms,
     Hands of doubt and feet of error!

Cheer her!   She is free at last,
With her back upon the past,
     With her foot upon the bars.
Hosts of freedom sorely prest,
Lo, a light is in the West,
     And a helmet full of Stars!

                    Wendell Phillips Stafford

THE whole country was transfigured.   The war was envisaged as a war to end war, and its purpose, in President Wilson's words, "to make the world safe for democracy."

THE NEW CRUSADE

LIFE is a trifle;
Honor is all;
Shoulder the rifle;
Answer the call.
"A nation of traders"!
We'll show what we are,
Freedom's crusaders
Who war against war.

Battle is tragic;
Battle shall cease;
Ours is the magic
Mission of Peace.
Gladly we barter
Gold of our youth
For Liberty's charter
Blood-sealed in truth.

Sons of the granite,
Strong be our stroke,
Making this planet
Safe for all folk.
Life is but passion,
Sunshine on dew.
Forward to fashion
The old world anew!

"A nation of traders"!
We'll show what we are,
Freedom's crusaders
Who war against war.

KATHARINE LEE BATES

CONGRESS passed a bill providing for a selective draft of all men between the ages of twenty-one and thirty, great training-camps were built throughout the country, and by September the training of a National Army of two million men was in full swing. The regular army was already overseas, and the National Guard regiments, which had received some training, were soon on their way to France.

YOUR LAD, AND MY LAD

DOWN toward the deep-blue water, marching to throb of
      drum,
From city street and country lane the lines of khaki come;
The rumbling guns, the sturdy tread, are full of grim appeal,
While rays of western sunshine flash back from burnished
      steel.
With eager eyes and cheeks aflame the serried ranks advance;
And your dear lad, and my dear lad, are on their way to
      France.

A sob clings choking in the throat, as file on file sweep by,
Between those cheering multitudes, to where the great ships
      lie;
The batteries halt, the columns wheel, to clear-toned bugle-
      call,
With shoulders squared and faces front they stand a khaki
      wall.
Tears shine on every watcher's cheek, love speaks in every
      glance;
For your dear lad, and my dear lad, are on their way to
      France.

Before them, through a mist of years, in soldier buff or blue,
Brave comrades from a thousand fields watch now in proud
      review;
The same old Flag, the same old Faith — the Freedom of the
      World —
Spells Duty in those flapping folds above long ranks unfurled.
Strong are the hearts which bear along Democracy's advance,
As your dear lad, and my dear lad, go on their way to France.

The word rings out; a million feet tramp forward on the road,
Along that path of sacrifice o'er which their fathers strode.
With eager eyes and cheeks aflame, with cheers on smiling
      lips,
These fighting men of '17 move onward to their ships.
Nor even love may hold them back, or halt that stern ad-
      vance,
As your dear lad, and my dear lad, go on their way to France.
                                        RANDALL PARRISH

GERMANY had boasted that an American army could never get to
Europe past her submarines, but only one transport was sunk during
the entire war.   Early in February, 1918, the Tuscania, carrying
2179 American soldiers, was torpedoed off the north coast of Ireland.
British destroyers rushed to the scene and rescued all but about two
hundred before the ship sank.   The bodies of nearly all of these were
washed ashore and were tenderly buried.

A CALL TO ARMS

[February 5, 1918]

IT IS I, America, calling!
Above the sound of rivers falling,
Above the whir of the wheels and the chime of bells in the
      steeple
— Wheels, rolling gold into the palms of the people —
Bells ringing silverly clear and slow
To church-going, leisurely steps on pavements below.
Above all familiar sounds of the life of a nation
I shout to you a name.
And the flame of that name is sped
Like fire into hearts where blood runs red —
The hearts of the land burn hot to the land's salvation
As I call across the long miles, as I, America, call to my
      nation
Tuscania! Tuscania!
Americans. remember the Tuscania!

Shall we not remember how they died
In their young courage and loyalty and pride,
Our boys — bright-eyed, clean lads of America's breed,
Hearts of gold, limbs of steel, flower of the nation indeed?
How they tossed their years to be
Into icy waters of a winter sea
That we whom they loved — that the world which they loved
     should be free?
Ready, ungrudging, they died, each one thinking, likely, as
     the moment was come
Of the dear, starry flag, worth dying for, and then of dear
     faces at home;
Going down in good order, with a song on their lips of the
     land of the free and the brave
Till each young, deep voice stopped — under the rush of a
     wave.
Was it like that?   And shall their memory ever grow pale?
Not ever, till the stars in the flag of America fail.
It is I, America, who swear it, calling
Over the sound of that deep ocean's falling,
Tuscania! Tuscania!
Arm, arm, Americans!   Remember the Tuscania!

Very peacefully they are sleeping
In friendly earth, unmindful of a nation's weeping,
And the kindly, strange folk that honored the long, full graves,
     we know;
And the mothers know that their boys are safe, now, from
     the hurts of a savage foe;
It is for us who are left to make sure and plain
That these dead, our precious dead, shall not have died in
     vain;
So that I, America, young and strong and not afraid,
I set my face across that sea which swallowed the bodies of
     the sons I made,
I set my eyes on the still faces of boys washed up on a distant
     shore
And I call with a shout to my own to end this horror forever-
     more!

In the boys' names I call a name,
And the nation leaps to fire in its flame
And my sons and my daughters crowd, eager to end the
　　shame —
It is I, America, calling,
Hoarse with the roar of that ocean falling,
Tuscania! Tuscania!
Arm, arm, Americans! And remember, remember, the
　　Tuscania!

MARY RAYMOND SHIPMAN ANDREWS

MEANWHILE, in France Americans were already taking part in the fighting. About the middle of October, the First Division had been sent to the front in Lorraine, and there, before dawn on the morning of November 3, came a swift German raid in which three Americans were killed. They were buried next day with touching ceremonies.

THE FIRST THREE

[November 3, 1917]

"SOMEWHERE in France," upon a brown hillside,
　　They lie, the first of our brave soldiers slain;
　　Above them flowers, now beaten by the rain,
　　Yet emblematic of the youths who died
　　In their fresh promise. They who, valiant-eyed,
　　Met death unfaltering have not fallen in vain;
　　Remembrance hallows those who thus attain
　　The final goal; their names are glorified.
　　Read then the roster! — Gresham! Enright! Hay! —
　　No bugle call shall rouse them when the flower
　　Of morning breaks above the hills and dells,
　　For they have grown immortal in an hour,
　　And we who grieve and cherish them would lay
　　Upon their hillside graves our immortelles!

CLINTON SCOLLARD

TRAINING proceeded rapidly, and the sectors where its final stages took place became more and more lively as the Americans were gradually given a freer and freer hand.

ROUGE BOUQUET
[March 7, 1918]

IN A wood they call the Rouge Bouquet
There is a new-made grave today,
Build by never a spade nor pick
Yet covered with earth ten meters thick
There lie many fighting men,
    Dead in their youthful prime,
Never to laugh nor love again
    Nor taste the Summertime.
For Death came flying through the air
And stopped his flight at the dugout stair.
Touched his prey and left them there,
    Clay to clay.
He hid their bodies stealthily
In the soil of the land they fought to free
    And fled away.
Now over the grave abrupt and clear
    Three volleys ring;
And perhaps their brave young spirits hear
    The bugle sing:
"Go to sleep!
Go to sleep!
Slumber well where the shell screamed and fell
Let your rifles rest on the muddy floor,
You will not need them any more.
Danger's past;
Now at last,
Go to sleep!"

There is on earth no worthier grave
To hold the bodies of the brave
Than this place of pain and pride
Where they nobly fought and nobly died.

Never fear but in the skies
   Saints and angels stand
Smiling with their holy eyes
   On this new-come band.
St. Michael's sword darts through the air
And touches the aureole on his hair
As he sees them stand saluting there,
   His stalwart sons:
And Patrick, Brigid, Columkill
Rejoice that in veins of warriors still
   The Gael's blood runs.
And up to Heaven's doorway floats,
   From the wood called Rouge Bouquet,
A delicate cloud of bugle notes
   That softly say:
"Farewell!
Farewell!
Comrades true, born anew, peace to you!
Your souls shall be where the heroes are
And your memory shine like the morning-star.
Brave and dear,
Shield us here.
Farewell!"

JOYCE KILMER

THE great summons came in the spring of 1918, for on March 21, the Germans began a series of terrific attacks which sent the French and British reeling back upon Paris. On March 31, an official order announced that "The Star-Spangled Banner will float beside the French and English flags in the plains of Picardy." On April 17, the order came for the First Division to move into the battle area.

MARCHING SONG

[April 17, 1918]

WHEN Pershing's men go marching into Picardy.
Marching, marching into Picardy —

With their steel aslant in the sunlight and their great gray
    hawks a-wing
And their wagons rumbling after them like thunder in the
    Spring —

    Tramp, tramp, tramp, tramp,
      Till the earth is shaken —
    Tramp, tramp, tramp, tramp,
      Till the dead towns waken!
And flowers fall and shouts arise from Chaumont to the sea —
When Pershing's men go marching, marching into Picardy.

Women of France, do you see them pass to the battle in the
    North?
And do you stand in the doorways now as when your own
    went forth?
Then smile to them and call to them, and mark how brave
    they fare
Upon the road to Picardy that only youth may dare!

    Tramp, tramp, tramp, tramp,
      Foot and horse and caisson —
    Tramp, tramp, tramp, tramp,
      Such is Freedom's passion —
And oh, take heart, ye weary souls that stand along the Lys,
For the New World is marching, marching into Picardy!

April's sun is in the sky and April's in the grass —
And I doubt not that Pershing's men are singing as they
    pass —
For they are very young men, and brave men, and free,
And they know why they are marching, marching into
    Picardy.

    Tramp, tramp, tramp, tramp,
      Rank and file together —
    Tramp, tramp, tramp, tramp,
      Through the April weather.

And never Spring has thrust such blades against the light
    of dawn.
As yonder waving stalks of steel that move so shining on!

I have seen the wooden crosses at Ypres and Verdun,
I have marked the graves of such as lie where the Marne
    waters run,
And I know their dust is stirring by hill and vale and lea,
And their souls shall be our captains who march to Picardy.

        Tramp, tramp, tramp, tramp,
          Hope shall fail us never —
        Tramp, tramp, tramp, tramp,
          Forward, and forever!
And God is in His judgment seat, and Christ is on His
    tree —
And Pershing's men are marching, marching into Picardy.
                       DANA BURNET

IN LATE September, the American army began its greatest battle in
an attack on the well-nigh impregnable German positions in the
Argonne Forest, which neither the French nor the British had ever
tried to capture. The struggle was a terrible one, lasting for nearly
two months, and the American losses were very heavy. But every
day the line was advanced a little nearer to the railways back of the
German positions, upon which their whole front depended.

ON AN AMERICAN SOLDIER OF FORTUNE
SLAIN IN FRANCE

    You, who sought the great adventure
      That the blind fates held in store,
  Have beyond our mortal censure
      Passed forever, evermore;
  Passed beyond all joy or sighing,
      Blush of eve or flush of dawn,
  Who beneath the sod are lying
      In the Forest of Argonne.

What it was that lured and led you
   Who shall venture, who shall say?
From the valley of the dead you
   Speak not, question as we may;
Yet somehow our thoughts have flowed to
   The remembrance of the debt.
That our land had so long owed to
   Rochambeau and Lafayette.

You, bereft of earthly raiment,
   Brave as they and theirs were brave,
Have made sacrificial payment
   For whate'er their valor gave.
As they came, with aid unsparing,
   When both fears and foes were rife,
So you went with dreams of daring
   And the offering of your life.

We, who cling to freedom, hail you,
   Son of never vanquished sires,
Knowing courage did not fail you
   When you faced the battle fires;
Knowing that no vaunt of Vandal
   Daunted your determined aim,
Though your breath failed as a candle
   'Neath a flash of morning flame.

All the brown Atlantic beaches
   From far Fundy to the Keys,
All the billowy prairie reaches
   Sweeping westward toward the seas,
Mount Katahdin and Mount Rainier,
   Lake and river great of girth,
Greet your spirit, bold disdainer
   Of the tyrannies of earth!

Thrones shall crumble, kings shall perish,
   Howsoe'er their legions strive,

But the liberties men cherish,
　　They shall triumph and survive.
You, blithe wraith, shall be beholder
　　Of the flowering of that dawn,
Though your pulseless clay may moulder
　　In the Forest of Argonne!

CLINTON SCOLLARD

IT WAS during this battle, that perhaps the most remarkable single exploit of the war was performed.   Corporal Alvin C. York, a young giant from the mountains of Tennessee, was sent forward with a small squad to clean up some machine-gun nests, killed single-handed twenty-eight Germans and came back with one hundred and thirty-two prisoners.

A BALLAD OF REDHEAD'S DAY

[October 8, 1918]

TALK of the Greeks at Thermopylæ!
　　They fought like mad till the last was dead;
But Alvin C. York, of Tennessee,
　　Stayed cool to the end though his hair was red,
Stayed mountain cool, yet blazed that gray
October the Eighth as Redhead's Day.

With rifle and pistol and redhead nerve
　　He captured one hundred and thirty-two;
A battalion against him, he did not swerve
　　From the Titans' task they were sent to do —
Fourteen men under Sergeant Early
And York, the blacksmith, big and burly.

Sixteen only, but fighters all,
　　They dared the brood of a devil's nest,
And three of those that did not fall
　　Were wounded and out of the scrap; the rest
Were guarding a bunch of Boche they'd caught,
When both were trapped by a fresh onslaught.

Excepting York, who smiled "Amen,"
   And, spotting the nests of spitting guns,
Potted some twenty birds, and then
   Did with his pistol for eight more Huns
Who thought they could crush a Yankee alive
In each red pound of two hundred and five.

That was enough for kill-babe Fritz:
   Ninety in all threw up their hands,
Suddenly tender as lamb at the Ritz,
   Milder than sheep to a York's commands;
And back to his line he drove the herd,
Gathering more on the way — Absurd!

Absurd, but true — ay, gospel fact;
   For here was a man with a level head,
Who, scorning to fail for the help he lacked,
   Helped himself till he won instead;
An elder was he in the Church of Christ,
Immortal at thirty; his faith sufficed.

RICHARD BUTLER GLAENZER

WHILE the Argonne offensive was in progress, the French and British
had been striking mighty blows at other portions of the German line.
To save themselves from imminent disaster, the Germans asked for
an armistice. It was offered on terms so drastic that many thought
they would not sign, but they did, and at eleven o'clock on the morn-
ing of November 11, 1918, firing ceased all along the front. The war
was won.

VICTORY BELLS

I HEARD the bells across the trees,
I heard them ride the plunging breeze
Above the roofs from tower and spire,
And they were leaping like a fire,
And they were shining like a stream
With sun to make its music gleam.

Deep tones as though the thunder tolled,
Cool voices thin as tinkling gold,
They shook the spangled autumn down
From out the tree-tops of the town;
They left great furrows in the air
And made a clangor everywhere
As of metallic wings.   They flew
Aloft in spirals to the blue
Tall tent of heaven and disappeared.
And others, swift as though they feared
The people might not heed their cry
Went shouting VICTORY up the sky.
They did not say that war is done,
Only that glory has begun
Like sunrise, and the coming day
Will burn the clouds of war away.
There will be time for dreams again,
And home-coming for weary men.

GRACE HAZARD CONKLING

AMERICA had lost nearly fifty thousand men killed in battle.   Some
were brought back to their little home burial-grounds.   The others
were gathered together in beautiful cemeteries in France, where their
graves would be reverently cared for.

OUR DEAD, OVERSEAS

IN ITALY, in Belgium, in France,
They sleep ensphered in glorious circumstance.

With high heroic heart
They did their valiant part.
They gave the flower-like glory of their youth
To lie in heaps abhorrent and uncouth.
For us they gave their life to its last breath —
For us they plunged on into the gulf of death.
They turned from these bright skies
To lie with dust and silence on their eyes.

Yet they have wages that we know not of —
Wages of honor and immortal love.
For they went down only to live again
In the eternal memory of men —
To be warm pulse-beats in the greatening soul
That drives the blind world onward to her goal.
They are not dead: life's flag is never furled:
They passed from world to world.
Their bodies sleep; but in some nobler land
Their spirits march under a new command;
New joys await them there
In hero heavens wrapt in immortal air.

Rejoice for them, rejoice:
They made the nobler choice.
How shall we honor their deed —
How speak our praise of this immortal breed?
Only by living nobly, as they died —
Toiling for truth denied,
Loyal to something bigger than we are —
Something that swings the spirit to a star.

EDWIN MARKHAM

THE great task of bringing home the American troops began immediately, and they were soon landing, division after division. America went wild welcoming them.

AMERICA'S WELCOME HOME

OH, GALLANTLY they fared forth in khaki and in blue,
America's crusading host of warriors bold and true;
They battled for the rights of men beside our brave Allies,
And now they're coming home to us with glory in their eyes.

Oh, it's home again, and home again, America for me!
Our hearts are turning home again and there we long to be,
In our beautiful big country beyond the ocean bars,
Where the air is full of sunlight and the flag is full of stars.

They bore our country's great word across the rolling sea,
"America swears brotherhood with all the just and free."
They wrote that word victorious on fields of mortal strife,
And many a valiant lad was proud to seal it with his life.

Oh, welcome home in Heaven's peace, dear spirits of the dead!
And welcome home ye living sons America hath bred!
The lords of war are beaten down, your glorious task is
    done;
You fought to make the whole world free, and the victory is
    won.

Now it's home again, and home again, our hearts are
        turning west,
Of all the lands beneath the sun America is best.
We're going home to our own folks, beyond the ocean bars,
Where the air is full of sunlight and the flag is full of stars.
                                    HENRY VAN DYKE

MEANWHILE, in Paris, President Wilson was hammering out the
peace terms with the ministers of the Allied Powers. He had sworn
that this should be a war to end war, and the American people had
listened and believed, but he found himself confronted by the most
astute and cynical diplomats of Europe, intent only on plundering
the enemy.

PEACE

THE cannon's voice is dumb,
The sword is sheathed again,
Homeward our legions come —
Is it peace for the sons of men?

Peace for the troubled earth
And the host of those that lie
In the lands that gave them birth
Or beneath a stranger sky?

Shall children laugh for aye
And the sound of weeping cease
At the call of those who cry
Peace — when there is no peace?

Peace? What is peace but a name
For the war that shall not end
While souls are wrought in flame
High heaven to defend? —

Peace is a living sword
Forged for the hand of man
At the smithy of the Lord
In the halls where life began.

Peace is a challenge blown
In the trumpet of the wind —
Till the stars are overthrown
Lift up your eyes, O blind!

And with your eyes mark well
God's banners swinging clear.
What do these banners tell?
To arms! For peace is here!
                    HAROLD TROWBRIDGE PULSIFER

PRESIDENT WILSON announced that America sought no indemnity
nor any territory; that she wanted only a just peace, which must
provide for the creation of a League of Nations to render future wars
impossible.

THE LEAGUE OF NATIONS

Lo, JOSEPH dreams his dream again,
And Joan leads her armies in the night,
And somewhere, the Master from His cross
Lifts his hurt hands and heals the world again!
For from the great red welter of the world,

Out from the tides of its red suffering
Comes the slow sunrise of the ancient dream —
Is flung the glory of its bright imaging.
See how it breaks in beauty on the world,
Shivers and shudders on its trembling way —
Shivers and waits and trembles to be born!

America, young daughter of the gods, swing out,
Strong in the beauty of virginity,
Fearless in thine unquestioned leadership,
And hold the taper to the nations' torch,
And light the hearthfires of the halls of home.
Thine must it be to break an unpathed way,
To life the torch for world's in-brothering —
To bring to birth this child of all the earth,
Formed of the marriage of all nations;
Else shall we go, the head upon the breast,
A Cain without a country, a Judas at the board!

MARY SIEGRIST

AFTER months of bitter controversy, President Wilson compelled
agreement to his plan for a League of Nations, but the treaty itself
took from Germany all her colonies, and imposed reparations so
enormous that they meant economic slavery for a century.

ARMISTICE DAY

I THINK I hear them stirring there today
Who have lain still
So long, so long beside the Aisne and Aire
On Verdun hill.

I think I hear them whispering today,
The young, the brave,
The gallant and the gay — unmurmuring long
There in the grave.

I think I hear them sighing there today,
    They sigh for all
The glory and the wonder that was life
    Beyond recall.

I think that their young eyes are wistfully
    On us who go
So gayly to our sports this holiday —
    I think they know!

I think that they are listening today....
    I feel them near!
Our orators declaim — they answer back,
    "Why lie we here?"

Across the fleet, forgetting years it comes
    Today, their cry,
"O world, O world, if it was all in vain,
    Why did we die?"

Above the earth's enduring hates they ask,
    "Was it for this?"
I think they are remembering this day
    Of Armistice.

And oh, I think I hear them weeping there
    Who should be sleeping....
A plaintive thing — to hear across the world,
    The young dead weeping!
            ROSELLE MERCIER MONTGOMERY

AMERICA began to realize that she had fought in vain; the world had not been made safe for democracy; and European hatreds, deeper than ever, were already preparing for another war.

LINES FOR THE HOUR

IF WHAT we fought for seems not worth the fighting,
    And if to win seems in the end to fail,

Know that the vision lives beyond all blighting
And every struggle rends another veil.

The tired hack, the cynic politician,
  Can dim, but cannot make us lose the goal,
Time moves with measured step upon her mission,
  Knowing the slow mutations of the soul.
                    HAMILTON FISH ARMSTRONG

So IN the end, America refused to ratify the treaty or to enter the
League of Nations, and made a separate peace with Germany.   She
had come to realize not only that the rôle of crusader is a thankless
one, but that every nation must in the end work out its own destiny.

"SEPARATE PEACE"

HAVE we, then, lost the war,
The valor, ardor; lost the noble deaths
Of them that gave their slender store,
Their loves, their passions, even their mortal breaths
  For what we hope to be, for what we are?

Have we then lost — forgot
The deeps of comfort in a duty done;
Duty transfiguring, tho' repaying not;
And of all duties this the imperious one?
  Is this to be our lot?

Ah, no, the soul that sweeps
A radiance from the onward-rolling dawn
Returns not ever to the sunless deeps,
But like a summit in the evening, keeps
  The glow of what has gone.
                    HARRISON S. MORRIS

On Armistice Day, November 11, 1921, the body of an American Unknown Soldier, brought from the battle-fields of France, was laid to rest at Arlington National Cemetery, on the Virginia hills overlooking Washington.

THE PASSING OF THE UNKNOWN SOLDIER

They are bearing him home through the old Virginia valley,
  Home to a hill where a Nation's heroes sleep;
Hushed are the hosts that honor his silent passing.
  Hushed is their grief and deep.
Lower him tenderly; vex not his gentle dreaming;
  Pillow his head on the kindly loam of France.
So shall his sleep be the sweeter, feeling thy nearness,
  Land of the Great Romance.

Souls of the mighty fallen stand at attention,
  Sheridan riding his shadowy steed of fame;
Heroes of Gettysburg, Shiloh, and grim Shenandoah,
  Scorched in the battle flame;
A hundred score of lads whose bodies were taken
  Maimed from the fields where the red Rappahannock runs;
Nameless as he, yet honored as he is honored;
  All of them Mothers' Sons!

He is the youth of America, taken untimely;
  Symbol of countless thousands who perished young;
Sinew and bone of a Nation, crushed in the making;
  The poet, his song half sung.
You, who dwell in a liberty bought by his passing,
  It is your Son, your Brother is buried here.
Pause for a moment, forgetting the day's occupation,
  Offer a prayer — a tear.

Vilda Sauvage Owens

So America gained a new shrine, which serves to recall the high ardors, the noble purpose, the singing spirit of the war years — and of these she can always think with pride.

AFTER THE WAR

After the war — I hear men ask — what then?
As though this rock-ribbed world, sculptured with fire,
And bastioned deep in the ethereal plan,
Can never be its morning self again
Because of this brief madness, man with man;
As though the laughing elements should tire,
The very seasons in their order reel;
As though indeed yon ghostly golden wheel
Of stars should cease from turning, or the moon
Befriend the night no more, or the wild rose
Forget the world, and June be no more June.

How many wars and long-forgotten woes
Unnumbered, nameless, made a like despair
In hearts long stilled; how many suns have set
On burning cities blackening the air, —
Yet dawn came dreaming back, her lashes wet
With dew, and daisies in her innocent hair.
Nor shall, for this, the soul's ascension pause,
Nor the sure evolution of the laws
That out of foulness lift the flower to sun,
And out of fury forge the evening star.

Deem not Love's building of the world undone —
Far Love's beginning was, her end is far;
By paths of fire and blood her feet must climb,
Seeking a loveliness she scarcely knows,
Whose meaning is beyond the reach of Time.

RICHARD LE GALLIENNE

She can be proud, too, of her brave inheritance, and of the ideals which have made her what she is, and which perhaps, some day, the other nations of the world may understand and share.

WHAT DOES IT MEAN TO BE AMERICAN?

What does it mean?   I look across the years....
I see them come, but through a mist of tears,
Our gallant forebears, full of hopes and fears.

I see them leave behind for conscience' sake,
The homes they loved, the ties so hard to break,
Their questing, wondering, westward way to take

I see them face and fight the wilderness,
Undaunted by its dangers, its duress,
And from its wildness, wrest and win success

I see them take their living from the soil,
The men and women joined in homely toil —
Where they then planted, now our heart-roots coil.

I see them build their homes, their house of prayer,
And when its bell rings out upon the air,
I see them kneel in simple worship there.

I hear the drums of war's alarum beat,
I see them seize their arms, rise to their feet
Their enemies — and liberty's — to meet.

I see them face and conquer every foe,
I see their cities rise, a nation grow,
To whose broad breast earth's eager pilgrims go.

To be American is to be one
In whom these brave inheritances run,
A worthy daughter, or a noble son....
                    Roselle Mercier Montgomery

MEANWHILE, she faces the future unafraid, confident of her destiny, and determined that "government of the people, by the people, for the people, shall not perish from the earth."

THE REPUBLIC

[From "The Building of the Ship"]

THOU, too, sail on, O Ship of State!
Sail on, O Union, strong and great!
Humanity with all its fears,
With all the hopes of future years,
Is hanging breathless on thy fate!
We know what Master laid thy keel,
What Workmen wrought thy ribs of steel,
Who made each mast, and sail, and rope,
What anvils rang, what hammers beat,
In what a forge and what a heat
Were shaped the anchors of thy hope!
Fear not each sudden sound and shock,
'Tis of the wave and not the rock;
'Tis but the flapping of the sail,
And not a rent made by the gale!
In spite of rock and tempest's roar,
In spite of false lights on the shore,
Sail on, nor fear to breast the sea!
Our hearts, our hopes, are all with thee,
Our hearts, our hopes, our prayers, our tears,
Our faith triumphant o'er our fears,
Are all with thee — are all with thee!

HENRY WADSWORTH LONGFELLOW

NOTES

NOTES

Page ii. AMERICA. This famous hymn was written in 1832, and was first sung publicly at a Sabbath school celebration at Park Street Church, Boston, July 4, 1832. The melody to which it has been set is the same as that of the British national anthem, "God Save the King," and is supposed to have been written by Henry Carey, an English song writer who died in 1743. Its author, Samuel Francis Smith, was a clergyman, and a member of the class of 1829 at Harvard, of which Dr. Oliver Wendell Holmes was also a member. At the class dinner of 1859, Dr. Holmes, as usual, recited a poem, and coined an epigram which has since become famous:

> And there's a nice youngster of excellent pith —
> Fate tried to conceal him by naming him Smith;
> But he shouted a song for the brave and the free —
> Just read on his medal, "My country," "of thee."

"America" is often referred to as the American national anthem, but this is not the case. "The Star-Spangled Banner" is used by both army and navy on all official occasions. It, too, strangely enough, has been set to a British air.

Page 4. *The Inquisition's mystic doom.* It was, of course, a serious question whether Columbus's great idea did not involve heresy, since it assumed that the earth was round — an assumption entirely at variance with the teachings of the Church.

Page 7. *The Gates of Hercules.* Gibraltar on the north and Cape Serra on the south, guarding the entrance to the Mediterranean, were called by the ancients the Pillars of Hercules, and were supposed to have been placed there by Hercules to mark the westward limit of his wanderings.

Page 9. *Viceroy they made him.* The stipulations for rewards and honors which had been made by Columbus were anything but modest, and for a time threatened to wreck the enterprise. He demanded that he be made Admiral of the Ocean Seas, Viceroy and Governor-General of all the lands he might discover, that he be given a tenth part of the profits resulting from such discoveries in perpetuity, and that all his heirs and descendants for ever were to possess the same privileges. Small wonder that Ferdinand hesitated, and that the nobles of his court resented the ambitions of this Italian upstart. But Columbus stood firm, and finally the king agreed.

Page 12. *As far back as Ptolemy.* Ptolemy was a celebrated astronomer of Alexandria, Egypt, of the first half of the second century, who believed that the earth was round, and that the sun and the planets revolved about it. He did not suspect the existence of the American continent, however, and calculated the circumference of the globe at about a third less than it actually is. Columbus was familiar with this estimate, and the error, which brought the east coast of Asia eight thousand miles nearer the western coast of Europe than is really the case, encouraged him to undertake the voyage which led to the discovery of America. If Ptolemy had computed the distance correctly, Columbus would never have dared attempt to cover it.

Page 14. THE FIRST VOYAGE OF JOHN CABOT. Cabot probably landed on what is now Cape Breton Island. Upon his return to England, Henry VII, being a frugal monarch, is said to have rewarded him for his discoveries with a gift of £10 — about fifty dollars. Cabot made two other voyages, in 1498 and 1499, and then disappears from history.

Page 14. *His swarthy sons beside him.* The most famous of them was Sebastian Cabot (1474–1557), who was afterwards Pilot-Major to Emperor Charles V of Spain, and who published an engraved map of the world in 1544.

Page 14. *Henry on his battle-wrested throne.* Henry VII had gained the English crown by defeating and slaying Richard III at Bosworth in 1485.

Page 15. SIR HUMPHREY GILBERT (1539–1583) was a step-brother of Sir Walter Raleigh, and this was his first important voyage.

Page 15. *Lo not fear.* The last words Sir Humphrey Gilbert is known to have spoken were the famous, "We are as near to heaven by sea as by land." They are said to have been heard on board the companion ship, the Hind, just before Gilber 's ship, the Squirrel, disappeared.

Page 16. *The fleet of Death.* Gilbert's ship is supposed to have been overwhelmed by icebergs.

Page 17. *St. George's ensign.* St. George was a Christian martyr who died in A.D. 303, and in the fourteenth century was adopted as the patron saint of England. The British flag showed the red cross of St. George on a white field. It was afterwards combined with the white cross of St. Andrew, the Scottish emblem, and the green cross of St. Patrick, the Irish emblem, into the Union Jack.

Page 17. *As e'er upon Arcadian lake were cast.* Arcadia was a district in Greece whose inhabitants were a simple, pastoral people; hence, any idyllic country.

Page 18. *Pocahontas.* This fanciful tale, from which all other narratives of the event are derived, appeared in the second chapter of the third book of Smith's *The Generall Historie of Virginia, New England, and the Summer Isles*, published at London in 1622.

Page 18. *Now they heap the funeral pyre.* This is merely Thackeray's imagination. Smith said nothing about either fire or stake.

Page 20. THE MARRIAGE OF POCAHONTAS. A contemporary account asserted that Rolfe married Pocahontas in spite of personal scruples and "for the good of the colony." Poets and romancers prefer to believe that he was captivated by her grace and beauty.

Page 21. THE LAST MEETING OF POCAHONTAS AND THE GREAT CAPTAIN. A reference to this meeting may be found in Smith's *True Relation of Virginia.*

Page 22. *Sparkling Water.* The English meaning of Pocahontas.

Page 24. *When Eolus scowls.* Eolus, the god of the winds.

Page 26. HENRY HUDSON'S QUEST. Hudson was an Englishman, who had taken employment with the Dutch, and on this voyage he demonstrated that there was no strait across North America. In 1610, he tried again, farther to the north, reached Hudson Strait and was caught in the ice in James's Bay. Here his men mutinied and set him and his son adrift in a small boat. They were never seen again.

Page 27. *An arm of sand.* Sandy Hook.

Page 27. *Onward they glide.* The Half Moon ascended the Hudson to the point where Albany now stands before her captain was convinced that the quest was fruitless.

Page 28. THE WORD OF GOD TO LEYDEN CAME. The Separatist congregation from the little town of Scrooby, about a hundred in number, in order to escape religious persecution, had fled from England to Amsterdam, and finally, in 1609, had settled at Leyden.

Page 29. *We leave Old England's shores behind.* There were originally two ships in the expedition, the Mayflower, carrying ninety persons, and a smaller vessel, the Speedwell, carrying thirty. They sailed together from Southampton August 15, but the Speedwell proved unseaworthy, and after twice putting back for repairs, twelve of her passengers were crowded on board the Mayflower, which finally got away on September 16. Note should be taken that this is the date according to the modern calendar. The Old Style date was September 6, and this is sometimes used, but the dates given throughout this book are New Style. Only about a third of the persons on the Mayflower were Pilgrims, the remainder being a nondescript collection of settlers, mostly from London.

Page 31. LANDING OF THE PILGRIM FATHERS. The Northern or Plymouth Branch of the Virginia Company, which had been chartered by James I in 1606, did, to some extent, for the north what its sister company did for the south. Sir Ferdinando Gorges was its Raleigh, and sent out a number of exploring ships, one of which made what is now reckoned the first permanent settlement in New England. Captain George Popham was in command, and in August, 1607, three months after the planting of Jamestown, built Fort Popham (afterwards Fort St. George), at the mouth of the Kennebec River.

Page 31. *On the stern and rock-bound coast.* Mrs. Hemans had never seen the coast where the Pilgrims landed, and this is merely her idea of what was fitting to the occasion. The coast is really low and sandy.

Page 32. *"Ho, Rose!" quoth the stout Miles Standish.* Myles Standish (1584–1656), was military captain of the colony, and did much to insure its success by keeping the Indians overawed with military display and the clank of arms. Rose Standish, his wife, lived only a little more than two months after that first washing-day, dying January 29, 1621. His unsuccessful courtship by proxy of the "Puritan maiden Priscilla," is the subject of one of Longfellow's most popular poems, which contains the famous line:

Why don't you speak for yourself, John?

Standish afterwards married his first wife's kinswoman, Barbara.

Page 33. *Bartholomew Gosnold's "headlands."* Gosnold commanded an expedition which, in 1602, discovered Cape Cod and Martha's Vineyard, both of which were named by him.

Page 35. *But Carver leads.* John Carver (1575?–1621), the leader of the Pilgrims, chosen governor of the colony in 1620; made a treaty with Massasoit, Chief of the Wampanoag Indians in March, 1621, which continued in force unbroken for fifty-four years; died a few months later as the result of sunstroke.

Page 37. *And therefore I, William Bradford.* William Bradford (1590–1657) was chosen governor of Plymouth in 1621, to succeed John Carver, and was reëlected every year, except for two short intervals at his own request, until his death.

Page 37. *And unto our feast the Sachem.* The Sachem was Massasoit, and he brought ninety of his warriors with him, and also five deer as their contribution to the larder.

Page 38. *To listen to Elder Brewster.* William Brewster (1560?–1644), the colony's teacher and preacher.

Page 40. *Bradford of Austerfield.* William Bradford was born at Austerfield, in Yorkshire, England.

Page 42. *When Winthrop's fleet from Yarmouth crept.* Charles I had come to the throne in 1625, with the expressed determination to harry the Puritans out of England, but when, in 1628, he confirmed the patent for a trading company which had been secured by John Endicott and a few others from the New England Council, he little suspected that he was providing them with an asylum. Such, however, was the case. No place had been stipulated for the meetings of the company by the royal charter to "The Governor and Company of the Massachusetts-Bay in New England," and the audacious plan was formed to remove the company, patents, charter and all, to New England. Secret meetings were held, the old officers got rid of, John Winthrop elected governor, and the transfer successfully made. Winthrop (1588–1649) left a manuscript Journal which was published in 1825, and which forms the most important source for all subsequent histories of New England.

Page 48. *The Bourbon's lilied blue.* The French flag showed three golden fleurs-de-lis, or lilies, on a blue or azure ground.

Page 48. *That was a brave old governor.* Peter Schuyler (1657–1724), first mayor of Albany, and for a year acting governor of New York.

Page 52. A BALLAD OF THE FRENCH FLEET. Rev. Thomas Prince was the pastor of the Old South Meeting House, in Boston in 1746, and Mr. Longfellow's poem is based upon a passage in Hutchinson's history. The poem was written at the suggestion of Dr. Edward Everett Hale, when efforts were being made to save the old church from destruction.

Page 54. THE SONG OF BRADDOCK'S MEN. This spirited song was written by an unknown rhymester in Braddock's army while on the march in the early summer of 1755. It shows how confident the army was of victory.

Page 54. *Brave Braddock leads the foremost.* Major General Edward

Braddock (1695-1755) was a gallant and experienced soldier, but his experience had been on the battle-fields of Europe, where war was conducted according to certain set and very ceremonious rules. He had been with the Coldstream Guards at Fontenoy, where, according to tradition, the French Guards were invited to fire first and had responded with the famous, "The French Guard never fires first!"

Page 55. *Who's your bold Berserker.* A Berserker was a wild warrior of heathen times in Scandinavia, and is applied to any extremely violent person.

Page 56. *Beaujeu and Pontiac.* Captain Beaujeu was the young Frenchman in charge of the assaulting party, the Indian detachment of which was led by the famous chief, Pontiac.

Page 57. *The war-songs of Rollo.* Rollo, a Norwegian Viking, born about 860, who, in 912, wrested Normandy from the French king.

Page 57. *Their fortalice proud.* The reference is to the old stone tower at Newport, R. I., which is really not of Norse origin, but probably the remains of a windmill built about 1676.

Page 57. *Came Robert of Jamestown.* Rev. Robert Hunt, the brave clergyman of the Jamestown colony, to whom, according to Captain John Smith's testimony, the colony owed everything.

Page 57. *To wed sweet Matoäka.* Matoäka was another name of Pocahontas.

Page 58. *The old lion.* England. The English arms show a lion and a unicorn.

Page 61. *Since Hebe served with nectar.* Hebe, in Greek mythology, was the cup-bearer of the gods.

Page 63. *Whig and Tory.* Tory was the name applied to Americans who supported the British. In British politics the Tories were the conservatives, supporting the old order and the power of the throne, especially in the reign of George III, while the Whigs were the liberals and progressives.

Page 63. *The rocky nook with hill-tops three.* The name first given to Boston was Tri-Mountain, because of the three hills upon and around which it is built — Beacon Hill, Fort Hill, and Copp's Hill. The name was changed to Boston in honor of the town in Lincolnshire, England, from which many of the settlers came.

Page 64. *Millions for self-government.* "Millions for defense, but not one cent for tribute," has been attributed erroneously to Charles C. Pinckney, Ambassador to France in 1796, when Talleyrand, the French Minister of Foreign Affairs, and the French Directory demanded an enormous bribe before receiving him as the representative of an independent power. It was really used by Robert Goodloe Harper, a member of Congress from South Carolina, in responding to a toast at a dinner given in honor of John Marshall upon his return from a mission to France in 1798. (See Beveridge, *Life of John Marshall*, II, 349.) This was twenty-five years after the Boston tea-party — but the spirit existed at that time, even if the phrase did not!

Page 65 *He told Lord North.* Lord Frederick North, First Lord of the Treasury under George III, a determined enemy of American independence.

Page 67. *Bound all the Old Thirteen.* The original thirteen colonies.

Page 67. LIBERTY TREE. On August 14, 1765, an effigy representing Andrew Oliver, distributer of stamps for Boston, was found hanging from a tree opposite the Boylston Market. A mob gathered when the sheriff tried to take down the effigy, the stamp office was demolished and Oliver was compelled to go to the tree and resign his commission. It was thenceforward called the Liberty Tree, and Liberty Trees were afterwards consecrated with various ceremonies in many other New England towns.

Page 69. PAUL REVERE'S RIDE. The publication of Mr. Longfellow's poem evoked a long controversy as to the accuracy of its details. It was probably based upon Revere's own account of the adventure in a letter to Dr. Jeremy Belknap. Paul Revere (1735–1818) was a goldsmith and engraver on silver. After the war he established a foundry to cast church-bells and cannon. He had a companion on that historic April night whom history has entirely lost sight of, for at the same time that Revere started by way of Charlestown to give the alarm, William Dawes was dispatched by way of Roxbury, Warren wishing to be sure that at least one messenger would get through. As it happened, they both got through, and Dawes played an important part in the events which followed. Dawes (1745–1799) was a tanner by trade, and prominent in anti-British agitation at Boston.

WHAT'S IN A NAME?

I am a wandering, bitter shade;
Never of me was a hero made;
Poets have never sung my praise,
Nobody crowned my brow with bays;
And if you ask me the fatal cause,
I answer only, "My name was Dawes."

'Tis all very well for the children to hear
Of the midnight ride of Paul Revere;
But why should my name be quite forgot,
Who rode as boldly and well, God wot?
Why should I ask? The reason is clear —
My name was Dawes and his Revere....

History rings with his silvery name;
Closed to me are the portals of fame.
Had he been Dawes and I Revere,
No one had heard of him, I fear.
No one has heard of me because
He was Revere and I was Dawes.

HELEN F. MORE.

Page 69. *He said to his friend.* There has always been disagreement both as to the identity of the friend and as to the church from whose tower the signals were hung.

Page 72. *It was one by the village clock.* Lexington is eleven miles north-west of Boston, and Concord seventeen miles.

Page 76. *Of man for man the sacrifice.* The British lost 65 killed, 180 wounded, 28 captured; the Americans lost 59 killed, 39 wounded, 5 missing.

Page 77. CONCORD HYMN. The first stanza of this poem is inscribed on the Battle Monument at Concord. Emerson's grandfather, William Emerson, was minister at Concord in 1775, and from his pulpit had strongly advocated resistance to the British. When the day of trial came, he took his place among the "embattled farmers," and urged them to stand their ground.

Page 79. *Stalwart Ethan Allen.* Ethan Allen (1737–1789), who had moved to Bennington, Vermont, from Connecticut, was made colonel of an armed force known as the "Green Mountain Boys," organized to fight not the British but the New York authorities, who were trying to drive the holders of land in Vermont from their farms, which were claimed by New York. Governor Tryon, of New York, declared him an outlaw, but after the war started, his regiment was incorporated in the American army.

Page 80. *The fort of Chiming Rills.* Ticonderoga was at first called Carillon.

Page 80. *Like the "going" in the mulberry trees that once King David heard.* "And when David inquired of the Lord, he said,... And let it be, when thou hearest the sound of a going in the tops of the mulberry trees, that then thou shalt bestir thyself: for then shall the Lord go out before thee, to smite the host of the Philistines." — II Samuel, v, 23–24.

Page 81. *In the name of the great Jehovah and the Continental Congress!* Legend has it that these words were really uttered by Allen upon this occasion, but historians are skeptical.

Page 82. *Yankee Doodle.* Accounts of the origin of "Yankee Doodle" are many and various. The air is very old, and nearly every country in Europe claims it. In the days of Charles I it was used in England for some verses beginning:

> Lydia Lockett lost her pocket,
> Kittie Fisher found it.

Afterwards, when Cromwell rode into Oxford on a pony, with his single plume fashioned into a sort of knot called a "macaroni," the Cavaliers used the same air for their derisive verses. The story goes that this fact was recalled by Dr. Richard Shuckburg, of the Seventeenth Foot, when the queerly garbed provincial levies presented themselves, in June, 1755, at the British camp at Albany, to take part in the campaign against the French. He wrote down the notes of the air and got the regimental band to play it. It was taken up by the Americans and became instantly popular. Verses innumerable were attached to it, the best known of which are "The Yankee's Return from Camp" and "The Battle of the Kegs."

Page 83. *Edward Bangs.* This is upon the authority of Dr. Edward Everett Hale, who states that "an autograph note of Judge Dawes, of the Harvard class of 1777, addressed to my father, says that the author of the well-known lines was Edward Bangs, who graduated with him. Mr. Bangs had, as a college boy, joined the Middlesex farmers in the pursuit of April 19, 1775. He was afterwards a judge in Worcester county."

Page 85. *Warren's Address.* For his bravery at Lexington, Dr. Joseph Warren had been made major-general of the Massachusetts troops, and was serving at Bunker Hill as a volunteer.

Page 85. *Fear ye foes who kill for hire?* The reference is to the "Hessians," hired by the British Government from the Duke of Brunswick and other German princes for service in America. There was none present at Bunker Hill, but before the war was over, almost thirty thousand had been brought to America. They were good soldiers, but were detested by the Colonials. A great many settled in America after the war was over.

Page 86. *While Phœbus blazed down.* Phœbus was the Greek name for Apollo, the Sun-God.

Page 87. *Howe, Burgoyne, Clinton, Gage.* The British generals in command of the attack.

Page 88. *From Bunker Hill and Breed.* Bunker Hill, 110 feet in height, and Breed's Hill, 75 feet in height, were connected by a ridge, and the American redoubt was on Breed's Hill. Bunker Hill Monument stands on Breed's Hill, at almost the exact spot where Warren fell.

Page 89. *With the dead and the dying.* The British loss was 1054; the American loss was 449, incurred mainly in the last hand-to-hand struggle.

Page 90. *Beneath our consecrated elm.* The old elm itself lasted until 1923, when a storm blew it over; but a scion from its top was planted in the same spot and is now flourishing.

Page 90. *Famed vaguely for that old fight in the wood.* Braddock's defeat, where Washington had tried to rally the flying regulars.

Page 94. Rodney's Ride. Cæsar Rodney, one of the delegates from Delaware to the Continental Congress, had obtained leave of absence for a journey through the southern part of the state to prepare the people for a change of government. The other two delegates from Delaware were divided on the question of independence, and by great exertion Rodney arrived just in time for the final discussion, and his affirmative vote secured the consent of the Delaware delegation to the Declaration, and effected that unanimity which was essential to the success of the measure.

Page 98. *What of Adams? What of Sherman?* John Adams, of Massachusetts, the foremost advocate of the adoption of the Declaration, and Roger Sherman, of Connecticut, the "learned shoemaker," one of the committee of five who helped draft the document.

Page 98. *Sat the bellman, old and gray.* The bellman was William Hurley, who died October 27, 1781, at the age of sixty, and whose grave is in the graveyard of the old Pine Street Church, at Philadelphia. The story is told in Rhoades's *Story of Philadelphia*, much as given in the poem, but probably with more poetry than truth. There seems to have been very little popular excitement when the Declaration was signed.

Page 99. *The old State House bell is silent.* The Liberty Bell was ordered by the Assembly of the Province of Pennsylvania, in 1751, to be hung in the tower of the new State House, and by an odd chance, which savors of inspiration, in the letter ordering it, written November 1, 1751, it was directed that it should be inscribed "with the following words well-shaped in large letters round it, viz: Proclaim Liberty through all the land to all the inhabitants thereof. — Levit., xxv, 10." It became badly cracked and was lowered from the belfry, and has since been carefully preserved in Independence Hall.

Page 101. THE MARYLAND BATTALION. The Maryland Battalion was organized at the opening of the Revolution by the young men of Baltimore. At the battle of Long Island, the battalion fought with great gallantry, checked the advance of Cornwallis and saved a portion of the army from capture. Of its four hundred members, two hundred and fifty-nine were left dead on the field.

Page 101. *Spruce Macaronis.* A Macaroni, in the London slang of the period, was a fop or dandy.

Page 102. *The cohorts of Grant.* General Grant, who commanded the British left wing, had declared in Parliament that the Americans would not fight, and that he could march from one end of the continent to the other with five thousand men.

Page 102. *Oh, Stirling, good Stirling!* William Alexander, commonly called Lord Stirling, who had fled to America upon the discovery of the Jacobite conspiracy of 1715. It was Stirling's command which the battalion saved from capture.

Page 102. *Brave Mordecai Gist.* The major in command of the battalion.

Page 103. NATHAN HALE. Nathan Hale was a great-grandson of John Hale, first minister of Beverly, Massachusetts. He was born in 1755 and graduated from Yale in 1773. Little is known of his personal history.

Page 104. *And the brutal guards withhold.* Hale was refused a Bible, the attendance of a clergyman, or permission to write any letters.

Page 104. *They burn, lest friendly eye.* A written message which he left was burned because, as one of his guards explained, it would give too much encouragement to his comrades.

Page 107. *Greene on the left.* General Nathanael Greene (1742–1786), second in command of the American army, and Washington's most trusted general.

Page 107. *The right was led by Sullivan.* General John Sullivan (1740–1795) was one of the eight brigadier-generals appointed by the Congress at the beginning of the war.

Page 108. *Cornwallis came fiercely.* Major-General Charles Cornwallis (1738–1805), Marquis and Earl, was sent with British troops to Boston in 1776, made second in command in America in 1778, and surrendered his army to Washington at Yorktown in 1781. He afterwards had a distinguished career in India, where he died in 1805.

Page 109. *Both St. Clair and Reed.* General Arthur St. Clair (1743–1818) had been with Wolfe at Quebec, and after the war was appointed governor of the Northwest Territory, where he was badly defeated by the

Indians in 1791. General James Reed (1724–1807) was at Ticonderoga and Bunker Hill.

Page 109. *Brave Mercer lay dead.* General Hugh Mercer (1720–1777) had taken part as a volunteer in Braddock's expedition. He led the column of attack at Trenton and the advance at Princeton. During the battle there, he was surrounded by the enemy, refused to surrender, and was repeatedly bayoneted and left for dead on the field. He died a few days later, and his funeral at Philadelphia was attended by over thirty thousand people. He was one of the most loved characters of the Revolution.

Page 109. *Redcoats by scores entered college.* A company of the British had barricaded itself in Nassau Hall, one of the college buildings, but surrendered as soon as Washington brought up a battery of guns and opened fire. The building is still standing and shows the marks of the bombardment.

Page 111. BETSY'S BATTLE-FLAG. Mrs. Elizabeth Griscom Ross (1752–1836) was a seamstress living in a little house at 239 Arch Street, Philadelphia, and according to her own story, was visited in June, 1776, by Washington and two other gentlemen, who requested her to make a flag after a design for which Washington provided a rough sketch. It was the "Stars and Stripes," as afterwards adopted by the Congress, but Mrs. Ross suggested several minor changes, one being that the stars should be five-pointed, instead of six-pointed, as shown on Washington's sketch. These details were all agreed to and Mrs. Ross proceeded to make the flag. There is a further story that Washington was acquainted with her because she had for a long time made the ruffles for his shirts. This statement was repeated by Mrs. Ross's daughter, as coming from her, and all that can be said about it is that no evidence to corroborate it has ever been discovered. The Betsy Ross house is still standing in Philadelphia, and is preserved as a national shrine.

Page 117. *We follow old John Stark.* General John Stark (1728–1822) fought at Bunker Hill, where his order, "Boys, aim at their waist-bands," made him famous. He served till the end of the war, and then retired to his farm and lived there in true republican simplicity until his death at the age of ninety-three.

Page 118. *To greet Parson Allen.* Rev. Thomas Allen (1743–1810), for forty-six years pastor of the church at Pittsfield, Massachusetts.

Page 118. *Or Molly Stark sleeps a widow.* Tradition has it that, as Stark led his men to the assault, he cried, "There they are, boys; we beat them today or Molly Stark's a widow."

Page 122. *The banner of the rampant unicorn.* The arms of England show the lion and the unicorn rampant, that is standing erect.

Page 126. MOLLY PITCHER. Her real name is said to have been Mary McCauley. Little is known about her except that she came from Carlisle, Pennsylvania, where a monument to her memory was erected in 1876.

Page 126. *Lee was beating a wild retreat.* General Charles Lee, in command of the advance guard, who, instead of pressing forward, ordered his men to retire. Washington, white with rage, rode up in the nick of time, ordered Lee to the rear, re-formed the troops and drove the British back.

Page 130. WAYNE AT STONY POINT. General Anthony Wayne (1745–1796) earned the nickname of "Mad Anthony" because he never refused a fight, no matter how great were the odds against him. He served throughout the Revolution, from Ticonderoga to Yorktown, and in 1793, opened the fertile country north of the Ohio to settlement by decisively defeating the Indians at a place called Fallen Timbers on the Maumee River, fifteen miles from what is now Toledo, Ohio.

Page 130. *Prone doth the leader fall.* General Wayne was convinced that he would not survive the attack on Stony Point, but nevertheless led the assault in person. He was struck in the head by a bullet, but, although he supposed himself mortally wounded, insisted on being carried into the fort at the head of his men. Fortunately, the bullet had struck a glancing blow, and he lived many years longer.

Page 132. *Caldwell of Springfield.* James Caldwell (1734–1781) was chaplain of the New Jersey brigade and known as the "Fighting Parson." He was shot by an American sentry during an altercation, and the sentry was tried for murder, convicted and hanged.

Page 133. *Boys, give 'em Watts!* Isaac Watts was the author of many hymns. The anecdote is well authenticated.

Page 134. *John Paulding was his name.* Paulding was born in New York City in 1758 and died there in 1818. His capture of André seems to have been his one noteworthy exploit. With him at the time were two comrades, Isaac Van Wart and David Williams, and the three were awarded medals by the Congress and an annuity of two hundred dollars for life. This ballad, written shortly after the event, was very popular.

Page 139. THE SWAMP FOX. General Francis Marion (1737–1795) was a native of South Carolina, and had taken a prominent part in the war against the Cherokee Indians. He had a rare courtesy and simplicity of manner, and the story of his serving only baked sweet potatoes to a British officer whom he had invited to dinner was a favorite one in the old school readers.

Page 139. *And when the troop of Tarleton rides.* Sir Banastre Tarleton (1754–1833) came to America with Cornwallis, and was one of the most active of the British generals.

Page 143. *It's up, Tench Tilghman.* Tench Tilghman (1744–1786) had entered the war at its beginning as lieutenant in a Philadelphia company, and in August, 1776, became Washington's military secretary and an aide on his staff, a position he held until the war was over. He was selected by Washington to carry the dispatch announcing the surrender of Cornwallis to the Congress, which was in session at Philadelphia. He left Yorktown October 19 and reached Philadelphia at midnight on the 23d. He was voted the thanks of the Congress, together with a sword and a horse with full accoutrements as a reward for the exploit.

Page 143. *The World Turned Upside Down.* A favorite military air of the day, to which many ballads were written.

Page 144. *Fierce called McKean.* Thomas McKean (1734–1817), one of the signers of the Declaration of Independence, and President of the Congress in 1781.

Page 146. *Who wrenched their rights from thee.* It is worth noting that the Revolution lasted eight years to a day, if it is assumed to have started with the battle of Lexington. Lexington was fought April 19, 1775, and the cessation of hostilities was, by order of General Washington, proclaimed in the American camp April 19, 1783.

Page 147. *Horeb's peak.* Horeb is another name for Mount Sinai. The reference is to Exodus, ii, 11–12: "And it came to pass in those days, when Moses was grown... he spied an Egyptian smiting a Hebrew, one of his brethren. And he looked this way and that way, and when he saw that there was no man, he slew the Egyptian and hid him in the sand."

Page 148. *The Vow of Washington.* Read in New York, April 30, 1889, at the centennial celebration of Washington's inauguration.

Page 150. *The Cincinnatus of the West.* Cincinnatus, the Roman dictator, who, after saving his country from a foreign foe, resigned his office and returned to his farm.

Page 152. *A Pharos in the night.* A famous lighthouse which stood on the island of Pharos; hence any remarkable lighthouse or beacon.

Page 155. *Adams and liberty.* Mr. Charles Prentiss, in his preface to the collected works of Robert Treat Paine, published in 1812, says: "There was, probably, never a political song more sung in America than this. It was sung at theaters, and on public and private occasions throughout the United States, and republished and applauded in Great Britain."

Page 155. *Rome's haughty victors.* The French, under Napoleon, occupied Italy in 1796 and 1797.

Page 156. *Like Leonidas' band.* Leonidas, King of Sparta, was leader of the band of three hundred Spartans who, until all of them were slain, defended the pass of Thermopylæ against the Persian army.

Page 157. HAIL COLUMBIA. Hopkinson himself told of the circumstances under which he wrote the song. (See Griswold's *Poets and Poetry of America.*) It was sung to the tune of the "President's March."

Page 160. *Out went Hull.* Isaac Hull (1773–1843) started to sea as a boy and was a captain at the age of twenty-one.

Page 160. *He'll catch Dacres and his pretty Guerrière.* Captain (afterwards Rear-Admiral) James Richard Dacres. Guerrière is the French word for warrior.

Page 163. *There's a fighting glint in Decatur's eye.* Stephen Decatur (1779–1820) was one of America's most famous sea-fighters.

Page 163. *And brave Old Glory floats out on high.* There are many accounts of the origin of the name "Old Glory" for the flag of the United States, none of them very convincing. The most probable is that the phrase was first used by Captain William Driver, of Salem, Massachusetts, in December, 1831, when, at the age of twenty-eight, he stood on the deck of a new ship of which he had just been appointed master. Some friends had presented him with an American flag, and as he saw it run up to the masthead, he christened it "Old Glory."

Page 165. *Since we fought here with Harrison.* General William Henry

Harrison (1773–1841), who, on November 7, 1811, defeated a force of five thousand Indians in a terrific battle near the Tippecanoe River, in Indiana, and was ever afterwards known as "Old Tippecanoe." He was elected president of the United States in 1840, but died a month after assuming office.

Page 166. *Was Lawrence there.* James Lawrence (1781–1813) had entered the navy as a midshipman at the age of seventeen.

Page 167. *Iron crimson-hot.* Cannon-balls were heated white-hot before being fired, in order to set fire to the enemy ship.

Page 167. *When Broke cast down his sword.* Sir Philip Bowes Vere Broke (1776–1841) was in command of the Shannon, and was severely wounded during the engagement.

Page 168. *Don't give up the ship.* That Lawrence uttered these words seems to rest on the testimony of Dr. John Dix, at the trial of Lieutenant Cox, April 14, 1814, to the effect "that Captain Lawrence ordered me to go on deck, and tell the men to fire faster and not give up the ship." A daughter of Benjamin Russell, editor of the Boston *Centinel* at the time, is authority for the statement that her father coined the phrase in his account of Lawrence's death. (Bombaugh, *Facts and Fancies for the Curious*, p. 388.) "Don't give up the ship!" was floated at the masthead of Commodore Oliver Hazard Perry's flagship, the Lawrence, during the battle of Lake Erie, September 10, 1813.

Page 169. *It was Thomas Macdonough.* Thomas Macdonough (1783–1825) entered the navy as a midshipman at the age of seventeen, and had a distinguished career.

Page 170. *And when he saw Downie.* George Downie, commander of the British fleet. He was killed during the action.

Page 171. *Thy blue waves, Patapsco.* The Patapsco River, near Baltimore.

Page 172. THE STAR-SPANGLED BANNER. The poem was really written at white heat, for Key made his first draft while the bombardment was actually in progress, and corrected it at Baltimore next day. Its meter was fashioned after the model set by Robert Treat Paine in his immensely popular "Adams and Liberty," with which Key was, of course, familiar. It was immediately struck off as a broadside and received with great enthusiasm. The air to which it is still sung was selected almost at random from a volume of flute music by an actor named Ferdinand Durang, and was known as "Anacreon in Heaven." Durang was playing at the famous Holliday Street Theater in Philadelphia, and the "Star-Spangled Banner" was first sung on the stage there. Although never officially designated by Congress as the National Anthem, it has been prescribed by formal order to be played in both the army and navy on occasions of ceremony, and may therefore be so regarded.

Page 174. *For I went down with Carroll.* William Carroll, major-general of the Tennessee militia.

Page 175. *As Jackson's voice was heard.* Andrew Jackson (1767–1845),

familiarly known as "Old Hickory," was one of the most genuine and pic-
turesque characters in American history.   After New Orleans, he waged a
successful campaign against the Cherokee Indians in Florida, and in 1828
was elected President of the United States.

Page 176. *'Twas Pakenham in person.* Sir Edward Michael Pakenham
(1778–1815), major general, a distinguished soldier who had led the Third
Division at the battle of Salamanca in 1812.   He was killed during the battle
at New Orleans.

Page 177. *And came, with Gibbs to head it.* Sir Samuel Gibbs, second in
command to Pakenham.   He also was killed during the battle.

Page 178. *It is the Baratarian.* The headquarters of Jean Lafitte, the
notorious pirate, at Barataria, an inlet of the Gulf of Mexico on the coast
of Louisiana, had been broken up only a short time before, and many of
his band captured and imprisoned.   They were subsequently released, and
under three of Lafitte's lieutenants, Dominique, You, and Bluche, hastened
to Jackson's aid before New Orleans, where they did good service, especially
with the artillery.

Page 180. *Our captain was married.* Charles Stewart (1778–1869), who
held the remarkable record of being seventy-one years in the service of the
American navy, and its senior officer for seventeen years.   He, also, was
called "Old Ironsides."   His daughter was mother of the famous Irish
patriot, Charles Stewart Parnell.

Page 182. *Parole they gave and parole they broke.* Only one of the prizes,
the Cyane, ever reached America.   The other, the Levant, put into the
neutral harbor of Port Praya, but was attacked there by a British fleet and
captured.

Page 182. OLD IRONSIDES. Oliver Wendell Holmes was only twenty-one
when he wrote these verses — his first famous poem.   It was written im-
petuously on a scrap of paper and sent to the *Boston Daily Advertiser*, signed
only with the initial "H."

Page 187. *The dark and bloody ground.* There is a popular belief that this
was the meaning of the Cherokee Indian word "Kentucky," but as a matter
of fact it meant simply "prairie" or "barrens."

Page 187. *Bold Putnam.* Rufus Putnam (1738–1824) founded the first
permanent settlement in Ohio at Marietta, in 1788.

Page 188. *As glides the Oyo's solemn flood.* Oyo, a spelling of Ohio.   It is
an Iroquois Indian word meaning "beautiful river."

Page 189. *From Darien to Davis.* Darien, the Isthmus of Panama;
Davis, Davis Strait, separating Greenland from Baffin Land.

Page 192. *And Travis, great Travis.* William Barrett Travis (1811–1836),
was only twenty-five years old when he commanded at the Alamo and met
his death there.

Page 192. *Then Bowie gasped.* James Bowie (1790–1836) was the in-
ventor of the "bowie knife," the first one, with which he killed a man in a
duel, having been made from a large file.

Page 192. *Crockett.* David Crockett (1786–1836), famous hunter and
frontiersman, and also member of Congress for a time.

Page 192. *Two thousand lay dead.* The Mexicans lost about five hundred, but even that was more than three times the number of the fort's defenders.

Page 192. *Save the gasp of a woman.* Every man of the garrison was killed but three women and three children survived.

Page 194. *And Sam Houston.* Sam Houston (1793–1863) was commander-in-chief of the Texan army, and President of the Republic of Texas.

Page 195. *We slew and slew.* Houston reported the Mexican loss to be 630 killed, 208 wounded, 730 captured. The American loss was 2 killed and 23 wounded. Santa Anna himself was captured next day.

Page 196. *Old Rough-and-Ready.* General Zachary Taylor (1784–1850) was known as "Old Rough-and-Ready." He was uncouth and uneducated, but a good soldier, and in 1848 was elected to the Presidency of the United States largely because of the popularity he had won by his victories in Mexico.

Page 196. *Lieutenant Blake.* Lieutenant George A. H. Blake (1812–1884) seems to have done nothing further to win distinction.

Page 207. *Pallas-born.* Pallas, or Minerva, the Goddess of Wisdom, who, according to Greek mythology, sprang "full-armed from the head of Jove."

Page 207. *Like the mother of the Gracchi.* Cornelia, the wife of Tiberius Sempronius Gracchus, when asked if she possessed any jewels, pointed to her sons, saying, "These are my jewels." The Gracchi, as they were called, became two of the greatest statesmen and patriots of Rome.

Page 210. Battle Hymn of the Republic. This poem, perhaps the loftiest strain of American patriotism, was inspired by a visit which Mrs. Howe paid to Washington in December, 1861. She heard the troops singing "John Brown's Body," and at the suggestion of James Freeman Clarke, determined to write some worthy words to replace the doggerel lines which went with the air. The poem was written almost at once, and was taken back to Boston by Mrs. Howe. She gave it to James T. Fields, editor of the *Atlantic Monthly,* and it was published in the issue of the magazine for February, 1862, being given the entire first page. Mr. Fields furnished the title. The poem attracted little attention until a copy of a newspaper containing it was smuggled into Libby prison. Chaplain Charles C. McCabe read it there, recognized its beauty, and presently the whole prison was singing it, to the astonishment of the Confederates. After his release, Chaplain McCabe continued to sing the song, and it became a great popular favorite. Theodore Roosevelt, while President, suggested that it be made the National Anthem.

Page 211. *On Freedom's southern line.* Mason and Dixon's line, which was the boundary established in 1767 between Pennsylvania and Maryland, and which, extended, marked the southern boundary of Kansas, was long regarded as the northern limit of slave territory.

Page 212. *Our Pilgrim gonfalon.* A gonfalon is an ensign, or flag, in the form a of streamer, attached to a spear.

Page 214. *Like Gideons we leapt.* Gideon was the mighty warrior who delivered Israel from the Midianites.

Page 214. *John Brown in Kansas settled.* John Brown (1800–1859) had joined the Free Soil party and settled with his five sons at Ossawatomie, Kansas, and hence was known as "Brown of Ossawatomie." He was a fanatical abolitionist and extremely erratic, but not insane in the strict meaning of the term. Two of his sons were murdered by slavery partisans, as recounted in the poem. Brown always denied that in capturing the arsenal at Harper's Ferry he had planned to arm the slaves and start an insurrection. He claimed that his only intention was to startle the country into action. But there is a good deal of evidence to the contrary.

Page 217. *Captain Stephens.* Aaron Dwight Stephens, a captain only in the sense that he was to be given that position in the negro army which Brown planned to organize.

Page 218. *Like the Emperor's coup d'état.* Napoleon III, who had been elected President of the French Republic in 1848, on December 2, 1851, seized the reins of power, threw an army into Paris, and proclaimed himself Emperor.

Page 219. *So they hurried off to Richmond for the Government Marines.* The marines arrived by train from Washington. Strangely, enough, they were under command of Colonel Robert E. Lee and Lieut. J. E. B. Stuart, destined to become famous leaders of the Confederate armies.

Page 219. *Fired their bullets in his clay.* The bodies of some of the dead were atrociously maltreated.

Page 219. *How they hastened on the trial.* The trial began October 26 and ended November 2. The proceedings, though swift, were not unseemly nor unduly summary, considering the excitement of the Virginians and the rumor that a rescue would be attempted from the North.

Page 220. *May trouble you more than ever.* A true prophecy. Alive, John Brown was merely a half-demented enthusiast; dead, he became a symbol of martyrdom.

Page 222. *We'll hang Jeff Davis.* Jefferson Davis (1808–1889) was President of the Confederacy. To the North he was always "Jeff" Davis, and his name was used as a bogie to frighten children.

Page 222. *Striking away with a heavy maul.* As a youth, Lincoln was famous for his prowess as a rail-splitter.

Page 222. *But the maul this time was a paddle.* Lincoln himself related that the first money he ever earned was for rowing two men and their baggage from the shore out to an Ohio river steamer. Each of them gave him a silver half-dollar.

Page 223. *A-pondering Coke and Story.* Coke and Story were two famous authors of lawbooks, which Lincoln borrowed from friendly lawyers.

Page 223. *The "Western Giant."* Stephen A. Douglas, known as the "Little Giant," with whom Lincoln had a famous series of debates on the slavery question in 1858, and whom he defeated for the Presidency in 1860.

Page 223. *A-writing the Proclamation.* The proclamation freeing the slaves, which was issued as a war measure.

Page 224. *When the Norn-Mother.* In Scandinavian mythology, the Norns were the three Fates, representing past, present, and future.

Page 227. *I'll find a way, or make it.* A phrase attributed to Hannibal, referring to his passage of the Alps.

Page 227. *In Helicon may slake it.* A mountain in Greece, the fabled retreat of Apollo and the muses.

Page 228. *Gave the soul of Henry Clay.* Henry Clay's birthday was April 12, 1777.

Page 231. *Annan. Shannon.* Annan, a river in Scotland. Shannon, the principal river of Ireland.

Page 233. DIXIE. Dan Emmett, a once-famous black-face minstrel, was the author of the original "Dixie," which was written in 1859, to an old plantation melody, and sung by him with great success. It was merely a bit of doggerel, the first stanza running:

> I wish I was in de land ob cotton,
> Old times dar am not forgotten;
>> Look away, look away, look away, Dixie land!
> In Dixie land whar I was born in,
> Early on one frosty mornin',
>> Look away, look away, look away, Dixie land!

It became the most popular of all the Southern war songs, the words used being those written by General Albert Pike, as given in the text. There are many stories as to the derivation of "Dixie," the generally accepted one being that the word originated at New Orleans, where ten-dollar bills were called "dixies," from the French word for ten, *dix.* It seems rather far-fetched, for in French *dix* is pronounced *deese*, to rhyme with *geese*.

Page 236. *The verdure climbs the Common.* Boston Common, the public square in the middle of the city.

Page 237. *My Maryland.* This poem, which divided with "Dixie" popularity among the southern troops, was written by Mr. Randall immediately upon hearing of the outbreak at Baltimore. The form of the poem was suggested by Mangan's "Karamanian Exile":

> I see thee ever in my dreams,
>> Karaman!
> Thy hundred hills, thy thousand streams,
>> Karaman, O Karaman.

It was wedded to the old college air, "Lauriger Horatius," by Miss Hattie Cary, of Baltimore. In 1898, the Sixth Massachusetts passed through Baltimore a second time, this time, on its way to Cuba; the whole town, headed by the mayor, turned out to welcome it, school-children drawn up along the line of march pelted the soldiers with flowers, each man was given a box containing cake, fruit and a love-letter, and a great banner strung across the principal street read, "Let the Welcome of '98 Efface the Memory of '61."

Page 238. *Sic semper.* The motto of the State of Virginia is *Sic semper tyrannis*, Thus always with tyrants.

Page 240. *Like the leaves of Vallombrosa.* Vallombrosa was a thickly wooded valley near Florence. "Thick as autumnal leaves that strew the brooks in Vallombrosa" was used first by Milton (*Paradise Lost*, bk. I, l. 302).

Page 243. *Then, like a kraken.* The kraken was a mythical sea-monster, said to appear at times off the coast of Norway.

Page 244. *Still floated our flag.* The Cumberland sank in shallow water, and the mainmast head, with the flag flying from it, was not covered.

Page 246. THE CRUISE OF THE MONITOR. The contract for the construction of the Monitor was given to John Ericsson, of New York, on October 4, 1861. It was to be an iron-plated raft, 172 feet over all, 41½ feet beam, and 11½ feet depth of hold, carrying a revolving iron turret containing two 11-inch Dahlgren guns. The ironclad was launched January 30, 1862, and handed over to the government on February 19th, an extraordinary feat in naval construction. Its cost was $275,000. At eleven o'clock on the morning of March 6, the queer craft started for Hampton Roads, to meet the Merrimac, word of whose completion had reached the United States government. That it did not founder on the voyage was little less than a miracle, but at nine o'clock on the evening of March 8, the Monitor reached Fort Monroe, her progress up the bay being lighted by the burning frigate Congress.

Page 248. *Bold Worden.* The Monitor was commanded by Lieutenant John Lorimer Worden, and the Merrimac by Lieutenant Catesby Jones, the latter's superior, Captain Franklin Buchanan, having been wounded by a rifle bullet the day before. Worden was injured during the action by a shell exploding against the sight-hole of the pilot-house, and was succeeded by Lieutenant Samuel Dana Green.

Page 249. *That story of Kearny.* General Philip Kearny (1815–1862), one of the most dashing officers of the Union army.

Page 250. *In the one hand still left.* Kearny had had his left arm amputated as the result of a wound received during the war with Mexico.

Page 250. *Received their yell.* The "Rebel yell" was the herald of every Confederate charge.

Page 257. BARBARA FRIETCHIE. In a note to the poem, Mr. Whittier stated that it had been written "in strict conformity to the account of the incident as I had it from respectable and trustworthy sources," but it has since been questioned by historians.

Page 259. THE VICTOR OF ANTIETAM. General George Brinton McClellan (1826–1885) was affectionately known as "Little Mac" to his soldiers, and was idolized by them. A great controversy has raged about his ability as a soldier. He was undoubtedly over-cautious, too insistent upon perfection of preparation, and too fond of complicated maneuvers which never got anywhere, but also undoubtedly he was vastly superior to many of the generals on the Union side, and the best commander which the Army of the Potomac ever had with the possible exception of Meade. He never returned to active service after being relieved of command following Antietam. He ran against Lincoln for President in 1864, and was badly defeated.

Page 264. *'Tis Meagher and his fellows.* Brigadier-General Thomas F.

Meagher commanded the second brigade of the First Division. It was called the "Irish Brigade," and Meagher himself had organized it. After Chancellorsville, it was so decimated that it was incorporated with other regiments.

Page 264. *The wild day is closed.* Burnside's attempt to carry the heights behind Fredericksburg was perhaps the most insane act of the war.

Page 265. *The earnest boy whose name was Grant.* General Ulysses S. Grant (1822–1885) had graduated from West Point, but had resigned from the army and was living at Galena, Ill., when the war began. He at once applied for a commission, and after he secured it, toiled doggedly away, refusing to be discouraged by any obstacle, and winning one victory after another, until he attracted Lincoln's attention. From that time on, he had the President's backing, and his advance was rapid. He was not generally regarded as a brilliant general, and there were bitter complaints about the terrible loss of life which his victories entailed, but his theory was that the shortest and most direct way was in the end the cheapest, and his success seemed to prove that he was right. He served two terms as President after the war.

Page 268. ALBERT SIDNEY JOHNSTON. General Albert Sidney Johnston (1803–1862), one of the best loved of the Southern leaders, was famed for his chivalry and courage. It was his chivalry caused his death. He had just sent his physician to the rear to care for some wounded Union soldiers, when a bullet severed an artery in his thigh. A little skill would probably have saved his life, but he bled to death while the members of his staff fumbled with the wound or looked helplessly on.

Page 268. *The flashing Stars and Bars.* The Confederate flag, as first adopted, consisted of a red field with a white stripe through the center, but in 1863 was changed to a white field with a blue star in the center. The "Stars and Bars" was hoisted for the first time on the State House at Montgomery, Ala., on March 4, 1861, the day of President Lincoln's inauguration.

Page 268. *Sherman and his legions.* William Tecumseh Sherman (1820–1891), next to Grant, the outstanding general on the Union side.

Page 269. *Beauregard.* General Pierre Beauregard (1818–1873) had served in the war with Mexico, was in command of the troops which attacked Fort Sumter, and commanded the Confederates at the first battle of Bull Run.

Page 274. TO JOHN C. FRÉMONT. John C. Frémont (1813–1890) explored the Rocky Mountains and the Pacific Coast, was in California when the war with Mexico began, and organized the American forces there. He was a vehement Free Soiler and was the Republican candidate for President in 1856 on an anti-slavery platform.

Page 274. *Since Roland wound his horn at Roncesvalles.* Roland was the most celebrated of the Paladins of Charlemagne, famous for his prowess. He was killed at the battle of Roncesvalles in 778.

Page 278. LAUS DEO! Praise to God!

Page 279. STONEWALL JACKSON'S WAY. General Thomas Jonathan Jackson (1824–1863) was the greatest leader the South possessed, next to Lee. He won his nickname of "Stonewall" at the first battle of Bull Run, when General Bee, to encourage his men, shouted, "Look at Jackson, standing like a stone wall." Jackson always claimed that it was his men whom. Bee meant and not himself, and that he did not merit the name, but it stuck to him to the end. He had resigned from the army and was professor of philosophy at the Virginia Military Institute when the war broke out. The verses, "Stonewall Jackson's Way," according to William Gilmore Simms, "were found, stained with blood, in the breast of a dead soldier of the old Stonewall Brigade, after one of Jackson's battles in the Shenandoah Valley." They were widely copied, but their authorship remained unknown for nearly a quarter of a century. The poem, perhaps, refers to the second battle of Manassas, August 30, 1862.

Page 280. *In forma pauperis.* In the form, or guise, of a pauper; as a poor man.

Page 287. *With Pickett leading grandly down.* Major General George Edward Pickett (1825-1875) commanded a division composed entirely of Virginians.

Page 291. *Of Burns of Gettysburg.* John Burns was seventy years of age in 1863. He had been among the first to volunteer for the War of 1812, and was present at the battles of Plattsburg, Queenstown and Lundy's Lane. He served through the war with Mexico, and volunteered promptly for the Civil War, was rejected because of his age, served for a time as a teamster, but was finally sent home to Gettysburg, where his townsmen made him constable to keep him busy and contented. When, in June, 1863, the Confederates occupied the town, Burns had to be locked up for asserting his civil authority in opposition to that of the Confederate provost guard. As soon as the Confederates left the town, Burns busied himself arresting Confederate stragglers. When the preliminary skirmishing at Gettysburg began, Burns borrowed a rifle and ammunition from a wounded Union soldier, went to the front and offered his services as volunteer. The colonel of the Seventh Wisconsin loaned him a long-range rifle, which he used with deadly effect all day, but he was badly wounded when the Union troops were forced back, was captured by the Confederates, and narrowly escaped being hanged as an un-uniformed combatant. He lived in his little home on the battlefield until 1872, and was visited by thousands of pilgrims to the scene of the great struggle.

Page 292. *From a stubborn Meade.* General George Gordon Meade (1815-1872) had replaced Hooker as commander of the Army of the Potomac only four days before.

Page 296. *Our grand young leader.* General John C. Pemberton (1814-1881.) It was to him, when he asked for terms, that Grant sent his famous message demanding unconditional surrender.

Page 301. *That battle in the cloud.* "The day had been one of dense mists and rains, and much of General Hooker's battle was fought above the clouds, on the top of Lookout Mountain." — General Meigs's Report.

Page 302. *Out on a crag walked something.* The flag was unfurled from Pulpit Rock, the extreme point of the mountain overlooking Chattanooga. It was from that "pulpit" that Jefferson Davis, three days before, had ad-dressed the troops, assuring them that all was well with the Confederacy.

Page 304. *That desperate day McPherson fell.* Mr. Garland is mistaken in stating that McPherson was killed at the battle of Peach Tree Creek. He was killed two days later at what is known as the battle of Atlanta. While hastening to join his troops, who had just been attacked by the Confederates, he ran full into the enemy's skirmish line and was shot while trying to escape. Sherman at once ordered General John A. Logan to assume command of the Army of Tennessee, and it was largely due to his skill and determination that the Union army was saved from serious disaster in the desperate battle which followed.

Page 306. SHERMAN'S MARCH TO THE SEA. General Sherman, in his Memoirs, says that on the afternoon of February 17, 1865, while overhauling his pockets, according to his custom, to read more carefully the various notes and memoranda received during the day, he found a paper which had been given him by a Union prisoner who had escaped from Columbia. It proved to be "Sherman's March to the Sea," composed by Adjutant S. H. M. Byers, of the Fifth Iowa Infantry, while a prisoner at Columbia. General Sherman was so impressed by the verses that he immediately sent for their author and attached him to his staff. The popular song of this campaign, however, was not Mr. Byers's verses, but a piece of doggerel by Henry Clay Work, called "Marching Through Georgia," which was sung not only during the war, but for many years after it. General Sherman detested the song and does not mention it. The first stanza runs:

Bring the good old bugle, boys, we'll sing another song —
Sing it with a spirit that will start the world along —
Sing it as we used to sing it, fifty thousand strong,
As we were marching through Georgia.

Page 311. *Let it reach the startled Huns.* The Huns were a savage and ruthless Mongolian race who invaded Europe, under the leadership of Attila, and were finally defeated by the Gauls, or French, at Chalons-sur-Marne in 451. The word was widely applied to the Germans during the World War because of their method of warfare.

Page 319. THE SURRENDER AT APPOMATTOX. Lee's army, at the time of the surrender, consisted of about twenty-eight thousand men, nearly half of whom were without arms. They had had little to eat for several days except parched corn, and were upon the verge of starvation. Immediately after the surrender, Grant sent 25,000 rations into the Confederate lines. His behavior was marked throughout with the greatest delicacy. He did not ask Lee's sword, promptly stopped salutes which were started after the surrender, did not require the Confederates to march out and stack arms, and did not enter their lines. The terms of surrender were so liberal that many partisans at the North took violent exception to them.

Page 321. O CAPTAIN! MY CAPTAIN! The murderer of the President, John Wilkes Booth, was a son of the famous tragedian Junius Brutus Booth, and a brother of Edwin Booth. He was twenty-six years old at the time of the assassination. He had broken one of his ankles in leaping from the President's box to the stage, but managed to mount a horse which was waiting, and to escape into Virginia. There he was finally cornered in a barn by a force sent in pursuit. There is some dispute as to whether he shot himself or whether he was struck by a bullet which a soldier called "Boston" Corbett fired at him. At any rate, he was brought out of the barn with a bullet in the base of his brain, and died the following morning. There were wild tales that he had escaped, but these were without foundation. Eight accomplices were arrested, tried by a military commission, and found guilty. Four, one a woman, were hanged, and the others, with one exception, sentenced to imprisonment for life. They were all obscure persons, and, in spite of many rumors to the contrary, no evidence was ever produced implicating any prominent Confederate leader in the crime. It was undoubtedly hatched and carried out by Booth himself and on his own responsibility.

Page 329. THE BLUE AND THE GRAY. This poem grew out of an item which appeared in the *New York Tribune* in 1867: "The women of Columbus. Mississippi, animated by nobler sentiments than many of their sisters, have shown themselves impartial in their offerings made to the memory of the dead. They strewed flowers alike on the graves of the Confederate and of the National Soldiers." The poem, prefaced by this item, was published in the *Atlantic Monthly* for September, 1867.

Page 335. *The elder dames, thy haughty peers.* The reference is to the nations of Europe, and remains so apropos that it is startling to realize that it was written in 1846.

Page 336. HOW CYRUS LAID THE CABLE. Mr. Field (1819–1892) had been working at this project since 1854. In 1858 he had succeeded in laying a cable across the ocean, and it was in operation from August 17 to September 4, when the signals became unintelligible and finally ceased. The work, therefore, had to be done all over again.

Page 339. *See the real Northern Thor.* Thor was the god of thunder, according to Scandinavian mythology. The thunder was produced when he hurled the mighty hammer he always carried, and which returned of itself to his hand.

Page 343. CUSTER'S LAST CHARGE. Custer was thirty-seven years old at the time of his death, and had served with distinction throughout the Civil War. He was bitterly censured for accepting battle upon the Little Big Horn, and there seems to be no doubt that he led his men into a trap through lack of proper precaution.

Page 344. *There lay the Sitting Bull's camp.* Sitting Bull was a famous Sioux chief, born about 1837, and killed during the last Sioux outbreak in 1890.

Page 355. *The Essex sailors.* The Essex, blockaded in the port of Valparaiso in 1814 by three British men-of-war, fought them and was finally compelled to surrender.

Page 356. *Fighting with him the gallant Ranger bore.* John Paul Jones (1747–1792), America's most daring sea-fighter during the Revolution, whose exploits, unfortunately for this book, remain strangely uncommemorated in worthy verse.

Page 356. *The dying Lawrence.* See page 168, and note thereto.

Page 356. *My grandfather fell on Vinegar Hill.* Vinegar Hill was the stronghold of the Irish revolutionists in 1798. It was attacked and carried by the British.

Page 359. *Iberian, palter no more!* Iberia, in ancient geography, was the peninsula which now includes Spain and Portugal.

Page 359. *Remember the Maine!* This phrase became the battle-cry of the war. But it is only fair to say that no evidence has ever been discovered linking the Spanish government with the ship's destruction, nor was it ever definitely determined how the explosion was caused.

Page 361. *Dewey at Manila.* Commodore George Dewey (1837–1917) came home to the greatest reception ever accorded an American, was made Admiral of the Navy, the only man ever to be given that title, with the exception of David Glasgow Farragut, but fell from the favor of the fickle populace because of political indiscretions, and ended his days in comparative neglect.

Page 361. *When the bold Olympia led.* The Olympia was Dewey's flagship.

Page 361. *Into Boca Grande gray.* The main channel into Manila Bay, south of Corregidor Island, which was strongly fortified. It means literally "large mouth."

Page 362. *O Montojo.* Admiral Patricio Montojo, commander of the Spanish naval forces in the Philippines.

Page 363. *Here within Cavité's lee.* Cavité, the capital of the province of the same name, on Manila Bay. It was off Cavité that the Spanish fleet was stationed.

Page 363. *You may fire when ready, Gridley.* Charles Vernon Gridley (1845–1898), Captain of the Olympia. Dewey's "You may fire when ready, Gridley," has become a classic.

Page 366. *As when beside Regillus Lake.* A lake near Rome where a great victory was won by Tarquin in 496 B.C.

Page 368. *Wheeler's Brigade.* "Fighting Joe" Wheeler (1836–1906) had been an active and successful cavalry leader on the Confederate side during the Civil War, and volunteered for active service at the outbreak of the war with Spain, an act which was hailed as a symbol that North and South were no longer divided.

Page 380. *The Duke of Alva's soul.* It was the Duke of Alva whom the King of Spain put in charge of the conquest of the Netherlands, in 1567, and who carried it out with unexampled ferocity.

Page 393. *"Silent upon a peak in Darien."* The last line of Keats's immortal sonnet, "On First Looking into Chapman's Homer."

Page 394. *Nuñez de Balboa,* who crossed the isthmus and discovered the Pacific in 1513.

Page 396. *The Day! The Day!* A toast of the German army and navy, meaning the day when war would start with England.

Page 396. *The Right Divine.* The divine right of kings, in which the German Kaiser so profoundly believed.

Page 396. *The Septentrional watershed.* The northern watershed, or watershed in northern France, which was the scene of the bitterest fighting.

Page 396. *O Reims, of ages heir.* The great Gothic cathedral at Reims, one of the most beautiful in the world, was bombarded and partially destroyed by the Germans.

Page 401. *The grim Titanic.* The great White Star steamship Titanic, on her maiden voyage to America, sank in mid-Atlantic, April 15, 1912, after colliding with an iceberg, and 1513 of her passengers and crew were drowned.

Page 403. *The Trail the Ghurkas found.* The Ghurkas were the best troops in the Anglo-Indian army.

Page 403. *The Anzac's glory road.* The "Anzacs" were the New Zealand troops, the word being a contraction of New Zealand Army Corps.

Page 412. *Patrick, Brigid, Columkill.* The three great Irish saints.

Page 416. *Were guarding a bunch of the Boche.* A word of uncertain origin employed quite generally by the Allies in speaking of the German soldiers.

Page 417. *Eight more Huns.* See note to page 311.

Page 417. *Lamb at the Ritz.* The Ritz is one of the most fashionable of the hotels of Paris.

Page 421. *Joan leads her armies.* Joan of Arc.

Page 422. *Beside the Aisne and Aire.* Two French rivers flowing through the battle-fields.

Page 425. *The kindly loam of France.* Soil brought from France was used to fill the grave.

ACKNOWLEDGMENTS

For permission to use the copyrighted material included in this volume, the compiler is indebted to the publishers and authors mentioned below, whose courtesy is here gratefully acknowledged. All rights to these poems are reserved by the holders of the copyright:

Messrs. D. Appleton & Co.: The poems by William Cullen Bryant, of whose work they are the authorized publishers.

The Bobbs Merrill Company: *The Fleet at Santiago*, by Charles E. Russell, from "Such Stuff as Dreams."

Brentano's: *Armistice Day*, by Roselle Mercier Montgomery, from "Ulysses Returns."

The Century Company: *How the Cumberland Went Down*, by S. Weir Mitchell and *What's In a Name*, by Helen F. More. From the Century Magazine: *The High Tide at Gettysburg*, by Will Henry Thompson.

Messrs. Henry T. Coates & Co.: *The Picket-Guard*, by Ethel Lynn Beers; *Monterey*, by Charles Fenno Hoffman.

Messrs. Dodd, Mead & Co.: *The Founders of Ohio* and *National Song*, by William Henry Venable.

Messrs. Doubleday Doran and Company: *Rouge Bouquet* and *The White Ships and the Red*, by Joyce Kilmer; *Lincoln*, and *Our Dead, Overseas*, by Edwin Markham.

Messrs. E. P. Dutton & Co.: *America the Beautiful* and *The New Crusade*, by Katherine Lee Bates.

Funk & Wagnalls Company: *The Defence of Lawrence*, by Richard Realf, from "Poems by Richard Realf."

Messrs. Harper & Brothers: *Parson Allen's Ride*, by Wallace Bruce; *Across the Delaware* and *Cuba to Columbia*, by Will Carleton; *The Storming of Stony Point*, by Arthur Guiterman; *Malvern Hill, The Victor of Antietam, The Cumberland, A Dirge for McPherson, The Fall of Richmond*, and *The Surrender at Appomattox*, by Herman Melville. From Harper's Magazine and Harper's Weekly: *Santiago*, by Thomas A. Janvier; *Assunpink and Princeton, The Battle of New Orleans*, and *Battle of the King's Mill*, by Thomas Dunn English.

Houghton Mifflin Company: *Unguarded Gates*, by Thomas Bailey Aldrich; *Concord Hymn, Boston Hymn, Boston*, by Ralph Waldo Emerson; *Cedar Mountain*, by Annie Fields; *Caldwell of Springfield, The Reveille, John Burns of Gettysburg, A Second Review of the Grand Army*, and *An Arctic Vision*, by Bret Harte; *A Ballad of the Boston Tea Party, Lexington, Old Ironsides, Brother Jonathan's Lament for Sister Caroline, The Flames of Liberty, Sherman's in Savannah*, and *After the Fire*, by Oliver Wendell Holmes; *Our Country, Battle Hymn of the Republic*, and *Robert E. Lee*, by Julia Ward Howe; *The Sinking of the Merrimack, The Nineteenth of April*, by Lucy Larcom; *Sir Humphrey Gilbert, A Ballad of the French Fleet, Paul Revere's Ride, The Cumberland, The Republic*, from "The Building of the Ship," *Decoration Day*, by Henry Wadsworth Longfellow; selections from "Under the Old Elm" and from "Ode Recited at the Harvard Commemoration," by James Russell Lowell; *On a Soldier Fallen in the Philippines*, by William Vaughn Moody;

ACKNOWLEDGMENTS

How Cyrus Laid the Cable, by John Godfrey Saxe; *How We Became a Nation* and *Can't*, by Harriet Prescott Spofford; *How Old Brown Took Harper's Ferry*, *Sumter*, and *Kearny at Seven Pines*, by Edmund Clarence Stedman; *To Spain — A Last Word*, by Edith M. Thomas; *The Ballad of Chickamauga*, by Maurice Thompson; *Columbus at the Convent*, by John Townsend Trowbridge; *Pentucket*, *Lexington*, *The Vow of Washington*, *The Kansas Emigrants*, *Brown of Ossawattomie*, *Barbara Frietchie*, *To John C. Frémont*, *Laus Deo*, *The Battle Autumn of 1862*, *Chicago*, and *Centennial Hymn*, by John Greenleaf Whittier; *Boy Brittan*, by Forceythe Willson.

J. B. Lippincott Company: *Dirge for a Soldier*, *The Battle of Lookout Mountain*, *The Cruise of the Monitor*, *Lincoln*, and *Before Vicksburg*, by George Henry Boker; *Separate Peace*, by Harrison S. Morris; *Valley Forge*, from "The Wagoner of the Alleghenies," and *Sheridan's Ride*, by Thomas Buchanan Read; *Our Left* and *Little Giffen*, by Francis Orrery Ticknor.

Messrs. Little, Brown and Company: *Columbus*, *The Ballad of Bunker Hill*, and *The Marching Song of Stark's Men*, by Edward Everett Hale, from "New England History in Ballads."

The Macmillan Company: *The Gold Seekers*, by Hamlin Garland; *The Islands of the Sea* and *Sonnets Written in the Fall of 1914*, by George Edward Woodberry; *Abraham Lincoln Walks at Midnight*, by Vachel Lindsay.

The Oliver Ditson Company: *Molly Pitcher*, by Kate Brownlee Sherwood.

Messrs. G. P. Putnam's Sons: *When the Great Gray Ships Come In*, by Guy Wetmore Carryl.

Messrs. Charles Scribner's Sons: *A Toast to Our Native Land*, by Robert Bridges ("Droch"), from "Bramble Brae"; *Romance*, by William Ernest Henley; *Keenan's Charge* and *Marthy Virginia's Hand*, by George Parsons Lathrop; *Panama*, *Washington*, *Jack Creamer*, *The Constitution's Last Fight*, and *Gettysburg*, by James Jeffrey Roche; *A Call to Arms*, by Mary Raymond Shipman Andrews; *America for Me* and *America's Welcome Home*, by Henry van Dyke.

Stewart Kidd Company: *The Mothers of the West*, by William D. Gallagher; *The Siege of Chapultepec* and *The Volunteers*, by William Haines Lytle.

Express personal permission has been received by the compiler from the following authors for the use of such of their poems as are included in this volume, and he wishes gratefully to acknowledge not only this courtesy, but also the helpful suggestions received from many of them:

Mary Raymond Shipman Andrews, Hamilton Fish Armstrong, Robert Bridges ("Droch"), Dana Burnet, Alice M. Trask (for Florence Earle Coates), Thomas and Joseph Butterworth (for Hezekiah Butterworth), Jeanne Robert Foster, Minna Irving, Daniel Henderson, Robert Underwood Johnson, Aline Kilmer (for Joyce Kilmer), Richard Le Gallienne, Edwin Markham, Roselle Mercier Montgomery, Harrison S. Morris, Margaret J. Preston (for Margaret Junkin Preston), David Proctor (for Edna Dean Proctor), Wallace Rice, Laura E. Richards, John Jerome Rooney, Clinton Scollard, Lewis Worthington Smith, Wendell Phillips Stafford, Mrs. Edith Trowbridge Vom Baur (for John Townsend Trowbridge), Henry van Dyke.

INDEX OF AUTHORS

INDEX OF FIRST LINES

INDEX OF TITLES